THE MYTHIC & MAGICKAL FOLKLORE OF PLANTS

BY

T.F. THISELTON-DYER

Original Publication, 1889

The Mythic & Magickal Folklore of Plants was first published in 1889 under the title *The Folklore of Plants*.

This *Samhain Song Press* edition of
The Mythic & Magickal Folklore of Plants
Copyright © 2008 by *Samhain Song Press*.

A *Samhain Song Press* publication
View the complete *Samhain Song Press*
catalog at www.SamhainSong.com

Editorial, sales and distribution, rights and permission inquiries should be sent via e-mail to SamhainSong@yahoo.com.

Thiselton-Dyer, T.F.
The Mythic & Magickal Folklore of Plants /by T.F. Thiselton-Dyer.

First *Samhain Song Press* Edition

ISBN 978-1-4357-3139-4

First Samhain Song Press Edition

1. Plants. 2. Folklore. 3. Herbalism. 4. Herbs
5. Botanical Folklore. 6. Herbal Magic 7. Title

PREFACE

Apart from botanical science, there is perhaps no subject of inquiry connected with plants of wider interest than that suggested by the study of folklore. This field of research has been largely worked of late years, and has obtained considerable popularity in this country, and on the Continent.

Much has already been written on the folklore of plants, a fact which has induced me to give, in the present volume, a brief systematic summary-- with a few illustrations in each case--of the many branches into which the subject naturally subdivides itself. It is hoped, therefore, that this little work will serve as a useful handbook for those desirous of gaining some information, in a brief concise form, of the folklore which, in one form or another, has clustered round the vegetable kingdom.

T.F. THISELTON-DYER.

November 19, 1888.

CONTENTS

CHAPTER I

PLANT LIFE

The fact that plants, in common with man and the lower animals, possess the phenomena of life and death, naturally suggested in primitive times the notion of their having a similar kind of existence. In both cases there is a gradual development which is only reached by certain progressive stages of growth, a circumstance which was not without its practical lessons to the early naturalist. This similarity, too, was held all the more striking when it was observed how the life of plants, like that of the higher organisms, was subject to disease, accident, and other hostile influences, and so liable at any moment to be cut off by an untimely end.[1] On this account a personality was ascribed to the products of the vegetable kingdom, survivals of which are still of frequent occurrence at the present day. It was partly this conception which invested trees with that mystic or sacred character whereby they were regarded with a superstitious fear which found expression in sundry acts of sacrifice and worship. According to Mr. Tylor,[2] there is reason to believe that, "the doctrine of the spirits of plants lay deep in the intellectual history of South-east Asia, but was in great measure superseded under Buddhist influence. The Buddhist books show that in the early days of their religion it was matter of controversy whether trees had souls, and therefore whether they might lawfully be injured. Orthodox Buddhism decided against the tree souls, and consequently against the scruple to harm them, declaring trees to have no mind nor sentient principle, though admitting that certain dewas or spirits do reside in the body of trees, and speak from within them." Anyhow, the notion of its being wrong to injure or mutilate a tree for fear of putting it to unnecessary pain was a widespread belief. Thus, the Ojibways imagined that trees had souls, and seldom cut them down, thinking that if they did so they would hear "the wailing of the trees when they suffered in this way."[3] In Sumatra[4] certain trees have special honours paid to them as being the embodiment of the spirits of the woods, and the Fijians[5] believe that "if an animal or a plant die, its soul immediately goes to Bolotoo." The Dayaks of Borneo[6] assert that rice has a living principle or spirit, and hold feasts to retain its soul lest the crops should decay. And the Karens affirm,[7] too, that plants as well as men and animals have their "la" or spirit. The Iroquois acknowledge the existence of spirits in trees and plants, and say that the spirit of corn, the spirit of beans, and the spirit of squashes are supposed to have the forms of three beautiful maidens.

According to a tradition current among the Miamis, one year when there was an unusual abundance of corn, the spirit of the corn was very angry because the children had thrown corn-cobs at each other in play, pretending to have suffered serious bodily injury in consequence of their sport[8]. Similarly, when the wind blows the long grass or waving corn, the German peasant will say, "the Grass-wolf," or "the Corn-wolf" is abroad. According to Mr. Ralston, in some places, "the last sheaf of rye is left as a shelter to the Roggenwolf or Rye-wolf during the winter's cold, and in many a summer or autumn festive rite that being is represented by a rustic, who assumes a wolf-like appearance. The corn spirit was, however, often symbolised under a human form."

Indeed, under a variety of forms this animistic conception is found among the lower races, and in certain cases explains the strong prejudice to certain herbs as articles of food. The Society Islanders ascribed a "varua" or surviving soul to plants, and the negroes of Congo adored a sacred tree called "Mirrone," one being generally planted near the house, as if it were the tutelar god of the dwelling. It is customary, also, to place calabashes of palm wine at the feet of these trees, in case they should be thirsty. In modern folklore there are many curious survivals of this tree-soul doctrine. In Westphalia,[9] the peasantry announce formally to the nearest oak any death that may have occurred in the family, and occasionally this formula is employed--"The master is dead, the master is dead." Even recently, writes Sir John Lubbock[10], an oak copse at Loch Siant, in the Isle of Skye, was held so sacred that no persons would venture to cut the smallest branch from it. The Wallachians, "have a superstition that every flower has a soul, and that the water-lily is the sinless and scentless flower of the lake, which blossoms at the gates of Paradise to judge the rest, and that she will inquire strictly what they have done with their odours."[11] It is noteworthy, also, that the Indian belief which describes the holes in trees as doors through which the special spirits of those trees pass, reappears in the German superstition that the holes in the oak are the pathways for elves;[12] and that various diseases may be cured by contact with these holes. Hence some trees are regarded with special veneration--particularly the lime and pine[13]--and persons of a superstitious turn of mind, "may often be seen carrying sickly children to a forest for the purpose of dragging them through such holes." This practice formerly prevailed in our own country, a well-knownillustration of which we may quote from White's "History of Selborne:"

"In a farmyard near the middle of the village," he writes, "stands at this day a row of pollard ashes, which by the seams and long cicatrices down their sides, manifestly show that in former times they had been cleft asunder. These trees, when young and flexible, were severed and held open by wedges, while ruptured children, stripped naked, were pushed through the apertures."[14]

In Somersetshire the superstition still lingers on, and in Cornwall the ceremony to be of value must be performed before sunrise; but the practice does not seem to have been confined to any special locality. It should also be added, as Mr. Conway[15] has pointed out, that in all Saxon countries in the Middle Ages a hole formed by two branches of a tree growing together was esteemed of highly efficacious value.

On the other hand, we must not confound the spiritual vitality ascribed to trees with the animistic conception of their being inhabited by certain spirits, although, as Mr. Tylor[16] remarks, it is difficult at times to distinguish between the two notions. Instances of these tree spirits lie thickly scattered throughout the folklore of most countries, survivals of which remain even amongst cultured races. It is interesting, moreover, to trace the same idea in Greek and Roman mythology. Thus Ovid[17] tells a beautiful story of Erisicthon's impious attack on the grove of Ceres, and it may be remembered how the Greek dryads and hamadryads had their life linked to a tree, and, "as this withers and dies, they themselves fall away and cease to be; any injury to bough or twig is felt as a wound, and a wholesale hewing down puts an end to them at once--a cry of anguish escapes them when the cruel axe comes near."

In "Apollonius Rhodius" we find one of these hamadryads imploring a woodman to spare a tree to which her existence is attached:

> "*Loud through the air resounds the woodman's stroke,*
> *When, lo! a voice breaks from the groaning oak,*
> *'Spare, spare my life! a trembling virgin spare!*
> *Oh, listen to the Hamadryad's prayer!*
> *No longer let that fearful axe resound;*
> *Preserve the tree to which my life is bound.*
> *See, from the bark my blood in torrents flows;*
> *I faint, I sink, I perish from your blows.'*"

Aubrey, referring to this old superstition, says:

"I cannot omit taking notice of the great misfortune in the family of the Earl of Winchelsea, who at Eastwell, in Kent, felled down a most curious grove of oaks, near his own noble seat, and gave the first blow with his own hands. Shortly after his countess died in her bed suddenly, and his eldest son, the Lord Maidstone, was killed at sea by a cannon bullet."

Modern European folklore still provides us with a curious variety of these spirit-haunted trees, and hence when the alder is hewn, "it bleeds, weeps, and begins to speak.[18]" An old tree in the Rugaard forest must not be felled for an elf dwells within, and another, on the Heinzenberg, near Zell, "uttered a complaint when the woodman cut it down, for in it was our Lady, whose chapel now stands upon the spot."[19]

An Austrian Märchen tells of a stately fir, in which there sits a fairy maiden waited on by dwarfs, rewarding the innocent and plaguing the guilty; and there is the German song of the maiden in the pine, whose bark the boy splits with a gold and silver horn. Stories again are circulated in Sweden, among the peasantry, of persons who by cutting a branch from a habitation tree have been struck with death. Such a tree was the "klinta tall" in Westmanland, under which a mermaid was said to dwell. To this tree might occasionally be seen snow-white cattle driven up from the neighbouring lake across the meadows. Another Swedish legend tells us how, when a man was on the point of cutting down a juniper tree in a wood, a voice was heard from the ground, saying, "friend, hew me not." But he gave another stroke, when to his horror blood gushed from the root[20]. Then there is the Danish tradition[21] relating to the lonely thorn, occasionally seen in a field, but which never grows larger. Trees of this kind are always bewitched, and care should be taken not to approach them in the night time, "as there comes a fiery wheel forth from the bush, which, if a person cannot escape from, will destroy him."

In modern Greece certain trees have their "stichios," a being which has been described as a spectre, a wandering soul, a vague phantom, sometimes invisible, at others assuming the most widely varied forms. It is further added that when a tree is "stichimonious" it is dangerous for a man, "to sleep beneath its shade, and the woodcutters employed to cut it down will lie upon the ground and hide themselves, motionless, and holding their breath, at the moment when it is about to fall, dreading lest the stichio at whose life the blow is aimed with each stroke of the axe, should avenge itself at the precise moment when it is dislodged."[22]

Turning to primitive ideas on this subject, Mr. Schoolcraft mentions an Indian tradition of a hollow tree, from the recesses of which there issued on a calm day a sound like the voice of a spirit. Hence it was considered to be the residence of some powerful spirit, and was accordingly deemed sacred. Among rude tribes trees of this kind are held sacred, it being forbidden to cut them. Some of the Siamese in the same way offer cakes and rice to the trees before felling them, and the Talein of Burmah will pray to the spirit of the tree before they begin to cut the tree down[23]. Likewise in the Australian bush demons whistle in the branches, and in a variety of other eccentric ways make their presence manifest--reminding us of Ariel's imprisonment:[24]

> *"Into a cloven pine; within which rift*
> *Imprison'd, thou didst painfully remain,*
> *A dozen years; ...*
> *... Where thou didst vent thy groans,*
> *As fast as mill-wheels strike."*

Similarly Miss Emerson, in her "Indian Myths" (1884, p. 134), quotes the story of "The Two Branches":

"One day there was a great noise in a tree under which Manabozho was taking a nap. It grew louder, and, at length exasperated, he leaped into the tree, caught the two branches whose war was the occasion of the din, and pulled them asunder. But with a spring on either hand, the two branches caught and pinioned Manabozho between them. Three days the god remained imprisoned, during which his outcries and lamentations were the subject of derision from every quarter--from the birds of the air, and from the animals of the woods and plains. To complete his sad case, the wolves ate the breakfast he had left beneath the tree. At length a good bear came to his rescue and released him, when the god disclosed his divine intuitions, for he returned home, and without delay beat his two wives."

Furthermore, we are told of the West Indian tribes, how, if any person going through a wood perceived a motion in the trees which he regarded as supernatural, frightened at the prodigy, he would address himself to that tree which shook the most. But such trees, however, did not condescend to converse, but ordered him to go to a boie, or priest, who would order him to sacrifice to their new deity.[25] From the same source we also learn[26] how among savage tribes those plants that produce great terrors, excitement, or a lethargic state, are supposed to contain a supernatural being. Hence in Peru, tobacco is known as the sacred herb, and from its invigorating effect superstitious veneration is paid to the weed. Many other plants have similar respect shown to them, and are used as talismans. Poisonous plants, again, from their deadly properties, have been held in the same repute;[27] and it is a very common practice among American Indians to hang a small bag containing poisonous herbs around the neck of a child, "as a talisman against diseases or attacks from wild beasts." It is commonly supposed that a child so protected is proof against every hurtful influence, from the fact of its being under the protection of the special spirits associated with the plant it wears.

Again, closely allied to beliefs of this kind is the notion of plants as the habitation of the departing soul, founded on the old doctrine of transmigration. Hence, referring to bygone times, we are told by

Empedocles that "there are two destinies for the souls of highest virtue -- to pass either into trees or into the bodies of lions."[28] Amongst the numerous illustrations of this mythological conception may be noticed the story told by Ovid,[29] who relates how Baucis and Philemon were rewarded in this manner for their charity to Zeus, who came a poor wanderer to their home. It appears that they not only lived to an extreme old age, but at the last were transformed into trees. Ovid, also, tells how the gods listened to the prayer of penitent Myrrha, and eventually turned her into a tree. Although, as Mr. Keary remarks, "she has lost understanding with her former shape, she still weeps, and the drops which fall from her bark (i.e., the myrrh) preserve the story of their mistress, so that she will be forgotten in no age to come."

The sisters of Phaëthon, bewailing his death on the shores of Eridanus, were changed into poplars. We may, too, compare the story of Daphne and Syrinx, who, when they could no longer elude the pursuit of Apollo and Pan, change themselves into a laurel and a reed. In modern times, Tasso and Spenser have given us graphic pictures based on this primitive phase of belief; and it may be remembered how Dante passed through that leafless wood, in the bark of every tree of which was imprisoned a suicide. In German folklore [30] the soul is supposed to take the form of a flower, as a lily or white rose; and according to a popular belief, one of these flowers appears on the chairs of those about to die. In the same way, from the grave of one unjustly executed white lilies are said to spring as a token of the person's innocence; and from that of a maiden, three lilies which no one save her lover must gather. The sex, moreover, it may be noted, is kept up even in this species of metempsychosis [31]. Thus, in a Servian folk-song, there grows out of the youth's body a green fir, out of the maiden's a red rose, which entwine together. Amongst further instances quoted by Grimm, we are told how, "a child carries home a bud which the angel had given him in the wood, when the rose blooms the child is dead. The Lay of Eunzifal makes a blackthorn shoot out of the bodies of slain heathens, a white flower by the heads of fallen Christians."

It is to this notion that Shakespeare alludes in "Hamlet," where Laertes wishes that violets may spring from the grave of Ophelia (v. I):

> "*Lay her in the earth,*
> *And from her fair and unpolluted flesh*
> *May violets spring.*"

A passage which is almost identical to one in the "Satires" of Persius (i. 39):

> "*E tumulo fortunataque favilla,*
> *Nascentur violae;*"

And an idea, too, which Tennyson seems to have borrowed:

> "*And from his ashes may be made,*
> *The violet of his native land.*"

Again, in the well-known story of "Tristram and Ysonde," a further reference occurs: "From his grave there grew an eglantine which twined about the statue, a marvel for all men to see; and though three times they cut it down, it grew again, and ever wound its arms about the image of the fair Ysonde[32]." In the Scottish ballad of "Fair Margaret and Sweet William," it is related--

"Out of her breast there sprang a rose,
And out of his a briar;
They grew till they grew unto the church top,
And there they tied in a true lovers' knot."

The same idea has prevailed to a large extent among savage races. Thus, some of the North-Western Indians believed that those who died a natural death would be compelled to dwell among the branches of tall trees. The Brazilians have a mythological character called Mani--a child who died and was buried in the house of her mother. Soon a plant sprang out of the grave, which grew, flourished, and bore fruit. This plant, says Mr. Dorman,[33] was the Mandioca, named from Mani, and Oca, house. By the Mexicans marigolds are known as "death-flowers," from a legend that they sprang up on the ground stained by, "the life-blood of those who fell victims to the love of gold and cruelty of the early Spanish settlers in America."

Among the Virginian tribes, too, red clover was supposed to have sprung from and to be coloured by the blood of the red men slain in battle, with which may be compared the well-known legend connected with the lily of the valley formerly current in St. Leonard's Forest, Sussex. It is reported to have sprung from the blood of St. Leonard, who once encountered a mighty worm, or "fire-drake," in the forest, engaging with it for three successive days. Eventually the saint came off victorious, but not without being seriously wounded; and wherever his blood was shed there sprang up lilies of the valley in profusion. After the battle of Towton a certain kind of wild rose is reported to have sprung up in the field where the Yorkists and Lancastrians fell, only there to be found:

"There still wild roses growing,
Frail tokens of the fray;
And the hedgerow green bears witness
Of Towton field that day." [33]

In fact, there are numerous legends of this kind; and it may be remembered how Defoe, in his "Tour through Great Britain," speaks of a certain camp called Barrow Hill, adding, "they say this was a Danish camp, and everything hereabout is attributed to the Danes, because of the neighbouring Daventry, which they suppose to be built by them. The road hereabouts too, being overgrown with Dane-weed, they fancy it sprung from the blood of Danes slain in battle, and that if cut upon a certain day in the year, it bleeds."[34]

Similarly, the red poppies which followed the ploughing of the field of Waterloo after the Duke of Wellington's victory were said to have sprung from the blood of the troops who fell during the engagement;[35] and the fruit of the mulberry, which was originally white, tradition tells us became empurpled through human blood, a notion which in Germany explains the colour of the heather. Once more, the mandrake, according to a superstition current in France and Germany, sprang up where the presence of a criminal had polluted the ground, and hence the old belief that it was generally found near a gallows. In Iceland it is commonly said that when innocent persons are put to death the sorb or mountain ash will spring up over their graves. Similar traditions cluster round numerous other plants, which, apart from being a revival of a very early primitive belief, form one of the prettiest chapters of our legendary tales. Although found under a variety of forms, and in some cases sadly corrupted from the dress they originally wore, yet in their main features they have not lost their individuality, but still retain their distinctive character.

In connection with the myths of plant life may be noticed that curious species of exotic plants, commonly known as "sensitive plants," and which have generally attracted considerable interest from their irritability when touched. Shelley has immortalised this curious freak of plant life in his charming poem, wherein he relates how,

> "*The sensitive plant was the earliest,*
> *Up-gathered into the bosom of rest;*
> *A sweet child weary of its delight,*
> *The feeblest and yet the favourite,*
> *Cradled within the embrace of night.*"

Who can wonder, on gazing at one of these wonderful plants, that primitive and uncultured tribes should have regarded such mysterious and inexplicable movements as indications of a distinct personal life.

Hence, as Darwin in his "Movements of Plants" remarks: "why a touch, slight pressure, or any other irritant, such as electricity, heat, or the absorption of animal matter, should modify the turgescence of the affected cells in such a manner as to cause movement, we do not know. But a touch acts in this manner so often, and on such widely distinct plants, that the tendency seems to be a very general one; and, if beneficial, it might be increased to any extent." If, therefore, one of the most eminent of recent scientific botanists confessed his inability to explain this strange peculiarity, we may excuse the savage if he regard it as another proof of a distinct personality in plant life. Thus, some years ago, a correspondent of the Botanical Register, describing the toad orchis (Megaclinium bufo), amusingly spoke as follows of its eccentric movements: "Let the reader imagine a green snake to be pressed flat like a dried flower, and then to have a road of toads, or some such speckled reptiles, drawn up along the middle in single file, their backs set up, their forelegs sprawling right and left, and their mouths wide open, with a large purple tongue wagging about convulsively, and a pretty considerable approach will be gained to an idea of this plant, which, if Pythagoras had but known of it, would have rendered all arguments about the transmigration of souls superfluous." But, apart from the vein of jocularity running through these remarks, such striking vegetable phenomena are scientifically as great a puzzle to the botanist as their movements are to the savage, the latter regarding them as the outward visible expression of a real inward personal existence.

But, to quote another kind of sympathy between human beings and certain plants, the Cingalese have a notion that the cocoa-nut plant withers away when beyond the reach of a human voice, and that the vervain and borage will only thrive near man's dwellings. Once more, the South Sea Islanders affirm that the scent is the spirit of a flower, and that the dead may be sustained by their fragrance, they cover their newly-made graves with many a sweet smelling blossom.

Footnotes:

1. See Tylor's "Primitive Culture," 1873, i. 474-5; also Dorman's "Primitive Superstitions," 1881, p. 294.
2. "Primitive Culture," i. 476-7.
3. Jones's "Ojibways," p. 104.
4. Marsden's "History of Sumatra," p. 301.
5. Mariner's "Tonga Islands," ii. 137.
6. St. John, "Far East," i. 187.
7. See Tylor's "Primitive Culture," i. 475.
8. Dorman's "Primitive Superstitions," p. 294; also Schoolcraft Indian Tribes."
9. See Thorpe's "Northern Mythology," iii. 61.
10. "Origin of Civilisation," 1870, p. 192. See Leslie Forbes' "Earl Races of Scotland," i. 171.
11. Folkard's "Plant-lore, Legends, and Lyrics," p. 463.
12. Conway's "Mystic Trees and Flowers," Blackwood's Magazine, 1870, p. 594.
13. Thorpe's "Northern Mythology," i. 212.
14. See Black's "Folk-Medicine."
15. "Mystic Trees and Flowers," p. 594.
16. "Primitive Culture," ii. 215.
17. Metam., viii. 742-839; also Grimm's Teut. Myth., 1883, ii. 953-4
18. Grimm's Teut. Myth., ii. 653.
19. Quoted in Tylor's "Primitive Culture," ii. 221.
20. Thorpe's "Northern Mythology," ii. 72, 73.
21. Ibid., p. 219.

22. "Superstitions of Modern Greece," by M. Le Baron d'Estournelles, in Nineteenth, Century, April 1882, pp. 394, 395.

23. See Dorman's "Primitive Superstitions," p. 288.

24. "The Tempest," act i. sc. 2.

25. Dorman's "Primitive Superstitions," p. 288.

26. Ibid., p. 295.

27. See chapter on Demonology.

28. See Keary's "Outlines of Primitive Belief," 1882, pp. 66-7.

29. Metam., viii. 714:--"Frondere Philemona Baucis, Baucida conspexit senior frondere Philemon. 'Valeque, O conjux!' dixere simul, simul abdita texit Ora frutex."

30. Thorpe's "Northern Mythology," i. 290, iii. 271.

31. Grimm's "Teut. Mythology," ii. 827.

32. Cox and Jones' "Popular Romances of the Middle Ages," 1880, p. 139

33. Smith's "Brazil," p. 586; "Primitive Superstitions," p. 293.

34. See Folkard's "Plant-lore, Legends, and Lyrics," p. 524.

35. See the Gardeners' Chronicle, 1875, p. 315.

36. According to another legend, forget-me-nots sprang up.

CHAPTER II

PRIMITIVE AND SAVAGE
NOTIONS RESPECTING PLANTS

The descent of the human race from a tree--however whimsical such a notion may seem--was a belief once received as sober fact, and even now-a-days can be traced amongst the traditions of many races.[1] This primitive idea of man's creation probably originated in the myth of Yggdrasil, the Tree of the Universe,[2] around which so much legendary lore has clustered, and for a full explanation of which an immense amount of learning has been expended, although the student of mythology has never yet been able to arrive at any definite solution on this deeply intricate subject. Without entering into the many theories proposed in connection with this mythical tree, it no doubt represented the life-giving forces of nature. It is generally supposed to have been an ash tree, but, as Mr. Conway[3] points out, "there is reason to think that through the confluence of traditions other sacred trees blended with it. Thus, while the ash bears no fruit, the Eddas describe the stars as the fruit of Yggdrasil."

Mr. Thorpe,[4] again, considers it identical with the "Robur Jovis," or sacred oak of Geismar, destroyed by Boniface, and the Irminsul of the Saxons, the Columna Universalis, "the terrestrial tree of offerings, an emblem of the whole world." At any rate the tree of the world, and the greatest of all trees, has long been identified in the northern mythology as the ash tree,[5] a fact which accounts for the weird character assigned to it amongst all the Teutonic and Scandinavian nations, frequent illustrations of which will occur in the present volume. Referring to the descent of man from the tree, we may quote the Edda, according to which all mankind are descended from the ash and the elm. The story runs that as Odhinn and his two brothers were journeying over the earth they discovered these two stocks "void of future," and breathed into them the power of life[6]:

> "Spirit they owned not,
> Sense they had not,
> Blood nor vigour,
> Nor colour fair.
> Spirit gave Odhinn,
> Thought gave Hoenir,
> Blood gave Lodr
> And colour fair."

This notion of tree-descent appears to have been popularly believed in olden days in Italy and Greece, illustrations of which occur in the literature of that period. Thus Virgil writes in the AEneid[7]:

> *"These woods were first the seat of sylvan powers,*
> *Of nymphs and fauns, and savage men who took*
> *Their birth from trunks of trees and stubborn oak."*

Romulus and Remus had been found under the famous Ficus Ruminalis, which seems to suggest a connection with a tree parentage. It is true, as Mr. Keary remarks,[8] that, "in the legend which we have received it is in this instance only a case of finding; but if we could go back to an earlier tradition, we should probably see that the relation between the mythical times and the tree had been more intimate."

Juvenal, it may be remembered, gives a further allusion to tree descent in his sixth satire[9]:

> *"For when the world was new, the race that broke*
> *Unfathered, from the soil or opening oak,*
> *Lived most unlike the men of later times."*

In Greece the oak as well as the ash was accounted a tree whence men had sprung; hence in the "Odyssey," the disguised hero is asked to state his pedigree, since he must necessarily have one; "for," says the interrogator, "belike you are not come of the oak told of in old times, nor of the rock."[10] Hesiod tells us how Jove made the third or brazen race out of ash trees, and Hesychius speaks of "the fruit of the ash the race of men." Phoroneus, again, according to the Grecian legend, was born of the ash, and we know, too, how among the Greeks certain families kept up the idea of a tree parentage; the Pelopidae having been said to be descended from the plane. Among the Persians the Achaemenidae had the same tradition respecting the origin of their house.[11] From the numerous instances illustrative of tree-descent, it is evident, as Mr. Keary points out, that, "there was once a fuller meaning than metaphor in the language which spoke of the roots and branches of a family, or in such expressions as the pathetic "Ah, woe, beloved shoot!" of Euripides."[12] Furthermore, as he adds, "Even when the literal notion of the descent from a tree had been lost sight of, the close connection between the prosperity of the tribe and the life of its fetish was often strictly held. The village tree of the German races was originally a tribal tree, with whose existence the life of the village was involved; and when we read of Christian saints and confessors, that they made a point of cutting down these half idols, we cannot wonder at the rage they called forth, nor that they often paid the penalty of their courage."

Similarly we can understand the veneration bestowed on the forest tree from associations of this kind. Consequently, as it has been remarked,[13] "At a time when rude beginnings were all that were of the builder's art, the human mind must have been roused to a higher devotion by the sight of lofty trees under an open sky, than it could feel inside the stunted structures reared by unskilled hands. When long afterwards the architecture peculiar to the Teutonic reached its perfection, did it not in its boldest creations still aim at reproducing the soaring trees of the forest? Would not the abortion of miserably carved or chiseled images lag far behind the form of the god which the youthful imagination of antiquity pictured to itself throned on the bowery summit of a sacred tree."

It has been asked whether the idea of the Yggdrasil and the tree-descent may not be connected with the "tree of life" of Genesis. Without, however, entering into a discussion on this complex point, it is worthy of note that in several of the primitive mythologies we find distinct counterparts of the biblical account of the tree of life; and it seems quite possible that these corrupt forms of the Mosaic history of creation may, in a measure, have suggested the conception of the world tree, and the descent of mankind from a tree. On this subject the late Mr. R.J. King[14] has given us the following interesting remarks in his paper on "Sacred Trees and Flowers":

"How far the religious systems of the great nations of antiquity were affected by the record of the creation and fall preserved in the opening chapters of Genesis, it is not, perhaps, possible to determine. There are certain points of resemblance which are at least remarkable, but which we may assign, if we please, either to independent tradition, or to a natural development of the earliest or primeval period. The trees of life and of knowledge are at once suggested by the mysterious sacred tree which appears in the most ancient sculptures and paintings of Egypt and Assyria, and in those of the remoter East. In the symbolism of these nations the sacred tree sometimes figures as a type of the universe, and represents the whole system of created things, but more frequently as a tree of life, by whose fruit the votaries of the gods (and in some cases the gods themselves) are nourished with divine strength, and are prepared for the joys of immortality. The most ancient types of this mystical tree of life are the date palm, the fig, and the pine or cedar."

By way of illustration, it may be noted that the ancient Egyptians had their legend of the "Tree of Life". It is mentioned in their sacred books that Osiris ordered the names of souls to be written on this tree of life, the fruit of which made those who ate it become as gods.[15] Among the most ancient traditions of the Hindoos is that of the tree of life--called Soma in Sanskrit--the juice of which imparted immortality; this marvellous tree being guarded by spirits. Coming down to later times, Virgil speaks of a sacred tree in a manner which Grimm[16] considers highly suggestive of the Yggdrasil:

"Jove's own tree,
High as his topmost boughs to heaven ascend,
So low his roots to hell's dominions tend."

As already mentioned, numerous legendary stories have become interwoven with the myth of the Yggdrasil, the following sacred one combining the idea of tree-descent. According to a trouvere of the thirteenth century,[17] "The tree of life was, a thousand years after the sin of the first man, transplanted from the Garden of Eden to the Garden of Abraham, and an angel came from heaven to tell the patriarch that upon this tree should hang the freedom of mankind. But first from the same tree of life Jesus should be born, and in the following wise. First was to be born a knight, Fanouel, who, through the scent merely of the flower of that living tree, should be engendered in the womb of a virgin; and this knight again, without knowing woman, should give birth to St. Anne, the mother of the Virgin Mary. Both these wonders fell out as they were foretold. A virgin bore Fanouel by smelling the tree; and Fanouel having once come unawares to that tree of life, and cut a fruit from it, wiped his knife against his thigh, in which he inflicted a slight wound, and thus let in some of the juice. Presently his thigh began to swell, and eventually St. Anne was born therefrom."

But turning to survivals of this form of animism among uncultured tribes, we may quote the Damaras, a South African race, with whom "a tree is supposed to be the universal progenitor, two of which divide the honour."[18] According to their creed, "In the beginning of things there was a tree, and out of this tree came Damaras, bushmen, oxen, and zebras. The Damaras lit a fire which frightened away the bushmen and the oxen, but the zebras remained."

Hence it is that bushmen and wild beasts live together in all sorts of inaccessible places, while the Damaras and oxen possess the land. The tree gave birth to everything else that lives. The natives of the Philippines, writes Mr. Marsden in his "History of Sumatra," have a curious tradition of tree-descent, and in accordance with their belief, "The world at first consisted only of sky and water, and between these two a glede; which, weary with flying about, and finding no place to rest, set the water at variance with the sky, which, in order to keep it in bounds, and that it should not get uppermost, loaded the water with a number of islands, in which the glede might settle and leave them at peace. Mankind, they said, sprang out of a large cane with two joints, that, floating about in the water, was at length thrown by the waves against the feet of the glede as it stood on shore, which opened it with its bill; the man came out of one joint, the woman out of the other. These were soon after married by the consent of their god, Bathala

Meycapal, which caused the first trembling of the earth,[19] and from thence are descended the different nations of the world."

Several interesting instances are given by Mr. Dorman, who tells us how the natives about Saginaw had a tradition of a boy who sprang from a tree within which was buried one of their tribe. The founders of the Miztec monarchy are said to be descended from two majestic trees that stood in a gorge of the mountain of Apoala. The Chiapanecas had a tradition that they sprang from the roots of a silk cotton tree; while the Zapotecas attributed their origin to trees, their cypresses and palms often receiving offerings of incense and other gifts. The Tamanaquas of South America have a tradition that the human race sprang from the fruits of the date palm after the Mexican age of water.[20]

Again, our English nursery fable of the parsley-bed, in which little strangers are discovered, is perhaps, "A remnant of a fuller tradition, like that of the woodpecker among the Romans, and that of the stork among our Continental kinsmen."[21] Both these birds having had a mystic celebrity, the former as the fire-singing bird and guardian genius of children, the latter as the baby-bringer.[22] In Saterland it is said "infants are fetched out of the cabbage," and in the Walloon part of Belgium they are supposed "to make their appearance in the parson's garden." Once more, a hollow tree overhanging a pool is known in many places, both in North and South Germany, as the first abode of unborn infants, variations of this primitive belief being found in different localities. Similar stories are very numerous, and under various forms are found in the legendary lore and folk-tales of most countries.

Footnotes:

1. See Keary's "Outlines of Primitive Belief," 1882, pp. 62-3.
2. See Grimm's "Teutonic Mythology," 1883, ii. 796-800; Quarterly Review, cxiv. 224; Thorpe's "Northern Mythology," i. 154; "Asgard and the Gods," edited by W. S. W. Anson, 1822, pp. 26, 27.
3. Fraser's Magazine, 1870, p. 597.
4. "Northern Mythology," i. 154-5.
5. See Max Miller's "Chips from a German Workshop."
6. See Keary's "Outlines of Primitive Belief," p. 64.
7. Book viii. p. 314.
8. "Outlines of Primitive Belief," p. 63.
9. Gifford.
10. Kelly's "Indo-European Folklore," p. 143.
11. Keary's "Outlines of Primitive Belief," p. 63; Fiske, "Myth and Myth Makers," 1873, pp. 64-5.

12. "Primitive Belief," p. 65.
13. Grimm's "Teutonic Mythology," i. 69.
14. Quarterly Review, 1863, cxiv. 214-15.
15. See Bunsen's "The Keys of St Peter," &c., 1867, p. 414.
16. "Teutonic Mythology."
17. Quoted by Mr. Keary from Leroux de Lincy, "Le Livre des égendes," p. 24.
18. Gallon's "South Africa," p. 188.
19. "Primitive Superstitions," p. 289.
20. Folkard's "Plant Lore," p. 311.
21. "Indo-European Folklore," p. 92.
22. Grimm's "Teutonic Mythology," ii. 672-3.

CHAPTER III

PLANT-WORSHIP

A form of religion which seems to have been widely-distributed amongst most races of mankind at a certain stage of their mental culture is plant-worship. Hence it holds a prominent place in the history of primitive belief, and at the present day prevails largely among rude and uncivilised races, survivals of which even linger on in our own country.

To trace back the history of plant-worship would necessitate an inquiry into the origin and development of the nature-worshipping phase of religious belief. Such a subject of research would introduce us to those pre-historic days when human intelligence had succeeded only in selecting for worship the grand and imposing objects of sight and sense. Hence, as Mr. Keary observes,[1] "The gods of the early world are the rock and the mountain, the tree, the river, the sea;" and Mr. Fergusson[2] is of opinion that tree-worship, in association with serpent-worship, must be reckoned as the primitive faith of mankind. In the previous chapter we have already pointed out how the animistic theory which invested the tree and grove with a conscious personality accounts for much of the worship and homage originally ascribed to them--identified, too, as they were later on, with the habitations of certain spirits. Whether viewed, therefore, in the light of past or modern inquiry, we find scattered throughout most countries various phases of plant-worship, a striking proof of its universality in days gone by.[3]

According to Mr. Fergusson, tree-worship has sprung from a perception of the beauty and utility of trees. "With all their poetry," he argues, "and all their usefulness, we can hardly feel astonished that the primitive races of mankind should have considered trees as the choicest gifts of the gods to men, and should have believed that their spirits still delighted to dwell among their branches, or spoke oracles through the rustling of their leaves." But Mr. McLennan[4] does not consider that this is conclusive, adding that such a view of the subject, "Does not at all meet the case of the shrubs, creepers, marsh-plants, and weeds that have been worshipped." He would rather connect it with Totemism,[5] urging that the primitive stages of religious evolution go to show that, "The ancient nations came, in pre-historic times, through the Totem stage, having animals, and plants, and the heavenly bodies conceived as animals, for gods before the anthropomorphic gods appeared;" While Mr. Herbert Spencer[6] again considers that, "Plant-worship, like the worship of idols and animals, is an aberrant species of ancestor-worship--a species somewhat more disguised externally, but having the same internal nature." Anyhow the subject is one concerning which the comparative mythologist has, at different times, drawn opposite theories; but of this there can be no doubt, that plant-worship was a primitive faith of mankind, a fact in connection with which we may quote Sir John Lubbock's words,[7] how, "By man in this stage of progress everything was regarded as having life, and being more or less a deity." Indeed, sacred rivers appear in the very earliest mythologies which have been recovered, and lingered among the last vestiges of heathenism long after the advent of a purer creed. As, too, it has been remarked,[8] "Either as direct objects of worship, or as forming the temple under whose solemn shadow other and remoter deities might be adored, there is no part of the world in which trees have not been regarded with especial reverence.

> 'In such green palaces the first kings reigned;
> Slept in their shade, and angels entertained.
> With such old counsellors they did advise,
> And by frequenting sacred shades grew wise.'

Even Paradise itself, says Evelyn, was but a kind of 'nemorous temple or sacred grove,' planted by God himself, and given to man tanquam primo sacerdoti; and he goes on to suggest that the groves which the patriarchs are recorded to have planted in different parts of Palestine may have been memorials of that first tree-shaded paradise from which Adam was expelled."

Briefly noticing the antecedent history of plant-worship, it would seem to have lain at the foundation of the old Celtic creed, although few records on this point have come down to us.[9] At any rate we have abundant evidence that this form of belief held a prominent place in the religion of these people, allusions to which are given by many of the early classical writers. Thus the very name of Druidism is a proof of the Celtic addiction to tree-worship, and De Brosses,[10] as a further evidence that this was so, would derive the word kirk, now softened into church, from quercus, an oak; that species having been peculiarly sacred. Similarly, in reviewing the old Teutonic beliefs, we come across the same references to tree-worship, in many respects displaying little or no distinction from that of the Celts. In explanation of this circumstance, Mr. Keary[11] suggests that, "The nature of the Teutonic beliefs would apply, with only some slight changes, to the creed of the predecessors of the Germans in Northern and Western Europe. Undoubtedly, in prehistoric days, the Germans and Celts merged so much one into the other that their histories cannot well be distinguished."

Mr. Fergusson in his elaborate researches has traced many indications of tree-adoration in Germany, noticing their continuance in the Christian period, as proved by Grimm, whose opinion is that, "the festal universal religion of the people had its abode in woods," while the Christmas tree of present German celebration in all families is "almost undoubtedly a remnant of the tree-worship of their ancestors."

According to Mr. Fergusson, one of the last and best-known examples of the veneration of groves and trees by the Germans after their conversion to Christianity, is that of the "Stock am Eisen" in Vienna, "The sacred tree into which every apprentice, down to recent times, before setting out on his "Wanderjahre", drove a nail for luck. It now stands in the centre of that great capital, the last remaining vestige of the sacred grove, round which the city has grown up, and in sight of the proud cathedral, which has superseded and replaced its more venerable shade."

Equally undoubted is the evidence of tree-worship in Greece — particular trees having been sacred to many of the gods. Thus we have the oak tree or beech of Jupiter, the laurel of Apollo, the vine of Bacchus. The olive is the well-known tree of Minerva. The myrtle was sacred to Aphrodite, and the apple of the Hesperides belonged to Juno.[12] As a writer too in the Edinburgh Review[13] remarks, "The oak grove at Dodona is sufficiently evident to all classic readers to need no detailed mention of its oracles, or its highly sacred character. The sacrifice of Agamemnon in Aulis, as told in the opening of the 'Iliad,' connects the tree and serpent worship together, and the wood of the sacred plane tree under which the sacrifice was made was preserved in the temple of Diana as a holy relic so late, according to Pausanias, as the second century of the Christian era." The same writer further adds that in Italy traces of tree-worship, if not so distinct and prominent as in Greece, are nevertheless existent. Romulus, for instance, is described as hanging the arms and weapons of Acron, King of Cenina, upon an oak tree held sacred by the people, which became the site of the famous temple of Jupiter.

Then, again, turning to Bible history,[14] the denunciations of tree-worship are very frequent and minute, not only in connection with the worship of Baal, but as mentioned in 2 Kings ix.: "And they (the children of Israel) set themselves up images and groves in every high hill, and under every green tree." These acts, it has been remarked, "may be attributable more to heretical idolatrous practices into which the Jews had temporarily fallen in imitation of the heathen around them, but at the same time they furnish ample proof of the existence of tree and grove worship by the heathen nations of Syria as one of their most solemn rites." But, from the period of King Hezekiah down to the Christian era, Mr. Fergusson finds no traces of tree-worship in Judea. In Assyria tree-worship was a common form of idolatrous veneration, as proved by Lord Aberdeen's black-stone, and many of the plates in the works of Layard and Botta.[15] Turning to India, tree-worship probably has always belonged to Aryan Hinduism, and as tree-worship did not belong to the aboriginal races of India, and was not adopted from them, "it must have formed part of the pantheistic worship of the Vedic system which endowed all created things with a spirit and life--a doctrine which modern Hinduism largely extended[16]."

Thus when food is cooked, an oblation is made by the Hindu to trees, with an appropriate invocation before the food is eaten. The Bo tree is extensively worshipped in India, and the Toolsee plant (Basil) is held sacred to all gods--no oblation being considered sacred without its leaves. Certain of the Chittagong hill tribes worship the bamboo,[17] and Sir John Lubbock, quoting from Thompson's "Travels in the Himalaya," tells us that in the Simla hills the Cupressus toridosa is regarded as a sacred tree. Further instances might be enumerated, so general is this form of religious belief. In an interesting and valuable paper by a Bengal civilian--intimately acquainted with the country and people[18]--the writer says:--"The contrast between the acknowledged hatred of trees as a rule by the Bygas,[19] and their deep veneration for certain others in particular, is very curious. I have seen the hillsides swept clear of forests for miles with but here and there a solitary tree left standing. These remain now the objects of the deepest veneration. So far from being injured they are carefully preserved, and receive offerings of food, clothes, and flowers from the passing Bygas, who firmly believe that tree to be the home of a spirit." To give another illustration[20], it appears that in Beerbhoom once a year the whole capital repairs to a shrine in the jungle, and makes simple offerings to a ghost who dwells in the Bela tree. The shrine consists of three trees--a Bela tree on the left, in which the ghost resides, and which is marked at the foot with blood; in the middle is a Kachmula tree, and on the right a Saura tree. In spite of the trees being at least seventy years old, the common people claim the greatest antiquity for the shrine, and tradition says that the three trees that now mark the spot neither grow thicker nor increase in height, but remain the same for ever.

A few years ago Dr. George Birwood contributed to the Athenaeum some interesting remarks on Persian flower-worship. Speaking of the Victoria Gardens at Bombay, he says:--"A true Persian in flowing robe of blue, and on his head his sheep-skin hat--black, glossy, curled, the fleece of Kar-Kal--would saunter in, and stand and meditate over every flower he saw, and always as if half in vision. And when the vision was fulfilled, and the ideal flower he was seeking found, he would spread his mat and sit before it until the setting of the sun, and then pray before it, and fold up his mat again and go home. And the next night, and night after night, until that particular flower faded away, he would return to it, and bring his friends in ever-increasing troops to it, and sit and play the guitar or lute before it, and they would all together pray there, and after prayer still sit before it sipping sherbet, and talking the most hilarious and shocking scandal, late into the moonlight; and so again and again every evening until the flower died. Sometimes, by way of a grand finale, the whole company would suddenly rise before the flower and serenade it, together with an ode from Hafiz, and depart." Tree-worship too has been more or less prevalent among the American Indians, abundant illustrations of which have been given by travelers at different periods. In many cases a striking similarity is noticeable, showing a common origin, a circumstance which is important to the student of comparative mythology when tracing the distribution of religious beliefs. The Dacotahs worship the medicine-wood, so called from a belief that it was a genius which protected or punished them according to their merits or demerits.[21] Darwin[22] mentions a tree near Siena de la Ventana to which the Indians paid homage as the altar of Walleechu; offerings of cigars, bread, and meat having been suspended upon it by threads. The tree was surrounded by bleached bones of horses that had been sacrificed. Mr. Tylor[23] speaks of an ancient cypress existing in Mexico, which he thus describes:--"All over its branches were fastened votive offerings of the Indians, hundreds of locks of coarse black hair, teeth, bits of coloured cloth, rags, and morsels of ribbon. The tree was many centuries old, and had probably had some mysterious influence ascribed to it, and been decorated with such simple offerings long before the discovery of America."

Once more, the Calchaquis of Brazil[24] have been in the habit of worshipping certain trees which were frequently decorated by the Indians with feathers; and Charlevoix narrates another interesting instance of tree-worship:--"Formerly the Indians in the neighbourhood of Acadia had in their country, near the sea-shore, a tree extremely ancient, of which they relate many wonders, and which was always laden with offerings.

After the sea had laid open its whole root, it then supported itself a long time almost in the air against the violence of the winds and waves, which confirmed those Indians in the notion that the tree must be the abode of some powerful spirit; nor was its fall even capable of undeceiving them, so that as long as the smallest part of its branches appeared above the water, they paid it the same honours as whilst it stood."

In North America, according to Franklin,[25] the Crees used to hang strips of buffalo flesh and pieces of cloth on their sacred tree; and in Nicaragua maize and beans were worshipped. By the natives of Carolina the tea-plant was formerly held in veneration above all other plants, and indeed similar phases of superstition are very numerous. Traces of tree-worship occur in Africa, and Sir John Lubbock [26] mentions the sacred groves of the Marghi--a dense part of the forest surrounded with a ditch--where in the most luxuriant and widest spreading tree their god, Zumbri, is worshipped. In his valuable work on Ceylon, Sir J. Emerson Tennent gives some interesting details about the consecration of trees to different demons to insure their safety, and of the ceremonies performed by the kattadias or devil-priests. It appears that whenever the assistance of a devil-dancer is required in extreme cases of sickness, various formalities are observed after the following fashion. An altar is erected, profusely adorned with garlands and flowers, within sight of the dying man, who is ordered to touch and dedicate to the evil spirit the wild flowers, rice, and flesh laid upon it.

Traces of plant-worship are still found in Europe. Before sunrise on Good Friday the Bohemians are in the habit of going into their gardens, and after falling on their knees before a tree, to say, "I pray, O green tree, that God may make thee good," a formula which Mr. Ralston[27] considers has probably been altered under the influence of Christianity "from a direct prayer to the tree to a prayer for it." At night they run about the garden exclaiming, "Bud, O trees, bud! or I will flog you." On the following day they shake the trees, and clank their keys, while the church bells are ringing, under the impression that the more noise they make the more fruit will they get. Traces, too, of tree-worship, adds Mr. Ralston,[28] may be found in the song which the Russian girls sing as they go out into the woods to fetch the birch tree at Whitsuntide, and to gather flowers for wreaths and garlands:

"Rejoice not, oaks;
Rejoice not, green oaks.
Not to you go the maidens;
Not to you do they bring pies,
Cakes, omelettes.
So, so, Semik and Troitsa [Trinity]!
Rejoice, birch trees, rejoice, green ones!
To you go the maidens!
To you they bring pies,
Cakes, omelettes."

The eatables here mentioned probably refer to the sacrifices offered in olden days to the birch--the tree of the spring. With this practice we may compare one long observed in our own country, and known as "wassailing." At certain seasons it has long been customary in Devonshire for the farmer, on the eve of Twelfth-day, to go into the orchard after supper with a large milk pail of cider with roasted apples pressed into it. Out of this each person in the company takes what is called a clome--i.e., earthenware cup--full of liquor, and standing under the more fruitful apple trees, address them in these words:

"Health to thee, good apple tree,
Well to bear pocket fulls, hat fulls,
Peck fulls, bushel bag fulls."

After the formula has been repeated, the contents of the cup are thrown at the trees.[29] There are numerous allusions to this form of tree-worship in the literature of the past; and Tusser, among his many pieces of advice to the husbandman, has not omitted to remind him that he should,

"Wassail the trees, that they may bear
You many a plum and many a pear;
For more or less fruit they will bring,
As you do them wassailing."

Survivals of this kind show how tenaciously old superstitious rites struggle for existence even when they have ceased to be recognised as worthy of belief.

Footnotes:

1. "Outlines of Primitive Belief," 1882, p. 54.
2. "Tree and Serpent Worship."
3. See Sir John Lubbock's "Origin of Civilisation," pp. 192-8.
4. Fortnightly Review, "The Worship of Animals and Plants," 1870,vii. 213.
5. Ibid., 1869, vi. 408.
6. "Principles of Sociology," 1885, i. p. 359.
7. "The Origin of Civilisation and Primitive Condition of Man."
8. Quarterly Review, cxiv. 212.
9. Keary's "Primitive Brlief," pp. 332-3; Edinburgh Review, cxxx.488-9.
10. "Du Culte des Dieux Fetiches," p. 169.
11. "Primitive Belief," pp. 332-3.
12. Fergusson's "Tree and Serpent Worship," p. 16.
13. cxxx. 492; see Tacitus' "Germania," ix.
14. See Edinburgh Review, cxxx. 490-1.
15. Edinburgh Review, cxxx. 491.
16. Mr. Fergusson's "Tree and Serpent Worship." See Edinburgh Review, cxxx. 498.
17. See Lewin's "Hill Tracts of Chittagong," p. 10.
18. Cornhill Magazine, November 1872, p. 598.
19. An important tribe in Central India.
20. See Sherring's "Sacred City of the Hindus," 1868, p. 89.
21. Dorman's "Primitive Superstitions," p. 291.
22. See "Researches in Geology and Natural History," p. 79.
23. "Anahuac," 215, 265.
24. Dorman's "Primitive Superstitions." p. 292.
25. "Journeys to the Polar Sea." i. 221.
26. "The Origin of Civilisation."
27. "Songs of the Russian People." p. 219.
28. Ibid., p. 238.
29. See my "British Popular Customs." p. 21.

CHAPTER IV

LIGHTNING PLANTS

Amongst the legends of the ancient world few subjects occupy a more prominent place than lightning, associated as it is with those myths of the origin of fire which are of such wide distribution.[1] In examining these survivals of primitive culture we are confronted with some of the most elaborate problems of primeval philosophy, many of which are not only highly complicated, but have given rise to various conjectures. Thus, although it is easy to understand the reasons which led our ancestors, in their childlike ignorance, to speak of the lightning as a worm, serpent, trident, arrow, or forked wand, yet the contrary is the case when we inquire why it was occasionally symbolised as a flower or leaf, or when, as Mr. Fiske[2] remarks, "we seek to ascertain why certain trees, such as the ash, hazel, white thorn, and mistletoe, were supposed to be in a certain sense embodiments of it."

Indeed, however satisfactory our explanations may apparently seem, in many cases they can only be regarded as ingenious theories based on the most probable theories which the science of comparative folklore may have suggested. In analysing, too, the evidence for determining the possible association of ideas which induced our primitive forefathers to form those mythical conceptions that we find embodied in the folk-tales of most races, it is necessary to unravel from the relics of the past the one common notion that underlies them. Respecting the origin of fire, for instance, the leading idea--as handed down to us in myths of this kind-- would make us believe that it was originally stolen. Stories which point to this conclusion are not limited to any one country, but are shared by races widely remote from one another. This circumstance is important, as helping to explain the relation of particular plants to lightning, and accounts for the superstitious reverence so frequently paid to them by most Aryan tribes. Hence, the way by which the Veda argues the existence of the palasa--a mystic tree with the Hindus — is founded on the following tradition:--The demons had stolen the heavenly soma, or drink of the gods, and cellared it in some mythical rock or cloud. When the thirsty deities were pining for their much-prized liquor, the falcon undertook to restore it to them, although he succeeded at the cost of a claw and a plume, of which he was deprived by the graze of an arrow shot by one of the demons. Both fell to the earth and took root; the claw becoming a species of thorn, which Dr. Kuhn identifies as the "Mimosa catechu," and the feather a "palasa tree," which has a red sap and scarlet blossoms. With such a divine origin—for the falcon was nothing less than a lightning god[3]--the trees naturally were incorporations,[4] "not only of the heavenly fire, but also of the soma, with which the claw and feather were impregnated."

It is not surprising, therefore, that extraordinary virtues were ascribed to these lightning plants, qualities which, in no small degree, distinguish their representatives at the present day. Thus we are told how in India the mimosa is known as the imperial tree on account of its remarkable properties, being credited as an efficacious charm against all sorts of malignant influences, such as the evil eye. Not unlike in colour to the blossom of the Indian palasa are the red berries of the rowan or mountain-ash (Pyrus aucuparia), a tree which has acquired European renown from the Aryan tradition of its being an embodiment of the lightning from which it was sprung. It has acquired, therefore, a mystic character, evidences of which are numerously represented throughout Europe, where its leaves are reverenced as being the most potent talisman against the darker powers. At the present day we still find the Highland milkmaid carrying with her a rowan-cross against unforeseen danger, just as in many a German village twigs are put over stables to keep out witches. Illustrations of this kind support its widespread reputation for supernatural virtues, besides showing how closely allied is much of the folklore of our own with that of continental countries. At the same time, we feel inclined to agree with Mr. Farrer that the red berries of the mountain-ash probably singled it out from among trees for worship long before our ancestors had arrived at any idea of abstract divinities. The beauty of its berries, added to their brilliant red colour, would naturally excite feelings of admiration and awe, and hence it would in process of time become invested with a sacred significance. It must be remembered, too, that all over the world there is a regard for things red, this colour having been once held sacred to Thor, and Grimm suggests that it was on this account the robin acquired its sacred character. Similarly, the Highland women tie a piece of red worsted thread round their cows' tails previous to turning them out to grass for the first time in spring, for, in accordance with an old adage:

"Rowan-ash, and red thread,
Keep the devils from their speed."

In the same way the mothers in Esthonia put some red thread in their babies' cradles as a preservative against danger, and in China something red is tied round children's wrists as a safeguard against evil spirits. By the aid of comparative folklore it is interesting, as in this case, to trace the same notion in different countries, although it is by no means possible to account for such undesigned resemblance. The common ash (Fraxinus excelsior), too, is a lightning plant, and, according to an old couplet:

"Avoid an ash,
It counts the flash."

Another tree held sacred to Thor was the hazel (Corylus avellana), which, like the mountain-ash, was considered an actual embodiment of the lightning. Indeed, "so deep was the faith of the people in the relation of this tree to the thunder god," says Mr. Conway,[5] "that the Catholics adopted and sanctioned it by a legend one may hear in Bavaria, that on their flight into Egypt the Holy Family took refuge under it from a storm."

Its supposed immunity from all damage by lightning has long caused special reverence to be attached to it, and given rise to sundry superstitious usages. Thus, in Germany, a twig is cut by the farm-labourer, in spring, and on the first thunderstorm a cross is made with it over every heap of grain, whereby, it is supposed, the corn will remain good for many years. Occasionally, too, one may see hazel twigs placed in the window frames during a heavy shower, and the Tyroleans regard it as an excellent lightning conductor. As a promoter of fruitfulness it has long been held in high repute--a character which it probably derived from its mythic associations--and hence the important part it plays in love divinations. According to a Bohemian belief, the presence of a large number of hazel-nuts betokens the birth of many illegitimate children; and in the Black Forest it is customary for the leader of a marriage procession to carry a hazel wand. For the same reason, in many parts of Germany, a few nuts are mingled with the seed corn to insure its being prolific. But leaving the hazel with its host of superstitions, we may notice the white-thorn, which according to Aryan tradition was also originally sprung from the lightning. Hence it has acquired a wide reverence, and been invested with supernatural properties. Like, too, the hazel, it was associated with marriage rites. Thus the Grecian bride was and is still decked with its blossoms, whereas its wood formed the torch which lighted the Roman bridal couple to their nuptial chamber on the wedding day. It is evident, therefore, that the white-thorn was considered a sacred tree long before Christian tradition identified it as forming the Crown of Thorns; a medieval belief which further enhanced the sanctity attached to it. It is not surprising, therefore, that the Irish consider it unlucky to cut down this holy tree, especially as it is said to be under the protection of the fairies, who resent any injury done to it. A legend current in county Donegal, for instance, tells us how a fairy had tried to steal one Joe M'Donough's baby, but the poor mother argued that she had never affronted the fairy tribe to her knowledge. The only cause she could assign was that Joe, "had helped Mr. Todd's gardener to cut down the old hawthorn tree on the lawn; and there's them that says that's a very bad thing to do;" adding how she "fleeched him not to touch it, but the master he offered him six shillings if he'd help in the job, for the other men refused." The same belief prevails in Brittany, where it is also "held unsafe to gather even a leaf from certain old and solitary thorns, which grow in sheltered hollows of the moorland, and are the fairies' trysting-places."[6]

Then there is the mistletoe, which, like the hazel and the white-thorn, was also supposed to be the embodiment of lightning; and in consequence of its mythical character held an exalted place in the botanical world. As a lightning-plant, we seem to have the key to its symbolical nature, in the circumstance that its branch is forked. On the same principle, it is worthy of note, as Mr. Fiske remarks [7] that, "the Hindu commentators of the Veda certainly lay great stress on the fact that the palasa is trident-leaved." We have already pointed out, too, how the red colour of a flower, as in the case of the berries of the mountain-ash, was apparently sufficient to determine the association of ideas. The Swiss name for mistletoe, donnerbesen, "thunder besom," illustrates its divine origin, on account of which it was supposed to protect the homestead from fire, and hence in Sweden it has long been suspended in farm-houses, like the mountain-ash in Scotland. But its virtues are by no means limited, for like all lightning-plants its potency is displayed in a variety of ways, its healing properties having from a remote period been in the highest repute. For purposes also of sorcery it has been reckoned of considerable importance, and as a preventive of nightmare and other night scares it is still in favour on the Continent.

One reason which no doubt has obtained for it a marked degree of honour is its parasitical manner of growth, which was in primitive times ascribed to the intervention of the gods. According to one of its traditionary origins, its seed was said to be deposited on certain trees by birds, the messengers of the gods, if not the gods themselves in disguise, by which this plant established itself in the branch of a tree. The mode of procedure, say the old botanists, was through the "mistletoe thrush." This bird, it was asserted, by feeding on the berries, surrounded its beak with the viscid mucus they contain, to rid itself of which it rubbed its beak, in the course of flying, against the branches of trees, and thereby inserted the seed which gave birth to the new plant. When the mistletoe was found growing on the oak, its presence was attributed specially to the gods, and as such was treated with the deepest reverence. It was not, too, by accident that the oak was selected, as this tree was honoured by Aryan tradition with being of lightning origin. Hence when the mistletoe was found on its branches, the occurrence was considered as deeply significant, and all the more so as its existence in such a locality was held to be very rare[8].

Speaking of the oak, it may be noted, that as sacred to Thor, it was under his immediate protection, and hence it was considered an act of sacrilege to mutilate it in ever so small a degree. Indeed, "it was a law of the Ostrogoths that anybody might hew down what trees he pleased in the common wood, except oaks and hazels; those trees had peace, i.e., they were not to be felled[9]." That profanity of this kind was not treated with immunity was formerly fully believed, an illustration of which is given us by Aubrey,[10] who says that, "to cut oakwood is unfortunate. There was at Norwood one oak that had mistletoe, a timber tree, which was felled about 1657. Some persons cut this mistletoe for some apothecaries in London, and sold them a quantity for ten shillings each time, and left only one branch remaining for more to sprout out. One fell lame shortly after; soon after each of the others lost an eye, and he that felled the tree, though warned of these misfortunes of the other men, would, notwithstanding, adventure to do it, and shortly afterwards broke his leg; as if the Hamadryads had resolved to take an ample revenge for the injury done to their venerable and sacred oak." We can understand, then, how the custom originated of planting the oak on the boundaries of lands, a survival of which still remains in the so-called gospel oaks of many of our English parishes. With Thor's tree thus standing our forefathers felt a sense of security which materially added to the peace and comfort of their daily life.

But its sacred attributes were not limited to this country, many a legend on the Continent testifying to the safety afforded by its sheltering branches. Indeed, so great are its virtues that, according to a Westphalian tradition, the Wandering Jew can only rest where he shall happen to find two oaks growing in the form of a cross. A further proof of its exalted character may be gathered from the fact that around its roots Scandinavian mythology has gathered fairyland, and hence in Germany the holes in its trunk are the pathways for elves. But the connection between lightning and plants extends over a wide area, and Germany is rich in legends relative to this species of folklore. Thus there is the magic springwort, around which have clustered so many curious lightning myths and talismanic properties. By reason of its celestial origin this much-coveted plant, when buried in the ground at the summit of a mountain, has the reputation of drawing down the lightning and dividing the storm. It is difficult, however, to procure, especially as there is no certainty as to the exact species of plants to which it belongs, although Grimm identifies it with the Euphorbia lathyris. At any rate, it is chiefly procurable by the woodpecker—a lightning-bearer; and to secure this much-prized treasure, its nest must be stopped up, access to which it will quickly gain by touching it with the springwort. But if one have in readiness a pan of water, a fire, or a red cloth, the bird will let the plant fall, which otherwise it would be a difficult work to obtain, "the notion, no doubt, being that the bird must return the mystic plant to the element from which it springs, that being either the water of the clouds or the lightning fire enclosed therein."[11]

Professor Gubernatis, referring to the symbolical nature of this tradition, remarks that, "this herb may be the moon itself, which opens the hiding-place of the night, or the thunderbolt, which opens the hiding-places of the cloud." According to the Swiss version of the story it is the hoopoe that brings the spring-wort, a bird also endowed with mystic virtues,[12] while in Iceland, Normandy, and ancient Greece it is an eagle, a swallow, or an ostrich. Analogous to the talismanic properties of the springwort are those of the famous luck or key-flower of German folklore, by the discovery of which the fortunate possessor effects an entrance into otherwise inaccessible fairy haunts, where unlimited treasures are offered for his acceptance. There then, again, the luck-flower is no doubt intended to denote the lightning, which reveals strange treasures, giving water to the parched and thirsty land, and, as Mr. Fiske remarks, "making plain what is doing under cover of darkness."[13]

The lightning-flash, too, which now and then, as a lesson of warning, instantly strikes dead those who either rashly or presumptuously essay to enter its awe-inspiring portals, is exemplified in another version of the same legend. A shepherd, while leading his flock over the Ilsentein, pauses to rest, but immediately the mountain opens by reason of the springwort or luck-flower in the staff on which he leans. Within the cavern a white lady appears, who invites him to accept as much of her wealth as he choses. Thereupon he fills his pockets, and hastening to quit her mysterious domains, he heeds not her enigmatical warning, "Forget not the best," the result being that as he passes through the door he is severed in twain amidst the crashing of thunder. Stories of this kind, howevr, are the exception, legendary lore generally regarding the lightning as a benefactor rather than a destroyer. "The lightning-flash," to quote Mr. Baring-Gould's words, "reaches the barren, dead, and thirsty land; forth gush the waters of heaven, and the parched vegetation bursts once more into the vigour of life restored after suspended animation."

That this is the case we have ample proof in the myths relating to plants, in many of which the life-giving properties of the lightning are clearly depicted. Hence, also, the extraordinary healing properties which are ascribed to the various lightning plants. Ash rods, for instance, are still used in many parts of England for the cure of diseased sheep, cows, and horses, and in Cornwall, as a remedy for hernia, children are passed through holes in ash trees. The mistletoe has the reputation of being an antidote for poisons and a specific against epilepsy. Culpepper speaks of it as a sure panacea for apoplexy, palsy, and falling sickness, a belief current in Sweden, where finger rings are made of its wood. An old-fashioned charm for the bite of an adder was to place a cross formed of hazel-wood on the wound, and the burning of a thorn-bush has long been considered a sure preventive of mildew in wheat. Without multiplying further illustrations, there can be no doubt that the therapeutic virtues of these so-called lightning plants may be traced to, in very many cases, their mythical origin. It is not surprising too that plants of this stamp should have been extensively used as charms against the influences of occult powers, their symbolical nature investing them with a potency such as was possessed by no ordinary plant.

Footnotes:

1. See an article on "Myths of the Fire Stealer," Saturday Review, June 2, 1883, p. 689; Tylor's "Primitive Culture." 2. "Myths and Myth Makers," p. 55.
3. See Keary's "Outlines of Primitive Belief," 1882, p. 98.
4. "Indo-European Tradition and Folklore," p. 159.
5. "Mystic Trees and Shrubs," Fraser's Magazine, Nov. 1870, p. 599.
6. "Sacred Trees and Flowers," Quarterly Review, July 1863, pp. 231, 232.
7. "Myths and Myth Makers," p. 55.
8. See "Flower Lore," pp. 38, 39.
9. Kelly's "Indo-European Folklore," p. 179.
10. "Natural History and Antiquities of Surrey," ii. 34.
11. Kelly's "Indo-European Folklore," p. 176; Grimm's "Teutonic Mythology," 1884, chap, xxxii.; Gubernatis' "Zoological Mythology," ii. 266-7. See Albertus Magnus, "De Mirab. Mundi," 1601, p. 225.
12. Gubernatis' "Zoological Mythology," ii. 230.
13. "Myths and Mythmakers," p. 58. See Baring-Gould's "Curious Myths of the Middle Ages," 1877, pp. 386-416.
14. Folkard's "Plant-lore Legends and Lyrics," p. 460. 15. See Kelly's "Indo-European Folklore," pp. 47-48.

CHAPTER V

PLANTS IN WITCHCRAFT

The vast proportions which the great witchcraft movement assumed in bygone years explains the magic properties which we find ascribed to so many plants in most countries. In the nefarious trade carried on by the representatives of this cruel system of sorcery certain plants were largely employed for working marvels, hence the mystic character which they have ever since retained. It was necessary, however, that these should be plucked at certain phases of the moon or seasons of the year, or from some spot where the sun was supposed not to have shone on it.[1] Hence Shakespeare makes one of his witches speak of "root of hemlock digg'd i' the dark," and of "slips of yew sliver'd in the moon's eclipse," a practice which was long kept up. The plants, too, which formed the witches' pharmacopoeia, were generally selected either from their legendary associations or by reason of their poisonous and soporific qualities. Thus, two of those most frequently used as ingredients in the mystic cauldron were the vervain and the rue, these plants having been specially credited with supernatural virtues. The former probably derived its notoriety from the fact of its being sacred to Thor, an honour which marked it out, like other lightning plants, as peculiarly adapted for occult uses. It was, moreover, among the sacred plants of the Druids, and was only gathered by them, "when the dog-star arose, from unsunned spots." At the same time, it is noteworthy that many of the plants which were in repute with witches for working their marvels were reckoned as counter-charms, a fact which is not surprising, as materials used by wizards and others for magical purposes have generally been regarded as equally efficacious if employed against their charms and spells.[2] Although vervain, therefore, as the "enchanters' plant," was gathered by witches to do mischief in their incantations, yet, as Aubrey says, it "hinders witches from their will," a circumstance to which Drayton further refers when he speaks of the vervain as "'gainst witchcraft much avayling." Rue, likewise, which entered so largely into magic rites, was once much in request as an antidote against such practices; and nowadays, when worn on the person in conjunction with agrimony, maiden-hair, broom-straw, and ground ivy, it is said in the Tyrol to confer fine vision, and to point out the presence of witches.

It is still an undecided question as to why rue should out of all other plants have gained its widespread reputation with witches, but M. Maury supposes that it was on account of its being a narcotic and causing hallucinations. At any rate, it seems to have acquired at an early period in this country a superstitious reverence, for, as Mr. Conway says,[3] "We find the missionaries sprinkling holy water from brushes made of it, whence it was called 'herb of grace'."

Respecting the rendezvous of witches, it may be noted that they very frequently resorted to hills and mountains, their meetings taking place "on the mead, on the oak sward, under the lime, under the oak, at the pear tree." Thus the fairy rings which are often to be met with on the Sussex downs are known as hag-tracks,[4] from the belief that "they are caused by hags and witches, who dance there at midnight."[5] Their love for sequestered and romantic localities is widely illustrated on the Continent, instances of which have been collected together by Grimm, who remarks how "the fame of particular witch mountains extends over wide kingdoms." According to a tradition current in Friesland,[6] no woman is to be found at home on a Friday, because on that day they hold their meetings and have dances on a barren heath. Occasionally, too, they show a strong predilection for certain trees, to approach which as night-time draws near is considered highly dangerous. The Judas tree (Cercis siliquastrum) was one of their favourite retreats, perhaps on account of its traditionary association with the apostle. The Neapolitan witches held their tryst under a walnut tree near Benevento,[7] and at Bologna the peasantry tell how these evil workers hold a midnight meeting beneath the walnut trees on St. John's Eve. The elder tree is another haunt under whose branches witches are fond of lurking, and on this account caution must be taken not to tamper with it after dark.[8] Again, in the Netherlands, experienced shepherds are careful not to let their flocks feed after sunset, for there are wicked elves that prepare poison in certain plants--nightwort being one of these. Nor does any man dare to sleep in a meadow or pasture after sunset, for, as the shepherds say, he would have everything to fear. A Tyrolese legend[9] relates how a boy who had climbed a tree, "overlooked the ghastly doings of certain witches beneath its boughs. They tore in pieces the corpse of a woman, and threw the portions in the air. The boy caught one, and kept it by him; but the witches, on counting the pieces, found that one was missing, and so replaced it by a scrap of alderwood, when instantly the dead came to life again."

Similarly, also, they had their favourite flowers, one having been the foxglove, nicknamed "witches' bells," from their decorating their fingers with its blossoms; while in some localities the hare-bell is designated the "witches' thimble." On the other hand, flowers of a yellow or greenish hue were distasteful to them.[10]

In the witchcraft movement it would seem that certain plants were in requisition for particular purposes, these workers of darkness having utilised the properties of herbs to special ends. A plant was not indiscriminately selected, but on account of possessing some virtue as to render it suitable for any design that the witches might have in view. Considering, too, how multitudinous and varied were their actions, they had constant need of applying to the vegetable world for materials with which to carry out their plans. But foremost amongst their requirements was the power of locomotion wherewith to enable them with supernatural rapidity to travel from one locality to another. Accordingly, one of their most favourite vehicles was a besom or broom, an implement which, it has been suggested, from its being a type of the winds, is an appropriate utensil "in the hands of the witches, who are windmakers and workers in that element.[11]" According to the Asiatic Register for 1801, the Eastern as well as the European witches "practise their spells by dancing at midnight, and the principal instrument they use on such occasions is a broom." Hence, in Hamburg, sailors, after long toiling against a contrary wind, on meeting another ship sailing in an opposite direction, throw an old broom before the vessel, believing thereby to reverse the wind.[12] As, too, in the case of vervain and rue, the besom, although dearly loved by witches, is still extensively used as a counter-charm against their machinations — it being a well-known belief both in England and Germany that no individual of this stamp can step over a besom laid inside the threshold. Hence, also, in Westphalia, at Shrovetide, white besoms with white handles are tied to the cows' horns; and, in the rites connected with the Midsummer fires kept up in different parts of the country, the besom holds a prominent place. In Bohemia, for instance, the young men collect for some weeks beforehand as many worn-out brooms as they can lay their hands on. These, after dipping in tar, they light--running with them from one bonfire to another--and when burnt out they are placed in the fields as charms against blight.[13] The large ragwort--known in Ireland as the "fairies' horse"--has long been sought for by witches when taking their midnight journeys. Burns, in his "Address to the Deil," makes his witches "skim the muirs and dizzy crags" on "rag-bred nags" with "wicked speed." The same legendary belief prevails in Cornwall, in connection with the Castle Peak, a high rock to the south of the Logan stone. Here, writes Mr. Hunt,[14] "many a man, and woman too, now quietly sleeping in the churchyard of St. Levan, would, had they the power, attest to have seen the witches flying into the Castle Peak on moonlight nights, mounted on the stems of the ragwort." Amongst other plants used for a similar purpose were the bulrush and reed, in connection with-which may be quoted the Irish tale of the rushes and cornstalks that "turn into horses the moment you bestride them[15]." In Germany[16] witches were said to use hay for transporting themselves through the air.

When engaged in their various occupations they often considered it expedient to escape detection by assuming invisibility, and for this object sought the assistance of certain plants, such as the fern-seed[17]. In

Sweden, hazel-nuts were supposed to have the power of making invisible, and it may be remembered how in one of Andersen's stories the elfin princess has the faculty of vanishing at will, by putting a wand in her mouth.[18] But these were not the only plants supposed to confer invisibility, for German folklore tells us how the far-famed luck-flower was endowed with the same wonderful property; and by the ancients the heliotrope was credited with a similar virtue, but which Boccaccio, in his humorous tale of Calandrino in the "Decameron," applies to the so-called stone. "Heliotrope is a stone of such extraordinary virtue that the bearer of it is effectually concealed from the sight of all present."

Dante in his "Inferno," xxiv. 92, further alludes to it:

"Amid this dread exuberance of woe
Ran naked spirits winged with horrid fear,
Nor hope had they of crevice where to hide,
Or heliotrope to charm them out of view."

In the same way the agate was said to render a person invisible, and to turn the swords of foes against themselves.[19] The Swiss peasants affirm that the Ascension Day wreaths of the amaranth make the wearer invisible, and in the Tyrol the mistletoe is credited with this property.

But some plants, as we have already pointed out, were credited with the magic property of revealing the presence of witches, and of exposing them engaged in the pursuit of plying their nefarious calling. In this respect the St. John's wort was in great request, and hence it was extensively worn as an amulet, especially in Germany on St. John's Eve, a time when not only witches by common report peopled the air, but evil spirits wandered about on no friendly errand. Thus the Italian name of "devil-chaser," from the circumstance of its scaring away the workers of darkness, by bringing their hidden deeds to light. This, moreover, accounts for the custom so prevalent in most European countries of decorating doorways and windows with its blossoms on St. John's Eve. In our own country Stowe[20] speaks of it as its having been placed over the doors together with green birch, fennel, orpine, and white lilies, whereas in France the peasantry still reverence it as dispersing every kind of unseen evil influence. The elder was invested with similar properties, which seem to have been more potent than even those attributed to the St. John's wort. According to an old tradition, any baptized person whose eyes were anointed with the green juice of its inner bark could see witches in any part of the world. Hence the tree was extremely obnoxious to witches, a fact which probably accounts for its having been so often planted near cottages. Its magic influence has also caused it to be introduced into various rites, as in Styria on Bertha Night (January 6th), when the devil goes about in great force.[21] As a safeguard, persons are recommended to make a magic circle, in the centre of which they should stand with elder-berries gathered on St. John's Night. By so doing the mystic fern seed may be obtained, which possesses the strength of thirty or forty men. In Germany, too, a species of wild radish is said to reveal witches, as also is the ivy, and saxifrage enables its bearer to see witches on Walpurgis Night.

But, in spite of plants of this kind, witches somehow or other contrived to escape detection by the employment of the most subtle charms and spells. They generally, too, took the precaution of avoiding such plants as were antagonistic to them, displaying a cunning ingenuity in most of their designs which it was by no means easy to forestall. Hence in the composition of their philtres and potions they infused the juices of the most deadly herbs, such as that of the nightshade or monkshood; and to add to the potency of these baleful draughts they considered it necessary to add as many as seven or nine of the most poisonous plants they could obtain, such, for instance, as those enumerated by one of the witches in Ben Jonson's "Masque of Queens," who says:--

"And I ha' been plucking plants among
Hemlock, Henbane, Adder's Tongue;
Nightshade, Moonwort, Libbard's bane,
And twice, by the dogs, was like to be ta'en."

Another plant used by witches in their incantations was the sea or horned poppy, known in mediaeval times as Ficus infernolis; hence it is further noticed by Ben Jonson in the "Witches' Song":

"Yes, I have brought to help our vows,
Horned poppy, cypress boughs,
The fig tree wild that grows on tombs,
And juice that from the larch tree comes."

Then, of course, there was the wondrous moonwort (Botrychium lunaria), which was doubly valuable from its mystic virtue, for, as Culpepper[22] tells us, it was believed to open locks and possess other magic virtues. The mullein, popularly termed the hag-taper, was also in request, and the honesty (Lunaria biennis), "in sorceries excelling," was equally employed. By Scotch witches the woodbine was a favourite plant,[23] who, in effecting magical cures, passed their patients nine times through a girth or garland of green woodbine.

Again, a popular means employed by witches of injuring their enemies was by the briony. Coles, in his "Art of Simpling," for instance, informs us how, "they take likewise the roots of mandrake, according to some, or, as I rather suppose, the roots of briony, which simple folk take for the true mandrake, and make thereof an ugly image, by which they represent the person on whom they intend to exercise their witchcraft." And Lord Bacon, speaking of the mandrake, says--"Some plants there are, but rare, that have a mossie or downy root, and likewise that have a number of threads, like beards, as mandrakes, whereof witches and impostours make an ugly image, giving it the form of a face at the top of the root, and leave those strings to make a broad beard down to the foot." The witchcraft literature of the sixteenth and seventeenth centuries contains numerous allusions to the diabolical practice--a superstition immortalised by Shakespeare. The mandrake, from its supposed mysterious character, was intimately associated with witches, and Ben Jonson, in his "Masque of Queens," makes one of the hags who has been gathering this plant say,

"I last night lay all alone
On the ground, to hear the mandrake groan;
And plucked him up, though he grew full low,
And, as I had done, the cock did crow."

We have already incidentally spoken of the vervain, St. John's wort, elder, and rue as antagonistic to witchcraft, but to these may be added many other well-known plants, such as the juniper, mistletoe, and blackthorn. Indeed, the list might be greatly extended--the vegetable kingdom having supplied in most parts of the world almost countless charms to counteract the evil designs of these malevolent beings. In our own country the little pimpernel, herb-paris, and cyclamen were formerly gathered for this purpose, and the angelica was thought to be specially noisome to witches. The snapdragon and the herb-betony had the reputation of averting the most subtle forms of witchcraft, and dill and flax were worn as talismans against sorcery. Holly is said to be antagonistic to witches, for, as Mr. Folkard[24] says, "in its name they see but another form of the word 'holy,' and its thorny foliage and blood-red berries are suggestive of the most Christian associations." Then there is the rowan-tree or mountain-ash, which has long been considered one of the most powerful antidotes against works of darkness of every kind, probably from its sacred associations with the worship of the Druids. Hence it is much valued in Scotland, and the following couplet, of which there are several versions, still embodies the popular faith:

"Rowan-tree and red thread,
Put the witches to their speed."

But its fame has not been confined to any one locality, and as far south as Cornwall the peasant, when he suspects that his cow has been "overlooked," twists an ashen twig round its horns. Indeed, so potent is the ash as a counter charm to sorcery, that even the smallest twig renders their actions impotent; and hence, in an old ballad entitled "Laidley Wood," in the "Northumberland Garland," it is said:

"The spells were vain, the hag returned
To the queen in sorrowful mood,
Crying that witches have no power,
Where there is row'n-tree wood."

Hence persons carry an ashen twig in their pocket, and according to a Yorkshire proverb:

"If your whipsticks made of row'n,
You may ride your nag through any town;"

But, on the other hand, "Woe to the lad without a rowan-tree gall." Possessed of such virtues, it is not surprising that the mystic ash should have been held in the highest repute, in illustration of which we find many an amusing anecdote. Thus, according to a Herefordshire tradition, some years ago two hogsheads full of money were concealed in an underground cellar belonging to the Castle of Penyard, where they were kept by supernatural force. A farmer, however, made up his mind to get them out, and employed for the purpose twenty steers to draw down the iron door of the vault. On the door being slightly opened, a jackdaw was seen sitting on one of the casks, but the door immediately closed with a bang--a voice being heard to say,

"Had it not been
For your quicken tree goad,
And your yew tree pin,
You and your cattle
Had all been drawn in."

Another anecdote current in Yorkshire is interesting, showing how fully superstitions of this kind are believed[25]:--"A woman was lately in my shop, and in pulling out her purse brought out also a piece of stick a few inches long. I asked her why she carried that in her pocket. 'Oh,' she replied, 'I must not lose that, or I shall be done for.' 'Why so?' I inquired. 'Well,' she answered, 'I carry that to keep off the witches; while I have that about me, they cannot hurt me.' On my adding that there were no witches nowadays, she instantly replied, 'Oh, yes! There are thirteen at this very time in the town, but so long as I have my rowan-tree safe in my pocket they cannot hurt me.'"

Occasionally when the dairymaid churned for a long time without making butter, she would stir the cream with a twig of mountain ash, and beat the cow with another, thus breaking the witch's spell. But, to prevent accidents of this kind, it has long been customary in the northern countries to make the churn-staff of ash. For the same reason herd-boys employ an ash-twig for driving cattle, and one may often see a mountain-ash growing near a house. On the Continent the tree is in equal repute, and in Norway and Denmark rowan branches are usually put over stable doors to keep out witches, a similar notion prevailing in Germany. No tree, perhaps, holds such a prominent place in witchcraft-lore as the mountain-ash, its mystic power having rarely failed to render fruitless the evil influence of these enemies of mankind.

In our northern counties witches are said to dislike the bracken fern, "because it bears on its root the initial C, which may be seen on cutting the root horizontally."[26] and in most places equally distasteful to them is the yew, perhaps for no better reason than its having formerly been much planted in churchyards. The herb-bennett (Geum urbanum), like the clover, from its trefoiled leaf, renders witches powerless, and the hazel has similar virtues. Among some of the plants considered antagonistic to sorcery on the Continent may be mentioned the water-lily, which is gathered in the Rhine district with a certain formula. In Tuscany, the lavender counteracts the evil eye, and a German antidote against the hurtful effects of any malicious influence was an ointment made of the leaves of the marsh-mallow. In Italy, an olive branch which has been blessed keeps the witch from the dwelling, and in some parts of the Continent the plum-tree is used. Kolb, writes Mr. Black,[27] who became one of the first "wonder-doctors" of the Tyrol, "when he was called to assist any bewitched person, made exactly at midnight the smoke of five different sorts of herbs, and while they were burning the bewitched was gently beaten with a martyr-thorn birch, which had to be got the same night. This beating the patient with thorn was thought to be really beating the hag who had caused the evil."

Some seasons, too, have been supposed to be closely associated with the witches, as in Germany, where all flax must be spun before Twelfth Night, for one who spins afterwards is liable to be bewitched.

Lastly, to counteract the spell of the evil eye, from which many innocent persons were believed to suffer in the witchcraft period, many flowers have been in requisition among the numerous charms used. Thus, the Russian maidens still hang round the stem of the birch-tree red ribbon, the Brahmans gather rice, and in Italy rue is in demand. The Scotch peasantry pluck twigs of the ash, the Highland women the groundsel, and the German folk wear the radish. In early times the ringwort was recommended by Apuleius, and later on the fern was regarded as a preservative against this baneful influence. The Chinese put faith in the garlic; and, in short, every country has its own special plants. It would seem, too, that after a witch was dead and buried, precautionary measures were taken to frustrate her baneful influence. Thus, in Russia, aspen is laid on a witch's grave, the dead sorceress being then prevented from riding abroad.

Footnotes:

1. See Moncure Conway's "Demonology and Devil Lore," 1880, ii. 324.
2. See Friend's "Flower Lore," ii. 529-30.
3. "Demonology and Devil Lore," ii. 324.
4. Grimm, "Teutonic Mythology," 1883, iii. 1051.
5. Folkard's "Plant Lore, Legends, and Lyrics," 1884, p. 91.
6. Thorpe's "Northern Mythology," iii. 19.
7. Grimm's "Teutonic Mythology," iii. 1052.
8. See Thorpe's "Northern Mythology," iii. 267.
9. See Folkard's "Plant Lore, Legends, and Lyrics," p. 209.
10. Ibid., p. 104.
11. See Kelly's "Indo-European Folklore," pp. 225-7.
12. See Hardwick's "Traditions, Superstitions, and Folklore," p. 117; also Grimm's "Teutonic Mythology," 1883, iii. 1083.
13. See Thorpe's "Northern Mythology," 1852, iii. 21, 137.
14. "Popular Romances of the West of England," 1871, p. 330.
15. Grimm's "Teutonic Mythology," iii. 1084.
16. See Thorpe's "Northern Mythology," iii. 208-9.
17. See chap. "Doctrine of Signatures."
18. See Yardley's "Supernatural in Romantic Fiction," 1880, pp. 131-2.
19. See Fiske, "Myths and Mythmakers," p. 44; also Baring-Gould's "Curious Myths of the Middle Ages," 1877, p. 398.
20. "Survey of London." See Mason's "Folklore of British Plants" in Dublin University Magazine, September 1873, p. 326-8.
21. Mr. Conway's "Mystic Trees and Flowers," Fraser's Magazine, 1870, 602.
22. "British Herbal."
23. See Folkard's "Plant-lore Legends and Lyrics," p. 380.
24. "Plant-lore Legends and Lyrics," p. 376.
25. Henderson's "Folklore of Northern Counties," 1879, p. 225.
26. "Folklore of Northern Counties," 1879.
27. "Folk-medicine," p. 202.

CHAPTER VI

PLANTS IN DEMONOLOGY

The association of certain plants with the devil forms an extensive and important division in their folklore, and in many respects is closely connected with their mystic history. It is by no means easy always to account for some of our most beautiful flowers having Satanic surroundings, although frequently the explanation must be sought in their poisonous and deadly qualities. In some cases, too, the student of comparative mythology may trace their evil reputation to those early traditions which were the expressions of certain primitive beliefs, the survivals of which nowadays are found in many an apparently meaningless superstition. Anyhow, the subject is a very wide one, and is equally represented in most countries. It should be remembered, moreover, that rudimentary forms of dualism--the antagonism of a good and evil deity[1]--have from a remote period occupied men's minds, a system of belief known even among the lower races of mankind. Hence, just as some plants would in process of time acquire a sacred character, others would do the reverse. Amongst the legendary stories and folktales of most countries we find frequent allusion to the devil as an active agent in utilising various flowers for his mischievous pursuits; and on the Continent we are told of a certain evil spirit named Kleure who transforms himself into a tree to escape notice, a superstition which under a variety of forms still lingers here and there.[2] It would seem, too, that in some of our old legends and superstitions the terms Puck and Devil are synonymous, a circumstance which explains the meaning, otherwise unintelligible, of many items of plant-lore in our own and other countries. Thus the word "Puck" has been identified with Pogge--toad, under which form the devil was supposed to be personified; and hence probably originated such expressions as toadstools, paddock-stools, &c. The thorns of the eglantine are said to point downwards, because when the devil was excluded from heaven he tried to regain his lost position by means of a ladder composed of its thorns. But when the eglantine was only allowed to grow as a bush, out of spite he placed its thorns in their present eccentric position. The seed of the parsley, "is apt to come up only partially, according as the devil takes his tithe of it."[3] In Germany "devil's oaks" are of frequent occurrence, and "one of these at Gotha is held in great regard."[4] and Gerarde, describing the vervaine, with its manifold mystic virtues, says that "the devil did reveal it as a secret and divine medicine." Belladonna, writes Mr. Conway, is esteemed in Bohemia a favourite plant of the devil, who watches it, but may be drawn from it on Walpurgis Night by letting loose a black hen, after which he will run. Then there is the sow-thistle, which in Russia is said to belong to the devil; and Loki, the evil spirit in northern mythology, is occasionally spoken of as sowing weeds among the good seed; from whence, it has been suggested, originated the popular phrase of "sowing one's wild oats."[5] The German peasantry have their "rye-wolf," a malignant spirit infesting the rye-fields; and in some parts of the Continent orchards are said to be infested by evil demons, who, until driven away by various incantations, are liable to do much harm to the fruit. The Italians, again, affirm that in each leaf of the fig-tree an evil spirit dwells; and throughout the Continent there are various other demons who are believed to haunt the crops. Evil spirits were once said to lurk in lettuce-beds, and a certain species was regarded with ill favour by mothers, a circumstance which, Mr. Folkard rightly suggests,[6] may account for a Surrey saying, "O'er much lettuce in the garden will stop a young wife's bearing." Among similar legends of the kind it is said that, in Swabia, fern-seed brought by the devil between eleven and twelve o'clock on Christmas night enables the bearer to do as much work as twenty or thirty ordinary men. According to a popular piece of superstition current in our southern counties, the devil is generally supposed to put his cloven foot upon the blackberries on Michaelmas Day, and hence after this date it is considered unlucky to gather them during the remainder of the year. An interesting instance of this superstition is given by Mrs. Latham in her "West Sussex Superstitions," which happened to a farmer's wife residing in the neighbourhood of Arundel. It appears that she was in the habit of making a large quantity of blackberry jam, and finding that less fruit had been brought to her than she required, she said to the charwoman, "I wish you would send some of your children to gather me three or four pints more." "Ma'am," exclaimed the woman in astonishment, "don't you know this is the 11th October?" "Yes," she replied. "Bless me, ma'am! And you ask me to let my children go out blackberrying! Why, I thought every one knew that the devil went round on the 10th October, and spat on all the blackberries, and that if any person were to eat on the 11th, he or some one belonging to him would either die or fall into great trouble before the year was out."

In Scotland the devil is said to but throw his cloak over the blackberries and render them unwholesome, while in Ireland he is said to stamp on them. Among further stories of this kind may be quoted one current in Devonshire respecting St. Dunstan, who, it is said, bought up a quantity of barley for brewing beer. The devil, knowing how anxious the saint would be to get a good sale for his beer, offered to blight the apple trees, so that there should be no cider, and hence a greater demand for beer, on condition that he sold himself to him. St. Dunstan accepted the offer, and stipulated that the trees should be blighted on the 17th, 18th, and 19th May. Should the apple-blossom be nipped by cold winds or frost about this time, many allusions are still made to St. Dunstan.

Of the plants associated personally with the evil one may be mentioned the henbane, which is known in Germany as the "devil's eye," a name applied to the stich-wort in Wales. A species of ground moss is also styled in Germany the "devil's claws;" one of the orchid tribe is "Satan's hand;" the lady's fingers is "devil's claws," and the plantain is "devil's head." Similarly the house-leek has been designated the "devil's beard," and a Norfolk name for the stinkhorn is "devil's horn." Of further plants related to his Satanic majesty is the clematis, termed "devil's thread," the toad-flax is his ribbon, the indigo his dye, while the scandix forms his darning-needles. The tritoma, with its brilliant red blossom, is familiar in most localities as the "devil's poker," and the ground ivy has been nicknamed the "devil's candlestick," the mandrake supplying his candle. The puff-balls of the lycoperdon form the devil's snuff-box, and in Ireland the nettle is his apron, and the convolvulus his garter; while at Iserlohn, in Germany,[7] "the mothers, to deter their children eating the mulberries, sing to them that the devil requires them for the purpose of blacking his boots." The Arum maculatum is "devil's ladies and gentlemen," and the Ranunculus arvensis is the "devil on both sides." The vegetable kingdom also has been equally mindful of his majesty's food, the spurge having long been named "devil's milk" and the briony the "devil's cherry." A species of fungus, known with us as "witches' butter," is called in Sweden "devil's butter," while one of the popular names for the mandrake is "devil's food." The hare-parsley supplies him with oatmeal, and the stichwort is termed in the West of England "devil's corn." Among further plants associated with his Satanic majesty may be enumerated the garden fennel, or love-in-a-mist, to which the name of "devil-in-a-bush" has been applied, while the fruit of the deadly nightshade is commonly designated "devil's berries." Then there is the "devil's tree," and the "devil's dung" is one of the nicknames of the assafoetida. The hawk-weed, like the scabious, was termed "devil's bit," because the root looks as if it had been bitten off. According to an old legend, "the root was once longer, until the devil bit away the rest for spite, for he needed it not to make him sweat who is always tormented with fear of the day of judgment." Gerarde further adds that, "The devil did bite it for envy, because it is an herb that hath so many great virtues, and is so beneficial to mankind." A species of ranunculus supplies his coach-wheels, and in some parts of the country ferns are said to supply his brushes. His majesty's wants, therefore, have been amply provided for by the vegetable kingdom, for even the wild garlic affords him a posy[8]. Once more, in Sweden, a rose-coloured flower, known as "Our Lady's hand," "has two roots like hands, one white, the other black, and when both are placed in water the black one will sink, this is called 'Satan's hand;' but the white one, called 'Mary's hand,' will float."[9] Hence this flower is held in deep and superstitious veneration among the peasantry; and in Crete the basil is considered an emblem of the devil, and is placed on most window-ledges, no doubt as a charm.

Some plants, again, have been used for exorcism from their reputed antagonism to all Satanic influence. Thus the avens or herb-bennett, when kept in a house, was believed to render the devil powerless, and the Greeks of old were in the habit of placing a laurel bough over their doorways to keep away evil spirits. The thistle has been long in demand for counteracting the powers of darkness, and in Esthonia it is placed on the ripening corn to drive and scare away malignant demons. In Poland, the disease known among the poorer classes as "elf-lock" is supposed to be the work of wicked spirits, but tradition says it will gradually disappear if one buries thistle seed.[10] The aloe, by the Egyptians, is reputed to resist any baleful influence, and the lunary or "honesty" is by our own country people said to put every evil influence to flight. In Germany the juniper disperses evil spirits, and in ancient times the black hellebore, peony, and mugwort were largely used for this purpose. According to a Russian belief the elder-tree drives away evil spirits, and hence this plant is held in high respect. Among further plants possessing the same quality are the nettle and milfoil, and then there is the famous St. John's wort, popularly nicknamed "devil's flight."

Closely allied with this part of our subject are those plants connected with serpents, here forming a very numerous class. Indeed, it was only natural that our ancestors, from their dread of the serpent on account of its poisonous sting, as well as from their antipathy to it as the symbol of evil, should ascertain those plants which seemed either attractive, or antagonistic, to this much-dreaded reptile. Accordingly certain plants, from being supposed to be distasteful to serpents, were much used as amulets to drive them away. Foremost among these may be mentioned the ash, to escape contact with which a serpent, it has been said, would even creep into the fire, in allusion to which Cowley thus writes:

"But that which gave more wonder than the rest,   Within an ash a serpent built her nest   And laid her eggs, when once to come beneath The very shadow of an ash was death."

Gerarde notices this curious belief, and tells us that, "the leaves of this tree are so great virtue against serpents that they dare not so much as touch the morning and evening shadows of the tree, but shun them afar off."

Hence ash-sap was a German remedy for serpent bites. Lucan, in his "Pharsalia" (915-921), has enumerated some of the plants burned for the purpose of expelling serpents:

> *"Beyond the farthest tents rich fires they build,*
> *That healthy medicinal odours yield,*
> *There foreign galbanum dissolving fries,*
> *And crackling flames from humble wallwort rise.*
> *There tamarisk, which no green leaf adorns,*
> *And there the spicy Syrian costos burns;*
> *There centaury supplies the wholesome flame,*
> *That from Therssalian Chiron takes its name;*
> *The gummy larch tree, and the thapsos there,*
> *Woundwort and maidenweed perfume the air,*
> *There the long branches of the long-lived hart*
> *With southernwood their odours strong impart,*
> *The monsters of the land, the serpents fell,*
> *Fly far away and shun the hostile smell."*

The smoke of the juniper was equally repellent to serpents, and the juice of dittany "drives away venomous beasts, and doth astonish them." In olden times, for serpent bites, agrimony, chamomile, and the fruit of the bramble, were held efficacious, and Gerarde recommends the root of the bugloss, "as it keepeth such from being stung as have drunk it before; the leaves and seeds do the same." On the other hand, some plants had the reputation of attracting serpents, one of these being the moneywort or creeping loosestrife, with which they were said to heal themselves when wounded. As far back as the time of Pliny serpents were supposed to be very fond of fennel, restoring to them their youth by enabling them to cast their old skins. There is a belief in Thuringia that the possession of fern seed causes the bearer to be pursued by serpents till thrown away; and, according to a curious Eussian proverb, "from all old trees proceeds either an owl or a devil," in reference, no doubt, to their often bare and sterile appearance.

Footnotes:

1. See Tylor's "Primitive Culture," ii. 316.
2. Thorpe's "Northern Mythology," iii. 193.
3. "Plant-lore Legends and Lyrics," p. 486.
4. Mr. Conway, Fraser's Magazine, 1870, p. 593.
5. Mr. Conway, Fraser's Magazine, 1870, p. 107.
6. "Plant-lore Legends and Lyrics," p. 411.
7. Folkard's "Plant-lore Legends and Lyrics," p. 448.
8. See Friend's "Flower-lore," i. 68.
9. Thorpe's "Northern Mythology," ii. 104.
10. "Mystic Trees and Flowers," Fraser's Magazine.

CHAPTER VII

PLANTS IN FAIRY-LORE

Many plants have gained a notoriety from their connection with fairyland, and although the belief in this romantic source of superstition has almost died out, yet it has left its traces in the numerous legends which have survived amongst us. Thus the delicate white flowers of the wood-sorrel are known in Wales as "fairy bells," from a belief once current that these tiny beings were summoned to their moonlight revels and gambols by these bells. In Ireland they were supposed to ride to their scenes of merrymaking on the ragwort, hence known as the "fairies' horse." Cabbage-stalks, too, served them for steeds, and a story is told of a certain farmer who resided at Dundaniel, near Cork, and was considered to be under fairy control. For a long time he suffered from "the falling sickness," owing to the long journeys which he was forced to make, night by night, with the fairy folk on one of his own cabbage stumps. Sometimes the good people made use of a straw, a blade of grass, or a fern, a further illustration of which is furnished by "The Witch of Fife:"

> "The first leet night, quhan the new moon set,
>   Quhan all was douffe and mirk,
> We saddled our naigis wi' the moon-fern leif,
>   And rode fra Kilmerrin kirk.
>
> Some horses were of the brume-cow framit,
>   And some of the greine bay tree;
> But mine was made of ane humloke schaw,
>   And a stour stallion was he." [1]

In some folk-tales fairies are represented as employing nuts for their mode of conveyance, in allusion to which Shakespeare, in "Romeo and Juliet," makes Mercutio speak of Queen Mab's arrival in a nut-shell. Similarly the fairies selected certain plants for their attire. Although green seems to have been their popular colour, yet the fairies of the moon were often clad in heath-brown or lichen-dyed garments, whence the epithet of "Elfin-grey." Their petticoats, for instance, were composed of the fox-glove, a flower in demand among Irish fairies for their gloves, and in some parts of that country for their caps, where it is nicknamed "Lusmore," while the Cuscuta epithymum is known in Jersey as "fairies' hair." Their raiment was made of the fairy flax, and the wood-anemone, with its fragile blossoms, was supposed to afford them shelter in wet weather. Shakespeare has represented Ariel reclining in "a cowslip's bell," and further speaks of the small crimson drops in its blossom as "gold coats spots"--"these be rubies, fairy favours." And at the present day the cowslip is still known in Lincolnshire as the "fairy cup." Its popular German name is "key-flower;" and no flower has had in that country so extensive an association with preternatural wealth. A well-known legend relates how "Bertha" entices some favoured child by exquisite primroses to a doorway overgrown with flowers. This is the door to an enchanted castle. When the key-flower touches it, the door gently opens, and the favoured mortal passes to a room with vessels covered over with primroses, in which are treasures of gold and jewels. When the treasure is secured the primroses must be replaced, otherwise the finder will be for ever followed by a "black dog."

Sometimes their mantles are made of the gossamer, the cobwebs which may be seen in large quantities on the furze bushes; and so of King Oberon we are told:

> *"A rich mantle did he wear,*
> *Made of tinsel gossamer,*
> *Bestarred over with a few*
> *Diamond drops of morning dew."*

Tulips are the cradles in which the fairy tribe have lulled their offspring to rest, while the Pyrus japonica serves them for a fire.[2] Their hat is supplied by the Peziza coccinea; and in Lincolnshire, writes Mr. Friend,[3] "A kind of fungus like a cup or old-fashioned purse, with small objects inside, is called a fairy-purse." When mending their clothes, the foxglove gives them thimbles; and many other flowers might be added which are equally in request for their various needs. It should be mentioned, however, that fairies, like witches, have a strange antipathy to yellow flowers, and rarely frequent localities where they grow.

In olden times, we read how in Scandinavia and Germany the rose was under the special protection of dwarfs and elves, who were ruled by the mighty King Laurin, the lord of the rose-garden:

> *"Four portals to the garden lead, and when the gates are closed,*
> *No living might dare touch a rose, 'gainst his strict command opposed;*
> *Whoe'er would break the golden gates, or cut the silken thread,*
> *Or who would dare to crush the flowers down beneath his tread,*
> *Soon for his pride would have to pledge a foot and hand;*
> *Thus Laurin, king of Dwarfs, rules within his land."*

We may mention here that the beautiful white or yellow flowers that grow on the banks of lakes and rivers in Sweden are called "neck-roses," memorials of the Neck, a water-elf, and the poisonous root of the water-hemlock was known as neck-root.[4]

In Brittany and in some parts of Ireland the hawthorn, or, as it is popularly designated, the fairy-thorn, is a tree most specially in favour. On this account it is held highly dangerous to gather even a leaf "from certain old and solitary thorns which grow in sheltered hollows of the moorlands," for these are the trysting-places of the fairy race. A trace of the same superstition existed in Scotland, as may be gathered from the subjoined extract from the "Scottish Statistical Report" of the year 1796, in connection with New parish:--"There is a quick thorn of a very antique appearance, for which the people have a superstitious veneration. They have a mortal dread to lop off or cut any part of it, and affirm with a religious horror that some persons who had the temerity to hurt it, were afterwards severely punished for their sacrilege."

One flower which, for some reason or other, is still held in special honour by them, is the common stichwort of our country hedges, and which the Devonshire peasant hesitates to pluck lest he should be pixy-led. A similar idea formerly prevailed in the Isle of Man in connection with the St. John's wort. If any unwary traveller happened, after sunset, to tread on this plant, it was said that a fairy-horse would suddenly appear, and carry him about all night. Wild thyme is another of their favourite plants, and Mr. Folkard notes that in Sicily rosemary is equally beloved; and that "the young fairies, under the guise of snakes, lie concealed under its branches." According to a Netherlandish belief, the elf-leaf, or sorceresses' plant, is particularly grateful to them, and therefore ought not to be plucked.[5]

The four-leaved clover is a magic talisman which enables its wearer to detect the whereabouts of fairies, and was said only to grow in their haunts; in reference to which belief Lover thus writes:

"I'll seek a four-leaved clover
In all the fairy dells,
And if I find the charmed leaf,
Oh, how I'll weave my spells!"

And according to a Danish belief, any one wandering under an elder-bush at twelve o'clock on Midsummer Eve will see the king of fairyland pass by with all his retinue. Fairies' haunts are mostly in picturesque spots (such as among the tufts of wild thyme); and the oak tree, both here and in Germany, has generally been their favourite abode, and hence the superstitious reverence with which certain trees are held, care being taken not to offend their mysterious inhabitants.

An immense deal of legendary lore has clustered round the so-called fairy-rings--little circles of a brighter green in old pastures — within which the fairies were supposed to dance by night. This curious phenomenon, however, is owing to the outspread propagation of a particular mushroom, the fairy-ringed fungus, by which the ground is manured for a richer following vegetation.[6] Amongst the many other conjectures as to the cause of these verdant circles, some have ascribed them to lightning, and others have maintained that they are produced by ants.[7] In the "Tempest" (v. i) Prospero invokes the fairies as the "demi-puppets" that:

"By moonshine do the green sour ringlets make,
Whereof the ewe not bites; and you, whose pastime
Is to make midnight mushrooms."

And in the "Merry Wives of Windsor" (v. 5) Mistress Quickly says:

"And nightly, meadow-fairies, look, you sing,
Like to the Garter's compass, in a ring;
The expressure that it bears, green let it be,
More fertile-fresh than all the field to see."

Drayton, in his "Nymphidia" (1. 69-72), tells how the fairies:

"In their courses make that round,
In meadows and in marshes found,
Of them so called the fayrie ground,
Of which they have the keeping."

These fairy-rings have long been held in superstitious awe; and when in olden times May-dew was gathered by young ladies to improve their complexion, they carefully avoided even touching the grass within them, for fear of displeasing these little beings, and so losing their personal charms. At the present day, too, the peasant asserts that no sheep nor cattle will browse on the mystic patches, a natural instinct warning them of their peculiar nature. A few miles from Alnwick was a fairy-ring, round which if people ran more than nine times, some evil was supposed to befall them.

It is generally agreed that fairies were extremely fond of dancing around oaks, and thus in addressing the monarch of the forest a poet has exclaimed:

"The fairies, from their nightly haunt,
In copse or dell, or round the trunk revered
Of Herne's moon-silvered oak, shall chase away
Each fog, each blight, and dedicate to peace
Thy classic shade."

In Sweden the miliary fever is said by the peasantry to be caused by the elf-mote or meeting with elves, as a remedy for which the lichen aphosus or lichen caninus is sought.

The toadstools often found near these so-called fairy-rings were also thought to be their workmanship, and in some localities are styled pixy-stools, and in the North of Wales "fairy-tables," while the "cheeses," or fruit of the mallow, are known in the North of England as "fairy-cheeses."

A species of wood fungus found about the roots of old trees is designated "fairy-butter," because after rain, and when in a certain degree of putrefaction, it is reduced to a consistency which, together with its colour, makes it not unlike butter. The fairy-butter of the Welsh is a substance found at a great depth in cavities of limestone rocks. Ritson, in his "Fairy Tales," speaking of the fairies who frequented many parts of Durham, relates how "a woman who had been in their society challenged one of the guests whom she espied in the market selling fairy-butter," an accusation, however, which was deeply resented.

Browne, in his "Britannia's Pastorals," makes the table on which they feast consist of:

"A little mushroom, that was now grown thinner
By being one time shaven for the dinner."

Fairies have always been jealous of their rights, and are said to resent any infringement of their privileges, one of these being the property of fruit out of season. Any apples, too, remaining after the crop has been gathered in, they claim as their own; and hence, in the West of England, to ensure their goodwill and friendship, a few stray ones are purposely left on the trees. This may partially perhaps explain the ill-luck of plucking flowers out of season[8]. A Netherlandish piece of folklore informs us that certain wicked elves prepare poison in some plants. Hence experienced shepherds are careful not to let their flocks feed after sunset. One of these plants, they say, is nightwort, "which belongs to the elves, and whoever touches it must die[9]." The disease known in Poland as "elf-lock" is said to be the work of evil fairies or demons, and is cured by burying thistle-seed in the ground. Similarly, in Iceland, says Mr. Conway, "the farmer guards the grass around his field lest the elves

abiding in them invade his crops." Likewise the globe-flower has been designated the troll-flower, from the malignant trolls or elves, on account of its poisonous qualities. On the other hand, the Bavarian peasant has a notion that the elves are very fond of strawberries; and in order that they may be good-humoured and bless his cows with abundance of milk, he is careful to tie a basket of this fruit
between the cow's horns.

Of the many legendary origins of the fairy tribe, there is a popular one abroad that mortals have frequently been transformed into these little beings through "eating of ambrosia or some peculiar kind of herb."[10]

According to a Cornish tradition, the fern is in some mysterious manner connected with the fairies; and a tale is told of a young woman who, when one day listlessly breaking off the fronds of fern as she sat resting by the wayside, was suddenly confronted by a "fairy widower," who was in search of some one to attend to his little son. She accepted his offer, which was ratified by kissing a fern leaf and repeating this formula:

"For a year and a day
I promise to stay."

Soon she was an inhabitant of fairyland, and was lost to mortal gaze until she had fulfilled her stipulated engagement.

In Germany we find a race of elves, somewhat like the dwarfs, popularly known as the Wood or Moss people. They are about the same size as children, "grey and old-looking, hairy, and clad in moss." Their lives, like those of the Hamadryads, are attached to the trees; and "if any one causes by friction the inner bark to loosen a Wood-woman dies."[11] Their great enemy is the Wild Huntsman, who, driving invisibly through the air, pursues and kills them. On one occasion a peasant, hearing the weird baying in a wood, joined in the cry; but on the following morning he found hanging at his stable door a quarter of a green Moss-woman as his share of the game. As a spell against the Wild Huntsman, the Moss-women sit in the middle of those trees upon which the woodcutter has placed a cross, indicating that they are to be hewn, thereby making sure of their safety. Then, again, there is the old legend which tells how Brandan met a man on the sea,[12] who was, "a thumb long, and floated on a leaf, holding a little bowl in his right hand and a pointer in his left; the pointer he kept dipping into the sea and letting water drop from it into the bowl; when the bowl was full, he emptied it out and began filling it again, his doom consisting in measuring the sea until the judgment-day." This floating on the leaf is suggestive of ancient Indian myths, and reminds us of Brahma sitting on a lotus and floating across the sea. Vishnu, when, after Brahma's death, the waters have covered all the worlds, sits in the shape of a tiny infant on a leaf of the fig tree, and floats on the sea of milk sucking the toe of his right foot.[13]

Another tribe of water-fairies are the nixes, who frequently assume the appearance of beautiful maidens. On fine sunny days they sit on the banks of rivers or lakes, or on the branches of trees, combing and arranging their golden locks:

"Know you the Nixes, gay and fair?
Their eyes are black, and green their hair,
They lurk in sedgy shores."

A fairy or water-sprite that resides in the neighbourhood of the Orkneys is popularly known as Tangie, so-called from tang,, the seaweed with which he is covered. Occasionally he makes his appearance as a little horse, and at other times as a man.[14]

Then there are the wood and forest folk of Germany, spirits inhabiting the forests, who stood in friendly relation to man, but are now so disgusted with the faithless world, that they have retired from it. Hence their precept--

"Peel no tree,
Relate no dream,
Pipe no bread, or
Bake no cumin in bread,
So will God help thee in thy need."

On one occasion a "forest-wife," who had just tasted a new baked-loaf, given as an offering, was heard screaming aloud:

"They've baken for me cumin bread,
That on this house brings great distress."

The prosperity of the poor peasant was soon on the wane, and before long he was reduced to abject poverty.[15] These legends, in addition to illustrating the fairy mythology of bygone years, are additionally interesting from their connection with the plants and flowers, most of which are familiar to us from our childhood.

Footnotes:

1. See Crofton Croker's "Fairy Legends and Traditions of the South of Ireland," 1862, p. 98.

2. Folkard's "Plant-lore Legends and Lyrics," p. 30.

3. Friend, "Flowers and Flower Lore," p. 34.

4. Thorpe's "Northern Mythology," ii. 81-2.

5. Thorpe's "Northern Mythology," iii. 266.

6. See "The Phytologist," 1862, p. 236-8.

7. "Folklore of Shakespeare," p. 15.

8. See Friend's "Flower Lore," i. 34.

9. Thorpe's "Northern Mythology," iii. 266.

10. Friend's "Flower Lore," i. 27.

11. See Keightley's "Fairy Mythology," p. 231.

12. Grimm's "Teut. Myth.," 1883, ii. 451;

13. "Asiatic Researches," i. 345.

14. See Keightley's "Fairy Mythology," p. 173.

15. Thorpe's "Northern Mythology," i. 251-3.

CHAPTER VIII

LOVE-CHARMS

Plants have always been largely used for testing the fidelity of lovers, and at the present day are still extensively employed for this purpose by the rustic maiden. As in the case of medical charms, more virtue would often seem to reside in the mystic formula uttered while the flower is being secretly gathered, than in any particular quality of the flower itself. Then, again, flowers, from their connection with certain festivals, have been consulted in love matters, and elsewhere we have alluded to the knowledge they have long been supposed to give in dreams, after the performance of certain incantations.

Turning to some of the well-known charm formulas, may be mentioned that known as "a clover of two," the mode of gathering it constituting the charm itself:

"A clover, a clover of two,
Put it in your right shoe;
The first young man you meet,
In field, street, or lane,
You'll get him, or one of his name."

Then there is the hempseed formula, and one founded on the luck of an apple-pip, which, when seized between the finger and thumb, is supposed to pop in the direction of the lover's abode; an illustration of which we subjoin as still used in Lancashire:

"Pippin, pippin, paradise,
Tell me where my true love lies,
East, west, north, and south,
Pilling Brig, or Cocker Mouth."

The old custom, too, of throwing an apple-peel over the head, marriage or single blessedness being foretold by its remaining whole or breaking, and of the peel so cast forming the initial of the future loved one, finds many adherents. Equally popular, too, was the practice of divining by a thistle blossom. When anxious to ascertain who loved her most, a young woman would take three or four heads of thistles, cut off their points, and assign to each thistle the name of an admirer, laying them under her pillow. On the following morning the thistle which has put forth a fresh sprout will denote the man who loves her most.

There are numerous charms connected with the ash-leaf, and among those employed in the North of England we may quote the following:

"The even ash-leaf in my left hand,
The first man I meet shall be my husband;
The even ash-leaf in my glove,
The first I meet shall be my love;
The even ash-leaf in my breast,
The first man I meet's whom I love best;
The even ash-leaf in my hand,
The first I meet shall be my man.

Even ash, even ash, I pluck thee,
This night my true love for to see,
Neither in his rick nor in his rear,
But in the clothes he does every day wear."

And there is the well-known saying current throughout the country:

"If you find an even ash or a four-leaved clover,
Rest assured you'll see your true love ere the day is over."

Longfellow alludes to the husking of the maize among the American colonists, an event which was always accompanied by various ceremonies, one of which he thus forcibly describes:

"In the golden weather the maize was husked, and the maidens
Blushed at each blood-red ear, for that betokened a lover,
But at the crooked laughed, and called it a thief in the corn-field:
Even the blood-red ear to Evangeline brought not her lover."

Charms of this kind are common, and vary in different localities, being found extensively on the Continent, where perhaps even greater importance is attached to them than in our own country. Thus, a popular French one--which many of our young people also practise--is for lovers to test the sincerity of their affections by taking a daisy and plucking its leaflets off one by one, saying, "Does he love me? — a little--much--passionately--not at all!" the phrase which falls to the last leaflet forming the answer to the inquiry:

"La blanche et simple Paquerette,
Que ton coeur consult surtout,
Dit, Ton amant, tendre fillette,
T'aime, un peu, beaucoup, point du tout."

Perhaps Brown alludes to the same species of divination when he writes of:

"The gentle daisy with her silver crown,
Worn in the breast of many a shepherd lass."

In England the marigold, which is carefully excluded from the flowers with which German maidens tell their fortunes as unfavourable to love, is often used for divination, and in Germany the star-flower and dandelion.

Among some of the ordinary flowers in use for love-divination may be mentioned the poppy, with its "prophetic leaf," and the old-fashioned "bachelor's buttons," which was credited with possessing some magical effect upon the fortunes of lovers. Hence its blossoms were carried in the pocket, success in love being indicated in proportion as they lost or retained their freshness.

Browne alludes to the primrose, which "maidens as a true-love in their bosoms place;" and in the North of England the kemps or spikes of the ribwort plantain are used as love-charms. The mode of procedure as practised in Northamptonshire is thus picturesquely given by Clare in his "Shepherd's Calendar:":

"Or trying simple charms and spells,
Which rural superstition tells,
They pull the little blossom threads
From out the knotweed's button heads,
And put the husk, with many a smile,
In their white bosom for a while;

Then, if they guess aright the swain
Their love's sweet fancies try to gain,
'Tis said that ere it lies an hour,
'Twill blossom with a second flower,
And from the bosom's handkerchief
Bloom as it ne'er had lost a leaf."

Then there are the downy thistle-heads, which the rustic maiden names after her lovers, in connection with which there are many old rhymes. Beans have not lost their popularity; and the leaves of the laurel still reveal the hidden fortune, having been also burnt in olden times by girls to win back their errant lovers.

The garden scene in "Faust" is a well-known illustration of the employment of the centaury or bluebottle for testing the faith of lovers, for Margaret selects it as the floral indication whence she may learn the truth respecting Faust:

> "And that scarlet poppies around like a bower,
> The maiden found her mystic flower.
> 'Now, gentle flower, I pray thee tell
> If my love loves, and loves me well;
> So may the fall of the morning dew
> Keep the sun from fading thy tender blue;
> Now I remember the leaves for my lot--
> He loves me not--he loves me--he loves me not--
> He loves me! Yes, the last leaf--yes!
> I'll pluck thee not for that last sweet guess;
> He loves me!' 'Yes,' a dear voice sighed;
> And her lover stands by Margaret's side."

Another mode of love-divination formerly much practised among the lower orders was known as "peascod-wooing." The cook, when shelling green peas, would, if she chanced to find a pod having nine, lay it on the lintel of the kitchen-door, when the first man who happened to enter was believed to be her future sweetheart; an allusion to which is thus given by Gay:

> "As peascod once I pluck'd, I chanced to see
> One that was closely fill'd with three times three,
> Which, when I cropp'd, I safely home couvey'd,
> And o'er the door the spell in secret laid.
> The latch mov'd up, when who should first come in,
> But, in his proper person, Lublerkin."

On the other hand, it was customary in the North of England to rub a young woman with pease-straw should her lover prove unfaithful:

> "If you meet a bonnie lassie,
>   Gie her a kiss and let her gae;
> If you meet a dirty hussey,
>   Fie, gae rub her o'er wi' strae!"

From an old Spanish proverb it would seem that the rosemary has long been considered as in some way connected with love:

> "Who passeth by the rosemarie
>   And careth not to take a spraye,
> For woman's love no care has he,
>   Nor shall he though he live for aye."

Of flowers and plants employed as love-charms on certain festivals may be noticed the bay, rosebud, and the hempseed on St. Valentine's Day, nuts on St. Mark's Eve, and the St. John's wort on Midsummer Eve.

In Denmark[1] many an anxious lover places the St. John's wort between the beams under the roof for the purpose of divination, the usual custom being to put one plant for herself and another for her sweetheart. Should these grow together, it is an omen of an approaching wedding. In Brittany young people prove the good faith of their lovers by a pretty ceremony. On St. John's Eve, the men, wearing bunches of green wheat ears, and the women decorated with flax blossoms, assemble round an old historic stone and place upon it their wreaths. Should these remain fresh for some time after, the lovers represented by them are to be united; but should they wither and die away, it is a certain proof that the love will as rapidly disappear.

Again, in Sicily it is customary for young women to throw from their windows an apple into the street, which, should a woman pick up, it is a sign that the girl will not be married during the year. Sometimes it happens that the apple is not touched, a circumstance which indicates that the young lady, when married, will ere long be a widow.

On this festival, too, the orpine or livelong has long been in request, popularly known as "Midsummer men," whereas in Italy the house-leek is in demand. The moss-rose, again, in years gone by, was plucked, with sundry formalities, on Midsummer Eve for love-divination, an allusion to which mode of forecasting the future, as practised in our own country, occurs in the poem of "The Cottage Girl:"

"The moss-rose that, at fall of dew,
Ere eve its duskier curtain drew,
Was freshly gathered from its stem,
She values as the ruby gem;
And, guarded from the piercing air,
With all an anxious lover's care,
She bids it, for her shepherd's sake,
Awake the New Year's frolic wake:
When faded in its altered hue,
She reads--the rustic is untrue!
But if its leaves the crimson paint,
Her sick'ning hopes no longer faint;
The rose upon her bosom worn,
She meets him at the peep of morn."

On the Continent the rose is still thought to possess mystic virtues in love matters, as in Thuringia, where girls foretell their future by means of rose-leaves.

A ceremony belonging to Hallowe'en is observed in Scotland with some trepidation, and consists in eating an apple before a looking-glass, when the face of the desired one will be seen. It is thus described by Burns:

"Wee Jenny to her granny says,
'Will ye gae wi' me, granny?
I'll eat the apple at the glass
I gat frae uncle Johnny.'
She fuff't her pipe wi' sic a lunt,

In wrath she was sae vap'rin,
She notic't na an aizle brunt
Her braw new worset apron
Out thro' that night.

'Ye little skelpie limmer's face!
I daur you try sic sportin'
As seek the foul thief ony place,
For him to spae your fortune;
Nae doubt but ye may get a sight!
Great cause ye hae to fear it,
For mony a ane has gotten a fright,
And lived and died deleeret
On sic a night.'"

Hallowe'en also is still a favourite anniversary for all kinds of nut-charms, and St. Thomas was long invoked when the prophetic onion named after him was placed under the pillow. Rosemary and thyme were used on St. Agnes' Eve with this formula:

"St. Agnes, that's to lovers kind,
Come, ease the troubles of my mind."

In Austria, on Christmas Eve, apples are used for divination. According to Mr. Conway, the apple must be cut in two in the dark, without being touched, the left half being placed in the bosom, and the right laid behind the door. If this latter ceremony be carefully carried out, the desired one may be looked for at midnight near the right half. He further tells us that in the Erzgebirge, the maiden, having slept on St. Andrew's, or Christmas, night with an apple under her pillow, "takes her stand with it in her hand on the next festival of the Church thereafter;

and the first man whom she sees, other than a relative, will become her husband."

Again, in Bohemia, on Christmas Eve, there is a pretty practice for young people to fix coloured wax-lights in the shells of the first nuts they have opened that day, and to float them in water, after silently assigning to each the name of some fancied wooer. He whose little barque is the first to approach the girl will be her future husband; but, on the other hand, should an unwelcome suitor seem likely to be the first, she blows against it, and so, by impeding its progress, allows the favoured barque to win.

In very early times flowers were mcuh in request as love-philtres, various allusions to which occur in the literature of most ages. Thus, in "A Midsummer Night's Dream," Oberon tells Puck to place a pansy on the eyes of Titania, in order that, on awaking, she may fall in love with the first object she encounters.

Gerarde speaks of the carrot as "serving for love matters," and adds that the root of the wild species is more effectual than that of the garden.

Vervain has long been in repute as a love-philtre, and in Germany now-a-days endive-seed is sold for its supposed power to influence the affections. The root of the male fern was in years gone by used in love-philtres, and hence the following allusion:

"'Twas the maiden's matchless beauty
That drew my heart a-nigh;
Not the fern-root potion,
But the glance of her blue eye."

Then there is the basil with its mystic virtues, and the cumin-see and cyclamen, which from the time of Theophrastus have been coveted for their magic virtues. The purslane, crocus, and periwinkle were thought to inspire love; while the agnus castus and the Saraca Indica (one of the sacred plants of India), a species of the willow, were supposed to drive away all feelings of love. Similarly in Voigtland, the common basil was regarded as a test of chastity, withering in the hands of the impure.

The mandrake, which is still worn in France as a love-charm, was employed by witches in the composition of their philtres; and in Bohemia, it is said that if a maiden can secretly put a sprig of the common clover into her lover's shoe ere he sets out on a journey, he will be faithful to her during his absence. As far back as the time of Pliny, the water-lily was regarded as an antidote to the love-philtre, and the amaranth was used for curbing the affections. On the other hand, Our Lady's bedstraw and the mallow were supposed to have the reverse effect, while the myrtle not only created love, but preserved it. The Sicilians still employ hemp to secure the affections of those they love, and gather it with various formalities,[2] fully believing in its potency. Indeed, charms of this kind are found throughout the world, every country having its own special plants in demand for this purpose.

However whimsical they may seem, they at any rate have the sanction of antiquity, and can claim an antecedent history certainly worthy of a better cause.

_____

Footnotes:

1. Thorpe's "Northern Mythology."
2. Fraser's Magazine, 1870, p. 720.

CHAPTER IX

DREAM-PLANTS

The importance attached to dreams in all primitive and savage culture accounts for the significance ascribed to certain plants found by visitors to dreamland. At the outset, it may be noticed that various drugs and narcotic potions have, from time immemorial, been employed for producing dreams and visions--a process still in force amongst uncivilised tribes. Thus the Mundrucus of North Brazil, when desirous of gaining information on any special subject, would administer to their seers narcotic drinks, so that in their dreams they might be favoured with the knowledge required. Certain of the Amazon tribes use narcotic plants for encouraging visions, and the Californian Indians, writes Mr. Tylor,[1] "would give children narcotic potions, to gain from the ensuing visions information about their enemies;" whilst, he adds, "the Darien Indians used the seeds of the Datura sanguinca to bring on in children prophetic delirium, in which they revealed hidden treasure." Similarly, the Delaware medicine-men used to drink decoctions of an intoxicating nature, "until their minds became wildered, so that they saw extraordinary visions."[2]

The North American Indians also held intoxication by tobacco to be supernatural ecstasy. It is curious to find a survival of this source of superstition in modern European folklore. Thus, on the Continent, many a lover puts the four-leaved clover under his pillow to dream of his lady-love; and in our own country, daisy-roots are used by the rustic maiden for the same purpose. The Russians are familiar with a certain herb, known as the son-trava, a dream herb, which has been identified with the Pulsatilla patens, and is said to blossom in April, and to have an azure-coloured flower. When placed under the pillow, it will induce dreams, which are generally supposed to be fulfilled. It has been suggested that it was from its title of "tree of dreams" that the elm became a prophetic tree, having been selected by Virgil in the Aeneid (vi.) as the roosting-place of dreams in gloomy Orcus:

"Full in the midst a spreading elm displayed
His aged arms, and cast a mighty shade;
Each trembling leaf with some light visions teems,
And leaves impregnated with airy dreams."

At the present day, the yarrow or milfoil is used by love-sick maidens, who are directed to pluck the mystic plant from a young man's grave, repeating meanwhile this formula:

"Yarrow, sweet yarrow, the first that I have found, In the name of Jesus Christ I pluck it from the ground; As Jesus loved sweet Mary and took her for His dear, So in a dream this night I hope my true love will appear."

Indeed, many other plants are in demand for this species of love-divination, some of which are associated with certain days and festivals. In Sweden, for instance, "if on Midsummer night nine kinds of flowers are laid under the head, a youth or maiden will dream of his or her sweetheart."[3] Hence in these simple and rustic love-charms may be traced similar beliefs as prevail among rude communities.

Again, among many of the American Indian tribes we find, according to Mr. Dorman,[4] "a mythical tree or vine, which has a sacredness connected with it of peculiar significance, forming a connecting-link and medium of communication between the world of the living and the dead. It is generally used by the spirit as a ladder to pass downward and upward upon; the Ojibways having possessed one of these vines, the upper end of which was twined round a star." He further adds that many traditions are told of attempts to climb these heavenly ladders; and, "if a young man has been much favoured with dreams, and the people believe he has the art of looking into futurity, the path is open to the highest honours. The future prophet puts down his dreams in pictographs, and when he has a collection of these, if they prove true in any respect, then this record of his revelations is appealed to as proof of his prophetic power." But, without enumerating further instances of these savage dream-traditions, which are closely allied with the animistic theories of primitive culture, we would turn to those plants which modern European folklore has connected with dreamland. These are somewhat extensive, but a brief survey of some of the most important ones will suffice to indicate their general significance.

Firstly, to dream of white flowers has been supposed to prognosticate death; with which may be compared the popular belief that "if a white rosebush puts forth unexpectedly, it is a sign of death to the nearest house;" dream-omens in many cases reflecting the superstitions of daily life. In Scotch ballads the birch is associated with the dead, an illustration of which we find in the subjoined lines:--

"I dreamed a dreary dream last nicht;
 God keep us a' frae sorrow!
I dreamed I pu'd the birk sae green,
 Wi' my true love on Yarrow.

I'll redde your dream, my sister dear,
I'll tell you a' your sorrow;
You pu'd the birk wi' your true love;
He's killed,--he's killed on Yarrow."

Of the many plants which have been considered of good omen when seen in dreams, may be mentioned the palm-tree, olive, jasmine, lily, laurel, thistle, thorn, wormwood, currant, pear, &c.; whereas the greatest luck attaches to the rose. On the other hand, equally numerous are the plants which denote misfortune. Among these may be included the plum, cherry, withered roses, walnut, hemp, cypress, dandelion, &c. Beans are still said to produce bad dreams and to portend evil; and according to a Leicestershire saying, "If you wish for awful dreams or desire to go crazy, sleep in a bean-field all night." Some plants are said to foretell long life, such as the oak, apricot, apple, box, grape, and fig; and sickness is supposed to be presaged by such plants as the elder, onion, acorn, and plum.

Love and marriage are, as might be expected, well represented in the dream-flora; a circumstance, indeed, which has not failed to impress the young at all times. Thus, foremost amongst the flowers which indicate success in love is the rose, a fact which is not surprising when it is remembered how largely this favourite of our gardens enters into love-divinations. Then there is the clover, to dream of which foretells not only a happy marriage, but one productive of wealth and prosperity. In this case, too, it must be remembered the clover has long been reckoned as a mystic plant, having in most European countries been much employed for the purposes of divination. Of further plants credited as auguring well for love affairs are the raspberry, pomegranate, cucumber, currant, and box; but the walnut implies unfaithfulness, and the act of cutting parsley is an omen that the person so occupied will sooner or later be crossed in love. This ill-luck attached to parsley is in some measure explained from the fact that in many respects it is an unlucky plant. It is a belief, as we have noticed elsewhere, widely spread in Devonshire, that to transplant parsley is to commit a serious offence against the guardian genius who presides over parsley-beds, certain to be punished either on the offender himself or some member of his family within the course of the year. Once more "to dream of cutting cabbage," writes Mr. Folkard,[5] "Denotes jealousy on the part of wife, husband, or lover, as the case may be. To dream of any one else cutting them portends an attempt by some person to create jealousy in the loved one's mind. To dream of eating cabbages implies sickness to loved ones and loss of money." The bramble, an important plant in folklore, is partly unlucky, and, "To dream of passing through places covered with brambles portends troubles; if they prick you, secret enemies will do you an injury with your friends; if they draw blood, expect heavy losses in trade." But to dream of passing through brambles unhurt denotes a triumph over enemies. To dream of being pricked with briars, says the "Royal Dream Book,"[6] "shows that the person dreaming has an ardent desire to something, and that young folks dreaming thus are in love, who prick themselves in striving to gather their rose."

Some plants are said to denote riches, such as the oak, marigold, pear and nut tree, while the gathering of nuts is said to presage the discovery of unexpected wealth. Again, to dream of fruit or flowers out of season is a bad omen, a notion, indeed, with which we find various proverbs current throughout the country. Thus, the Northamptonshire peasant considers the blooming of the apple-tree after the fruit is ripe as a certain omen of death--a belief embodied in the following proverb:

"A bloom upon the apple-tree when the apples are ripe,
Is a sure termination to somebody's life."

And once more, according to an old Sussex adage--

"Fruit out of season
Sounds out of reason."

On the other hand, to dream of fruit or any sort of crop during its proper season is still an indication of good luck.[7] Thus it is lucky to dream of daisies in spring-time or summer, but just the reverse in autumn or winter. Without enumerating further instances of this kind, we may quote the subjoined rhyme relating to the onion, as a specimen of many similar ones scattered here and there in various countries:[8]

"To dream of eating onions means
Much strife in thy domestic scenes,
Secrets found out or else betrayed,
And many falsehoods made and said."

Many plants in dream-lore have more than one meaning attached to them. Thus from the, "Royal Dream Book" we learn that yellow flowers "predict love mixed with jealousy, and that you will have more children to maintain than what justly belong to you." To dream of garlic indicates the discovery of hidden treasures, but the approach of some domestic quarrel.

Cherries, again, indicate inconstancy; but one would scarcely expect to find the thistle regarded as lucky; for, according to an old piece of folklore, to dream of being surrounded by this plant is a propitious sign, foretelling that the person will before long have some pleasing intelligence. In the same way a similar meaning in dream-lore attaches to the thorn.

According to old dream-books, the dreaming of yew indicates the death of an aged person, who will leave considerable wealth behind him; while the violet is said to devote advancement in life. Similarly, too, the vine foretells prosperity, "for which," says a dream interpreter, "we have the example of Astyages, king of the Medes, who dreamed that his daughter brought forth a vine, which was a prognostic of the grandeur, riches, and felicity of the great Cyrus, who was born of her after this dream."

Plucking ears of corn signifies the existence of secret enemies, and Mr. Folkard quotes an old authority which tells us that the juniper is potent in dreams. Thus, "it is unlucky to dream of the tree itself, especially if the person be sick; but to dream of gathering the berries, if it be in winter, denotes prosperity. To dream of the actual berries signifies that the dreamer will shortly arrive at great honours and become an important person. To the married it foretells the birth of a male child."

Again, eating almonds signifies a journey, its success or otherwise being denoted by their tasting sweet or the contrary. Dreaming of grass is an auspicious omen, provided it be green and fresh; but if it be withered and decayed, it is a sign of the approach of misfortune and sickness, followed perhaps by death. Woe betide, too, the person who dreams that he is cutting grass.

Certain plants produce dreams on particular occasions. The mugwort and plantain have long been associated with Midsummer; and, according to Thomas Hill in his "Natural and Artificial Conclusions," a rare coal is to be found under these plants but one hour in the day, and one day in the year. When Aubrey happened to be walking behind Montague House at twelve o'clock on Midsummer day, he relates how he saw about twenty-two young women, most of them well dressed, and apparently all very busy weeding. On making inquiries, he was informed that they were looking for a coal under the root of a plantain, to put beneath their heads that night, when they would not fail to dream of their future husbands. But, unfortunately for this credulity, as an old author long ago pointed out, the coal is nothing but an old dead root, and that it may be found almost any day and hour when sought for. By lovers the holly has long been supposed to have mystic virtues as a dream-plant when used on the eve of any of the following festivals:

Christmas,
New Year's Day,
Midsummer, and
All Hallowe'en.

According to the mode of procedure practised in the northern counties, the anxious maiden, before retiring to rest, places three pails full of water in her bedroom, and then pins to her night-dress three leaves of green holly opposite to her heart, after which she goes to sleep. Believing in the efficacy of the charm, she persuades herself that she will be roused from her first slumber by three yells, as if from the throats of three bears, succeeded by as many hoarse laughs. When these have died away, the form of her future husband will appear, who will show his attachment to her by changing the position of the water-pails, whereas if he have no particular affection he will disappear without even touching them.

Then, of course, from time immemorial all kinds of charms have been observed on St. Valentine's Day to produce prophetic dreams. A popular charm consisted of placing two bay leaves, after sprinkling them with rose-water, across the pillow, repeating this formula:--

"Good Valentine, be kind to me,
In dream let me my true love see."

St. Luke's Day was in years gone by a season for love-divination, and among some of the many directions given we may quote the subjoined, which is somewhat elaborate:--

"Take marigold flowers, a sprig of
marjoram, thyme, and a little wormwood; dry them before a fire, rub them
to powder, then sift it through a fine piece of lawn; simmer these with
a small quantity of virgin honey, in white vinegar, over a slow fire;
with this anoint your stomach, breasts, and lips, lying down, and repeat
these words thrice:--

'St Luke, St. Luke, be kind to me,
In dream let me my true love see!'

This said, hasten to sleep, and in the soft slumbers of night's repose, the very
man whom you shall marry shall appear before you."

Lastly, certain plants have been largely used by gipsies and fortune-tellers for invoking dreams, and in many a country village these are plucked and given to the anxious inquirer with various formulas.

Footnotes:

1. "Primitive Culture," 1873, ii. 416, 417.
2. See Dorman's "Primitive Superstition," p. 68.
3. Thorpe's "Northern Mythology," 1851, ii. 108.
4. "Primitive Superstitions," p. 67.
5. "Plant-lore Legends and Lyrics," p. 265.
6. Quoted in Brand's "Popular Antiquities," 1849, iii. 135.
7. See Friend's "Flower-Lore," i. 207.
8. Folkard's "Plant-lore Legends and Lyrics," p. 477.

CHAPTER X

PLANTS AND THE WEATHER

The influence of the weather on plants is an agricultural belief which is firmly credited by the modern husbandman. In many instances his meteorological notions are the result of observation, although in some cases the reason assigned for certain pieces of weather-lore is far from obvious. Incidental allusion has already been made to the astrological doctrine of the influence of the moon's changes on plants--a belief which still retains its hold in most agricultural districts. It appears that in years gone by "neither sowing, planting, nor grafting was ever undertaken without a scrupulous attention to the increase or waning of the moon;"[1] and the advice given by Tusser in his "Five Hundred Points of Husbandry" is not forgotten even at the present day:--

"Sow peas and beans in the wane of the moon,
Who soweth them sooner, he soweth too soon,
That they with the planet may rest and rise,
And flourish with bearing, most plentiful-wise."

Many of the old gardening books give the same advice, although by some
it has been severely ridiculed.

Scott, in his "Discoverie of Witchcraft," notes how, "the poor husbandman perceiveth that the increase of the moon maketh plants fruitful, so as in the full moone they are in best strength, decaying in the wane, and in the conjunction do entirely wither and fade." Similarly the growth of mushrooms is said to be affected by the weather, and in Devonshire apples "shrump up" if picked during a waning moon.[2]

One reason, perhaps, for the attention so universally paid to the moon's changes in agricultural pursuits is, writes Mr. Farrer, "that they are far more remarkable than any of the sun's, and more calculated to inspire dread by the nocturnal darkness they contend with, and hence are held in popular fancy nearly everywhere, to cause, portend, or accord with changes in the lot of mortals, and all things terrestrial."[3]

On this assumption may be explained the idea that the, "moon's wane makes things on earth to wane; when it is new or full it is everywhere the proper season for new crops to be sown." In the Hervey Islands cocoa-nuts are generally planted in the full of the moon, the size of the latter being regarded as symbolical of the ultimate fulness of the fruit.

In the same way the weather of certain seasons of the year is supposed to influence the vegetable world, and in Rutlandshire we are told that "a green Christmas brings a heavy harvest;" but a full moon about Christmas Day is unlucky, hence the adage:

"Light Christmas, light wheatsheaf,
Dark Christmas, heavy wheatsheaf."

If the weather be clear on Candlemas Day "corn and fruits will then be dear," and "whoever doth plant or sow on Shrove Tuesday, it will always remain green." According to a piece of weather-lore in Sweden, there is a saying that to strew ash branches in a field on Ash Wednesday is equivalent to three days' rain and three days' sun. Rain on Easter Day foretells a good harvest but poor hay crop, while thunder on All Fool's Day "brings good crops of corn and hay." According to the "Shepherd's Calendar," if, "Midsummer Day be never so little rainy the hazel and walnut will be scarce; corn smitten in many places; but apples, pears, and plums will not be hurt." And we are further reminded:--

"Till St. James's Day be come and gone,
There may be hops or there may be none."

Speaking of hops, it is said, "plenty of ladybirds, plenty of hops." It is also a popular notion among our peasantry that if a drop of rain hang on an oat at this season there will be a good crop. Another agricultural adage says:--

"No tempest, good July, lest corn come off bluely."

Then there is the old Michaelmas rhyme:--

"At Michaelmas time, or a little before,
Half an apple goes to the core;
At Christmas time, or a little after,
A crab in the hedge, and thanks to the grafter."

On the other hand, the blossoming of plants at certain times is said to be an indication of the coming weather, and so when the bramble blooms early in June an early harvest may be expected; and in the northern counties the peasant judges of the advance of the year by the appearance of the daisy, affirming that "spring has not arrived till you can set your foot on twelve daisies." We are also told that when many hawthorn blossoms are seen a severe winter will follow; and, according to Wilsford, "the broom having plenty of blossoms is a sign of a fruitful year of corn." A Surrey proverb tells us that "It's always cold when the blackthorn comes into flower;" and there is the rhyme which reminds us that:--

"If the oak is out before the ash,
'Twill be a summer of wet and splash;
But if the ash is before the oak,
'Twill be a summer of fire and smoke."

There are several versions of this piece of weather-lore, an old Kentish one being "Oak, smoke; ash, quash;" and according to a version given in Notes and Queries (1st Series v. 71):--

"If the oak's before the ash, then you'll only get a splash,
If the ash precedes the oak, then you may expect a soak."

From the "Shepherd's Calendar" we learn that, "If in the fall of the leaf in October many leaves wither on the boughs and hang there, it betokens a frosty winter and much snow," with which may be compared a Devonshire saying:--

"If good apples you would have
The leaves must go into the grave."

Or, in other words, "you must plant your trees in the fall of the leaf." And again, "Apples, pears, hawthorn-quick, oak; set them at All-hallow-tide and command them to prosper; set them at Candlemas and entreat them to grow."

In Germany,[4] too, there is a rhyme which may be thus translated:--

"When the hawthorn bloom too early shows,
We shall have still many snows."

In the same way the fruit of trees and plants was regarded as a prognostication of the ensuing weather, and Wilsford tells us that "great store of walnuts and almonds presage a plentiful year of corn, especially filberts." The notion that an abundance of haws betokens a hard winter is still much credited, and has given rise to the familiar Scotch proverb:--

"Mony haws,
Mony snaws."

Another variation of the same adage in Kent is, "A plum year, a dumb year," and, "Many nits, many pits," implying that the abundance of nuts in the autumn indicates the "pits" or graves of those who shall succumb to the hard and inclement weather of winter; but, on the other hand, "A cherry year, a merry year." A further piece of weather-lore tells us:--

"Many rains, many rowans;
Many rowans, many yawns,"

The meaning being that an abundance of rowans--the fruit of the mountain-ash--denote a deficient harvest.

Among further sayings of this kind may be noticed one relating to the onion, which is thus:--

"Onion's skin very thin,
Mild-winter's coming in;
Onion's skin thick and tough,
Coming winter cold and rough."

Again, many of our peasantry have long been accustomed to arrange their farming pursuits from the indications given them by sundry trees and plants. Thus it is said--

"When the sloe tree is as white as a sheet,
Sow your barley whether it be dry or wet."

With which may be compared another piece of weather-lore:--

"When the oak puts on his gosling grey,
'Tis time to sow barley night or day."

The leafing of the elm has from time immemorial been made to regulate agricultural operations, and hence the old rule:--

"When the elmen leaf is as big as a mouse's ear,
Then to sow barley never fear.
When the elmen leaf is as big as an ox's eye,
Then say I, 'Hie, boys, hie!'"

A Warwickshire variation is:--

"When elm leaves are big as a shilling,
Plant kidney beans, if to plant 'em you're willing.
When elm leaves are as big as a penny,
You must plant kidney beans if you mean to have any."

But if the grass grow in January, the husbandman is recommended to *"lock his grain in the granary,"* while a further proverb informs us that:--

"On Candlemas Day if the thorns hang a drop,
You are sure of a good pea crop."

In bygone times the appearance of the berries of the elder was held to indicate the proper season for sowing wheat:--

"With purple fruit when elder branches bend,
And their high hues the hips and cornels lend,
Ere yet chill hoar-frost comes, or sleety rain,
Sow with choice wheat the neatly furrowed plain."

The elder is not without its teaching, and according to a popular old proverb:--

"When the elder is white, brew and bake a peck,
When the elder is black, brew and bake a sack."

According to an old proverb, "You must look for grass on the top of the oak tree," the meaning being, says Ray, that "the grass seldom springs well before the oak begins to put forth."

In the Western Counties it is asserted that frost ceases as soon as the mulberry tree bursts into leaf, with which may be compared the words of Autolycus in the "Winter's Tale" (iv. 3):--

"When daffodils begin to peer,
With heigh! the doxy over the dale,
Why, then conies in the sweet o' the year."

The dairyman is recommended in autumn to notice the appearance of the fern, because:--

"When the fern is as high as a ladle,
You may sleep as long as you are able.
When the fern begins to look red,
Then milk is good with brown bread."

Formerly certain agricultural operations were regulated by the seasons, and an old rule tells the farmer--

"Upon St. David's Day, put oats and barley in the clay."

Another version being:--

"Sow peas and beans on David and Chad,
Be the weather good or bad."

A Somersetshire piece of agricultural lore fixes an earlier date, and bids the farmer to "sow or set beans in Candlemas waddle." In connection with the inclement weather that often prevails throughout the spring months it is commonly said, "They that go to their corn in May may come weeping away," but "They that go in June may come back with a merry tune." Then there is the following familiar pretty couplet, of which there are several versions:--

"The bee doth love the sweetest flower,
So doth the blossom the April shower."

In connection with beans, there is a well-known adage which says:--

"Be it weal or be it woe,
Beans should blow before May go."

Of the numerous other items of plant weather-lore, it is said that "March wind wakes the ether (i. e., adder) and blooms the whin;" and many of our peasantry maintain that:--

"A peck of March dust and a shower in May,
Makes the corn green and the fields gay."

It should also be noted that many plants are considered good barometers. Chickweed, for instance, expands its leaves fully when fine weather is to follow; but "if it should shut up, then the traveller is to put on his greatcoat."[5] The same, too, is said to be the case with the pimpernel, convolvulus, and clover; while if the marigold does not open its petals by seven o'clock in the morning, either rain or thunder may be expected in the course of the day. According to Wilsford, "tezils, or fuller's thistle, being gathered and hanged up in the house, where the air may come freely to it, upon the alteration of cold and windy weather will grow smoother, and against rain will close up its prickles." Once more, according to the "Shepherd's Calendar," "Chaff, leaves, thistle-down, or such light things whisking about and turning round foreshows tempestuous winds;" And Coles, in his introduction to the "Knowledge of Plants," informs us that, "If the down flieth off colt's-foot, dandelion, and thistles when there is no wind, it is a sign of rain."

Some plants, again, have gained a notoriety from opening or shutting their flowers at the sun's bidding; in allusion to which Perdita remarks in the "Winter's Tale" (iv. 3):--

"The marigold, that goes to bed with the sun, and with him
rises weeping."

It was also erroneously said, like the sun-flower, to turn its blossoms to the sun, the latter being thus described by Thomson:--

"The lofty follower of the sun,
Sad when he sets, shuts up her yellow leaves,
Drooping all night, and, when he warm returns,
Points her enamour'd bosom to his ray."

Another plant of this kind is the endive, which is said to open its petals at eight o'clock in the morning, and to close them at four in the afternoon. Thus we are told how:--

"On upland slopes the shepherds mark
The hour when, to the dial true,
Cichorium to the towering lark,
Lifts her soft eye, serenely blue."

And as another floral index of the time of day may be noticed the goat's-beard, opening at sunrise and closing at noon--hence one of its popular names of "Go to bed at noon." This peculiarity is described by Bishop Mant:--

"And goodly now the noon-tide hour,
When from his high meridian tower
The sun looks down in majesty,
What time about, the grassy lea.
The goat's-beard, prompt his rise to hail,
With broad expanded disk, in veil
Close mantling wraps its yellow head,
And goes, as peasants say, to bed."

The dandelion has been nicknamed the peasant's clock, its flowers opening very early in the morning; while its feathery seed-tufts have long been in requisition as a barometer with children:--

"Dandelion, with globe of down,
The schoolboy's clock in every town,
Which the truant puffs amain
To conjure lost hours back again."

Among other flowers possessing a similar feature may be noticed the wild succory, creeping mallow, purple sandwort, small bindweed, common nipplewort, and smooth sow-thistle. Then of course there is the pimpernel, known as the shepherd's clock and poor man's weather-glass; while the small purslane and the common garden lettuce are also included in the flower-clock.[6]

Among further items of weather-lore associated with May, we are told how he that "sows oats in May gets little that way," and "He who mows in May will have neither fruit nor hay." Calm weather in June "sets corn in tune;" and a Suffolk adage says:--

"Cut your thistles before St. John,
You will have two instead of one."

But "Midsummer rain spoils hay and grain," whereas it is commonly said that,

"A leafy May, and a warm June,
Bring on the harvest very soon."

Again, boisterous wet weather during the month of July is to be deprecated, for, as the old adage runs:--

"No tempest, good July,
Lest the corn look surly."

Flowers of this kind are very numerous, and under a variety of forms prevail largely in our own and other countries, an interesting collection of which have been collected by Mr. Swainson in his interesting little volume on "Weather Folklore," in which he has given the parallels in foreign countries. It must be remembered, however, that a great number of these plant-sayings originated very many years ago--long before the alteration in the style of the calendar--which in numerous instances will account for their apparent contradictory character. In noticing, too, these proverbs, account must be taken of the variation of climate in different countries, for what applies to one locality does not to another. Thus, for instance, according to a Basque proverb, "A wet May, a fruitful year," whereas it is said in Corsica, "A rainy May brings little barley and no wheat." Instances of this kind are of frequent occurrence, and of course are in many cases explained by the difference of climate. But in comparing all branches of folklore, similar variations, as we have already observed, are noticeable, to account for which is often a task full of difficulty.

Of the numerous other instances of weather-lore associated with agricultural operations, it is said in relation to rain:--

"Sow beans in the mud, and they'll grow like wood."

And a saying in East Anglia is to this effect:--

"Sow in the slop (or sop), heavy at top."

A further admonition advises the farmer to

"Sow wheat in dirt, and rye in dust;"

While, according to a piece of folklore current in East Anglia, "Wheat well-sown is half-grown." The Scotch have a proverb warning the farmer against premature sowing:--

"Nae hurry wi' your corns,
 Nae hurry wi' your harrows;
Snaw lies ahint the dyke,
 Mair may come and fill the furrows."

And according to another old adage we are told how:--

"When the aspen leaves are no bigger than your nail,
Is the time to look out for truff and peel." [7]

In short, it will be found that most of our counties have their items of weather-lore; many of which, whilst varying in some respect, are evidently modifications of one and the same belief. In many cases, too, it must be admitted that this species of weather-wisdom is not based altogether on idle fancy, but in accordance with recognised habits of plants under certain conditions of weather. Indeed, it has been pointed out that so sensitive are various flowers to any change in the temperature or the amount of light, that it has been noticed that there is as much as one hour's difference between the time when the same flower opens at Paris and Upsala. It is, too, a familiar fact to students of vegetable physiology that the leaves of Porleria hygrometrica fold down or rise up in accordance with the state of the atmosphere. In short, it was pointed out in the Standard, in illustration of the extreme sensitiveness of certain plants to surrounding influences, how the Haedysarums have been well known ever since the days of Linnseus to suddenly begin to quiver without any apparent cause, and just as suddenly to stop. Force cannot initiate the movement, though cold will stop it, and heat will set in motion again the suspended animation of the leaves. If artificially kept from moving they will, when released, instantly begin their task anew and with redoubled energy. Similarly the leaves of the Colocasia esculenta--the tara of the Sandwich Islands--will often shiver at irregular times of the day and night, and with such energy that little bells hung on the petals tinkle. And yet, curious to say, we are told that the keenest eye has not yet been able to detect any peculiarity in these plants to account for these strange motions. It has been suggested that they are due to changes in the weather of such a slight character that, "our nerves are incapable of appreciating them, or the mercury of recording their accompanying oscillations."

Footnotes:

1. Tylor's "Primitive Culture," 1873, i. 130.
2. See "English Folklore," pp. 42, 43.
3. "Primitive Manners and Customs," p. 74.
4. Dublin University Magazine, December 1873, p. 677.
5. See Swainson's "Weather-lore," p. 257.
6. See "Flower-lore," p. 226.
7. See Notes and Queries, 1st Ser. II. 511.

CHAPTER XI

PLANT PROVERBS

A host of curious proverbs have, from the earliest period, clustered round the vegetable world, most of which--gathered from experience and observation--embody an immense amount of truth, besides in numerous instances conveying an application of a moral nature. These proverbs, too, have a very wide range, and on this account are all the more interesting from the very fact of their referring to so many conditions of life. Thus, the familiar adage which tells us that "nobody is fond of fading flowers," has a far deeper signification, reminding us that everything associated with change and decay must always be a matter of regret. To take another trite proverb of the same kind, we are told how "truths and roses have thorns about them," which is absolutely true; and there is the well-known expression "to pipe in an ivy leaf," which signifies "to go and engage in some futile or idle pursuit" which cannot be productive of any good. The common proverb, "He hath sown his wild oats," needs no comment; and the inclination of evil to override good is embodied in various adages, such, as, "The weeds o'ergrow the corn," while the tenacity with which evil holds its ground is further expressed in such sayings as this--"The frost hurts not weeds." The poisonous effects, again, of evil is exemplified thus--"One ill-bred mars a whole pot of pottage," and the rapidity with which it spreads has, amongst other proverbs, been thus described, "Evil weeds grow apace." Speaking of weeds in their metaphorical sense, we may quote one further adage respecting them:--

"A weed that runs to seed
Is a seven years' weed."

And the oft-quoted phrase, "It will be a nosegay to him as long as he lives," implies that disagreeable actions, instead of being lost sight of, only too frequently cling to a man in after years, or, as Ray says, "stink in his nostrils." The man who abandons some good enterprise for a worthless, or insignificant, undertaking is said to "cut down an oak and plant a thistle," of which there is a further version, "to cut down an oak and set up a strawberry." The truth of the next adage needs no comment--"Usurers live by the fall of heirs, as swine by the droppings of acorns." Things that are slow but sure in their progress are the subject of a well-known Gloucestershire saying:--

"It is as long in coming as Cotswold barley."

"The corn in this cold country," writes Ray, "exposed to the winds, bleak and shelterless, is very backward at the first, but afterwards overtakes the forwardest in the country, if not in the barn, in the bushel, both for the quantity and goodness thereof." According to the Italians, "Every grain hath its bran," which corresponds with our saying, "Every bean hath its black," The meaning being that nothing is without certain imperfections. A person in extreme poverty is often described as being "as bare as the birch at Yule Even," and an ill-natured or evil-disposed person who tries to do harm, but cannot, is commonly said to:--

"Jump at it like a cock at a gooseberry."

Then the idea of durableness is thus expressed in a Wiltshire proverb:--

"An eldern stake and a blackthorn ether [hedge],
Will make a hedge to last for ever"--

an elder stake being commonly said to last in the ground longer than an iron bar of the same size.[1]
A person who is always on the alert to make use of opportunities, and never allows a good thing to escape his grasp, is said to "have a ready mouth for a ripe cherry." The rich beauty, too, of the cherry, which causes it to be gathered, has had this moral application attached to it:--

"A woman and a cherry are painted for their own harm."

Speaking of cherries, it may be mentioned that the awkwardness of eating them on account of their stones, has given rise to sundry proverbs, as the following:--

"Eat peas with the king, and cherries with the beggar,"

and:--

"Those that eat cherries with great persons shall have their eyes
squirted out with the stones."

A man who makes a great show without a corresponding practice is said to be like "fig-tree fuel, much smoke and little fire," and another adage says:--

"Peel a fig for your friend, and a peach for your enemy."

This proverb, however, is not quite clear when applied to this country. "To peel a fig, so far as we are concerned," writes Mr. Hazlitt[2], "can have no significance, except that we should not regard it as a friendly service; but, in fact, the proverb is merely a translation from the Spanish, and in that language and country the phrase carries a very full meaning, as no one would probably like to eat a fig without being sure that the fruit had not been tampered with. The whole saying is, however, rather unintelligible. 'Peeling a peach' would be treated anywhere as a dubious attention."

Of the many proverbs connected with thorns, there is the true one which tells us how,

"He that goes barefoot must not plant thorns,"

The meaning of which is self-evident, and the person who lives in a chronic state of uneasiness is said to, "sit on thorns." Then there is the oft-quoted adage:--

"While thy shoe is on thy foot, tread upon the thorns."

On the other hand, that no position in life is exempt from trouble of some kind is embodied in this proverb:--

"Wherever a man dwells he shall be sure to have a thorn bush near his door,"

which Ray also explains in its literal sense, remarking that there "are few places in England where a man can dwell, but he shall have one near him." Then, again, thorns are commonly said to "make the greatest crackling," and "the thorn comes forth with its point forward."

Many a great man has wished himself poor and obscure in his hours of adversity, a sentiment contained in the following proverb:--

"The pine wishes herself a shrub when the axe is at her root."

A quaint phrase applied to those who expect events to take an unnatural turn is:--

"Would you have potatoes grow by the pot-side?"

Amongst some of the other numerous proverbs may be mentioned a few relating to the apple; one of these reminding us that,

"An apple, an egg, and a nut,
You may eat after a slut."

Selfishness in giving is thus expressed:--

"To give an apple where there is an orchard."

And the idea of worthlessness is often referred to as when it is said that "There is small choice in rotten apples," with which may be compared another which warns us of the contagious effects of bad influence:--

"The rotten apple injures its neighbour."

The utter dissimilarity which often exists between two persons, or things, is jocularly enjoined in the familiar adage:--

"As like as an apple is to a lobster,"

And the folly of taking what one knows is paltry or bad has given rise to an instructive proverb:--

"Better give an apple than eat it."

The folly of expecting good results from the most unreasonable causes is the subject of the following old adage:--

"Plant the crab where you will, it will never bear pippins."

The crab tree has also been made the subject of several amusing rhymes, one of which is as follows:--

"The crab of the wood is sauce very good for the crab of the sea,
But the wood of the crab is sauce for a drab that will not her
husband obey."

The coolness of the cucumber has long ago become proverbial for a person of a cold collected nature, "As cool as a cucumber," and the man who not only makes unreasonable requests, but equally expects them to be gratified, is said to "ask an elm-tree for pears." Then, again, foolish persons who have no power of observation, are likened to "a blind goose that knows not a fox from a fern bush."

The willow has long been a proverbial symbol of sadness, and on this account it was customary for those who were forsaken in love to wear a garland made of willow. Thus in "Othello," Desdemona (Act iv. sc. 3) anticipating her death, says:--

"My mother had a maid called Barbara:
She was in love; and he she loved proved mad,
And did forsake her: she had a song of willow;
An old thing 'twas, but it expressed her fortune,
And she died singing it: that song to-night
Will not go from my mind."

According to another adage:--

"Willows are weak, yet they bind other wood,"

The significance of which is clear. Then, again, there is the not very complimentary proverbial saying, of which there are several versions:--

"A spaniel, a woman, and a walnut-tree,
The more they're beaten, the better they be."

Another variation, given by Moor in his "Suffolk Words" (p. 465), is this:--

"Three things by beating better prove:
A nut, an ass, a woman;
The cudgel from their back remove,
And they'll be good for no man."

A curious phrase current in Devonshire for a young lady who jilts a man is, "She has given him turnips;" and an expressive one for those persons who in spite of every kindness are the very reverse themselves is this:--

"Though you stroke the nettle
ever so kindly, yet it will sting you;"

With which may be compared a similar proverb equally suggestive:--

"He that handles a nettle tenderly is soonest stung."

The ultimate effects of perseverance, coupled with time, is thus shown:--

*"With time and patience the leaf of the mulberry tree
becomes satin."*

A phrase current, according to Ray, in Gloucestershire for those "who always have a sad, severe, and terrific countenance," is, "He looks as if he lived on Tewkesbury mustard"--this town having been long noted for its "mustard-balls made there, and sent to other parts." It may be remembered that in "2 Henry IV." (Act ii. sc. 4) Falstaff speaks of "wit as thick as Tewkesbury mustard." Then there is the familiar adage applied to the man who lacks steady application, "A rolling stone gathers no moss," with which may be compared another, "Seldom mosseth the marble-stone that men [tread] oft upon."

Among the good old proverbs associated with flax may be mentioned the following, which enjoins the necessity of faith in our actions:--

"Get thy spindle and thy distaff ready, and God will send the flax."

A popular phrase speaks of "An owl in an ivy-bush," which perhaps was originally meant to denote the union of wisdom with conviviality, equivalent to "Be merry and wise." Formerly an ivy-bush was a common tavern sign, and gave rise to the familiar proverb, "Good wine needs no bush," this plant having been selected probably from having been sacred to Bacchus.

According to an old proverb respecting the camomile, we are told that "the more it is trodden the more it will spread," an allusion to which is made by Falstaff in "I Henry IV." (Act ii. sc. 4):--

*"For though the camomile, the more it is trodden on, the faster it
grows; yet youth, the more it is wasted, the sooner it wears."*

There are many proverbs associated with the oak. Referring to its growth, we are told that "The willow will buy a horse before the oak will pay for a saddle," the allusion being, of course, to the different rates at which trees grow. That occasionally some trifling event may have the most momentous issues is thus exemplified:--

"The smallest axe may fell the largest oak;"

Although, on the other hand, it is said that:--

"An oak is not felled at one chop."

A further variation of the same idea tells us how:--

"Little strokes fell great oaks,"

In connection with which may be quoted the words of Ovid to the same effect:--

"Quid magis est durum saxo? Quid mollius unda?
Dura taneu molli saxa cavantur aqua?"

Then, again, it is commonly said that:--

"Oaks may fall when seeds brave the storm."

And to give one more illustration:--

"The greatest oaks have been little acorns."

Similarly, with trees in general, we find a good number of proverbs. Thus one informs us that "Wise men in the world are like timber trees in a hedge, here and there one." That there is some good in every one is illustrated by this saying--"There's no tree but bears some fruit." The familiar proverb, that "The tree is no sooner down but every one runs for his hatchet," explains itself, whereas "The highest tree hath the greater fall," which, in its moral application, is equally true. Again, an agricultural precept enjoins the farmer to "Set trees poor and they will grow rich; set them rich and they will grow poor," that is, remove them out of a more barren into a fatter soil. That success can only be gained by toil is illustrated in this proverb--"He that would have the fruit must climb the tree," and once more it is said that "He who plants trees loves others beside himself."

In the Midland counties there is a proverbial saying that "if there are no kegs or seeds in the ash trees, there will be no king within the twelvemonth," the ash never being wholly destitute of kegs. Another proverb refers to the use of ash-wood for burning:--

"Burn ash-wood green,
'Tis a fire for a queen,
Burn ash-wood dear,
'Twill make a man swear;"

The meaning being that the ash when green burns well, but when dry or withered just the reverse.

A form of well-wishing formerly current in Yorkshire was thus:--

"May your footfall be by the root of an ash,"

In allusion, it has been suggested, to the fact that the ash is a capital tree for draining the soil in its vicinity.

But leaving trees, an immense number of proverbs are associated with corn, many of which are very varied. Thus, of those who contrive to get a good return for their meagre work or money, it is said:--

"You have made a long harvest for a little corn,"

With which may be compared the phrase:--

"You give me coloquintida (colocynth) *for Herb-John."*

Those who reap advantage from another man's labour are said to "put their sickle into another man's corn," and the various surroundings of royalty, however insignificant they may be, are generally better, says the proverb, than the best thing of the subjects:--

"The king's chaff is better than other people's corn."

Among the proverbs relating to grass may be mentioned the popular one, "He does not let the grass grow under his feet;" another old version of which is, "No grass grows on his heel." Another well-known adage reminds us that:--

"The higher the hill the lower the grass."

And equally familiar is the following:--

"While the grass groweth the seely horse starveth."

In connection with hops, the proverb runs that "hops make or break;" and no hop-grower, writes, Mr. Hazlitt,[3] "will have much difficulty in appreciating this proverbial dictum. An estate has been lost or won in the course of a single season; but the hop is an expensive plant to rear, and a bad year may spoil the entire crop."

Actions which produce different results to what are expected are thus spoken of:--

"You set saffron and there came up wolfsbane."

In Devonshire it may be noted that this plant is used to denote anything of value; and it is related of a farmer near Exeter who, when praising a certain farm, remarked, "'Tis a very pretty little place; he'd let so dear as saffron."

Many, again, are the proverbial sayings associated with roses--most of these being employed to indicate what is not only sweet and lovely, but bright and joyous. Thus, there are the well-known phrases, "A bed of roses," and "As sweet as a rose," and the oft-quoted popular adage:--

"The rose, called by any other name, would smell as sweet,"

Which, as Mr. Hazlitt remarks, "although not originally proverbial, or in its nature, or even in the poet's intention so, has acquired that character by long custom."

An old adage, which is still credited by certain of our country folk, reminds us that:--

"A parsley field will bring a man to his saddle
and a woman to her grave,"

A warning which is not unlike one current in Surrey and other southern counties:--

"Where parsley's grown in the garden, there'll be a death before the year's out."

In Devonshire it has long been held unlucky to transplant parsley, and a poor woman in the neighbourhood of Morwenstow attributed a certain stroke with which one of her children had been afflicted after whooping-cough to the unfortunate undoing of the parsley bed. In the "Folklore Record," too, an amusing instance is related of a gardener at Southampton, who, for the same reason, refused to sow some parsley seed. It may be noted that from a very early period the same antipathy has existed in regard to this plant, and it is recorded how a few mules laden with parsley threw into a complete panic a Greek force on its march against the enemy. But the plant no doubt acquired its ominous significance from its having been largely used to bestrew the tombs of the dead; the Greek term "dehisthai selinou"--to be in need of parsley-- was a common phrase employed to denote those on the point of death. There are various other superstitions attached to this plant, as in Hampshire, where the peasants dislike giving any away for fear of some ill-luck befalling them. Similarly, according to another proverb:--

"Sowing fennel is sowing sorrow."

But why this should be so it is difficult to explain, considering that by the ancients fennel was used for the victor's wreath, and, as one of the plants dedicated to St. John, it has long been placed over doors on his vigil. On the other hand, there is a common saying with respect to rosemary, which was once much cultivated in kitchen gardens:--

"Where rosemary flourishes the lady rules."

Vetches, from being reputed a most hardy grain, have been embodied in the following adage:--

"A thetch will go through
The bottom of an old shoe,"

Which reminds us of the proverbial saying:--

"Like a camomile bed,
The more it is trodden
The more it will spread."

The common expression:--

"Worth a plum,"

is generally said of a man who is accredited with large means, and another adage tells us that,

"The higher the plum-tree, the riper the plum."

To live in luxury and affluence is expressed by the proverbial phrase "To live in clover," with which may be compared the saying "Do it up in lavender," applied to anything which is valuable and precious. A further similar phrase is "Laid up in lavender," in allusion to the old-fashioned custom of scenting newly-washed linen with this fragrant plant. Thus Shenstone says:--

"Lavender, whose spikes of azure bloom
Shall be, erewhile, in arid bundles bound,

To lurk amidst the labours of her loom,
And crown her kerchiefs clean with micklc rare perfume."

According to Gerarde, the Spartans were in the habit of eating cress with their bread, from a popular notion very generally held among the ancients, that those who ate it became noted for their wit and decision of character. Hence the old proverb:--

"Eat cress to learn more wit."

Of fruit proverbs we are told that,

"If you would enjoy the fruit, pluck not the flower."

And again:--

"When all fruit fails, welcome haws."

And "If you would have fruit, you must carry the leaf to the grave;" which Ray explains, "You must transplant your trees just about the fall of the leaf," and then there is the much-quoted rhyme:--

"Fruit out of season,
Sorrow out of reason."

Respecting the vine, it is said:--

"Make the vine poor, and it will make you rich,"

That is, prune off its branches; and another adage is to this effect: "Short boughs, long vintage." The constant blooming of the gorse has given rise to a popular Northamptonshire proverb:--

"When gorse is out of bloom, kissing is out of season."

The health-giving properties of various plants have long been in the highest repute, and have given rise to numerous well-known proverbs, which are still heard in many a home. Thus old Gerarde, describing the virtues of the mallow, tells us:--

"If that of health you have any special care,
Use French mallows, that to the body wholesome are."

Then there is the time-honoured adage which says that:--

"He that would live for aye
Must eat sage in May."

And Aubrey has bequeathed us the following piece of advice:--

"Eat leeks in Lide, and ramsines in May,
And all the year after physicians may play."

There are many sayings of this kind still current among our country-folk, some of which no doubt contain good advice; and of the plaintain, which from time immemorial has been used as a vulnerary, it is said:--

"Plantain ribbed, that heals the reaper's wounds."

In Herefordshire there is a popular rhyme associated with the aul (Alnus glutinosus):--

"When the bud of the aul is as big as the trout's eye,
Then that fish is in season in the river Wye."

A Yorkshire name for the quaking grass (Briza media) is "trembling jockies," and according to a local proverb:--

"A trimmling jock i' t' house,
An' you weeant hev a mouse,"

This plant being, it is said, obnoxious to mice. According to a Warwickshire proverb:--

"Plant your sage and rue together,
The sage will grow in any weather."

This list of plant proverbs might easily be extended, but the illustrations quoted in the preceding pages are a fair sample of this portion of our subject. Whereas many are based on truth, others are more or less meaningless. At any rate, they still thrive to a large extent among our rural community, by whom they are regarded as so many household sayings.

Footnotes:
1. See Akerman's "Wiltshire Glossary," p. 18.
2. "English Proverbs and Proverbial Phrases," pp. 327-8.
3. "Proverbs and Proverbial Phrases," p. 207.

CHAPTER XII

PLANTS AND THEIR CEREMONIAL USE

In the earliest period of primitive society flowers seem to have been largely used for ceremonial purposes. Tracing their history downwards up to the present day, we find how extensively, throughout the world, they have entered into sacred and other rites. This is not surprising when we remember how universal have been the love and admiration for these choice and lovely productions of nature's handiwork. From being used as offerings in the old heathen worship they acquired an additional veneration, and became associated with customs which had important significance. Hence the great quantity of flowers required, for ceremonial purposes of various kinds, no doubt promoted and encouraged a taste for horticulture even among uncultured tribes. Thus the Mexicans had their famous floating gardens, and in the numerous records handed down of social life, as it existed in different countries, there is no lack of references to the habits and peculiarities of the vegetable world.

Again, from all parts of the world, the histories of bygone centuries have contributed their accounts of the rich assortment of flowers in demand for the worship of the gods, which are valuable as indicating how elaborate and extensive was the knowledge of plants in primitive periods, and how magnificent must have been the display of these beautiful and brilliant offerings. Amongst some tribes, too, so sacred were the flowers used in religious rites held, that it was forbidden so much as to smell them, much less to handle them, except by those whose privileged duty it was to arrange them for the altar. Coming down to the historic days of Greece and Rome, we have abundant details of the skill and care that were displayed in procuring for religious purposes the finest and choicest varieties of flowers; abundant allusions to which are found in the old classic writings.

The profuseness with which flowers were used in Rome during triumphal processions has long ago become proverbial, in allusion to which Macaulay says:--

"On they ride to the Forum,
 While laurel boughs, and flowers,
From house-tops and from windows,
 Fell on their crests in showers."

Flowers, in fact, were in demand on every conceivable occasion, a custom which was frequently productive of costly extravagance. Then there was their festival of the Floralia, in honour of the reappearance of spring-time, with its hosts of bright blossoms, a survival of which has long been kept up in this country on May Day, when garlands and carols form the chief feature of the rustic merry-making. Another grand ceremonial occasion, when flowers were specially in request, was the Fontinalia, an important day in Rome, for the wells and fountains were crowned with flowers:--

"Fontinalia festus erat dies Romae, quo in fontes
coronas projiciebant, puteosque coronabant, ut a quibus pellucidos
liquores at restinguendam sitim acciperent, iisdem gratiam referre hoc
situ viderentur."

A pretty survival of this festival has long been observed in the well-dressing of Tissington on Ascension Day, when the wells are most beautifully decorated with leaves and flowers, arranged in fanciful devices, interwoven into certain symbols and texts. This floral rite is thus described in "The Fleece":--

"With light fantastic toe, the nymphs
Thither assembled, thither every swain;
And o'er the dimpled stream a thousand flowers,
Pale lilies, roses, violets and pinks,
Mix'd with the greens of bouret, mint, and thyme,
And trefoil, sprinkled with their sportive arms,
Such custom holds along th' irriguous vales,
From Wreken's brow to rocky Dolvoryn,
Sabrina's early haunt."

With this usage may be compared one performed by the fishermen of Weymouth, who on the first of May put out to sea for the purpose of scattering garlands of flowers on the waves, as a propitiatory offering to obtain food for the hungry. "This link," according to Miss Lambert, "is but another link in the chain that connects us with the yet more primitive practice of the Red Indian, who secures passage across the Lake Superior, or down the Mississippi, by gifts of precious tobacco, which he wafts to the great spirit of the Flood on the bosom of its waters."

By the Romans a peculiar reverence seems to have attached to their festive garlands, which were considered unsuitable for wearing in public. Hence, any person appearing in one was liable to punishment, a law which was carried out with much rigour. On one occasion, Lucius Fulvius, a banker, having been convicted at the time of the second Punic war, of looking down from the balcony of a house with a chaplet of roses on his head, was thrown into prison by order of the Senate, and here kept for sixteen years, until the close of the war. A further case of extreme severity was that of P. Munatius, who was condemned by the Triumviri to be put in chains for having crowned himself with flowers from the statue of Marsyas.

Allusions to such estimation of garlands in olden times are numerous in the literature of the past, and it may be remembered how Montesquieu remarked that it was with two or three hundred crowns of oak that Rome conquered the world.

Guests at feasts wore garlands of flowers tied with the bark of the linden tree, to prevent intoxication; the wreath having been framed in accordance with the position of the wearer. A poet, in his paraphrase on Horace, thus illustrates this custom:--

"*Nay, nay, my boy, 'tis not for me*
This studious pomp of Eastern luxury;
Give me no various garlands fine
  With linden twine;
Nor seek where latest lingering blows
  The solitary rose."

Not only were the guests adorned with flowers, but the waiters, drinking-cups, and room, were all profusely decorated.[1] "In short," as the author of "Flower-lore" remarks, "it would be difficult to name the occasions on which flowers were not employed; and, as almost all plants employed in making garlands had a symbolical meaning, the garland was composed in accordance with that meaning." Garlands, too, were thrown to actors on the stage, a custom which has come down to the present day in an exaggerated form.

Indeed, many of the flowers in request nowadays for ceremonial uses in our own and other countries may be traced back to this period; the symbolical meaning attached to certain plants having survived after the lapse of many centuries. For a careful description of the flowers thus employed, we would refer the reader to two interesting papers contributed by Miss Lambert to the Nineteenth Century,[2] in which she has collected together in a concise form all the principal items of information on the subject in past years. A casual perusal of these papers will suffice to show what a wonderful knowledge of botany the ancients must have possessed; and it may be doubted whether the most costly array of plants witnessed at any church festival supersedes a similar display witnessed by worshippers in the early heathen temples. In the same way, we gain an insight into the profusion of flowers employed by heathen communities in later centuries, showing how intimately associated these have been with their various forms of worship. Thus, the Singhalese seem to have used flowers to an almost incredible extent, and one of their old chronicles tells us how the Ruanwellé dagoba--270 feet high--was festooned with garlands from pedestal to pinnacle, till it had the appearance of one uniform bouquet. We are further told that in the fifteenth century a certain king offered no less than 6,480,320 sweet-smelling flowers at the shrine of the tooth; and, among the regulations of the temple at Dambedenia in the thirteenth century, one prescribes that "every day an offering of 100,000 blossoms, and each day a different kind of flower," should be presented. This is a striking instance, but only one of many.

"With regard to Greece, there are few of our trees and flowers," writes Mr. Moncure Conway,[3] "which were not cultivated in the gorgeous gardens of Epicurus, Pericles, and Pisistratus." Among the flowers chiefly used for garlands and chaplets in ceremonial rites we find the rose, violet, anemone, thyme, melilot, hyacinth, crocus, yellow lily, and yellow flowers generally. Thucydides relates how, in the ninth year of the Peloponnesian War, the temple of Juno at Argos was burnt down owing to the priestess Chrysis having set a lighted torch too near the garlands and then fallen asleep. The garlands caught fire, and the damage was irremediable before she was conscious of the mischief. The gigantic scale on which these floral ceremonies were conducted may be gathered from the fact that in the procession of Europa at Corinth a huge crown of myrtle, thirty feet in circumference, was borne. At Athens the myrtle was regarded as the symbol of authority, a wreath of its leaves having been worn by magistrates. On certain occasions the mitre of the Jewish high priest was adorned with a chaplet of the blossoms of the henbane. Of the further use of garlands, we are told that the Japanese employ them very freely;[4] both men and women wearing chaplets of fragrant blossoms. A wreath of a fragrant kind of olive is the reward of literary merit in China. In Northern India the African marigold is held as a sacred flower; they adorn the trident emblem of Mahádivá with garlands of it, and both men and women wear chaplets made of its flowers on his festivals. Throughout Polynesia garlands have been habitually worn on seasons of "religious solemnity or social rejoicing," and in Tonga they were employed as a token of respect. In short, wreaths seem to have been from a primitive period adopted almost universally in ceremonial rites, having found equal favour both with civilised as well as uncivilised communities. It will probably, too, always be so.

Flowers have always held a prominent place in wedding ceremonies, and at the present day are everywhere extensively used. Indeed, it would be no easy task to exhaust the list of flowers which have entered into the marriage customs of different countries, not to mention the many bridal emblems of which they have been made symbolical. As far back as the time
of Juno, we read, according to Homer's graphic account, how:--

"Glad earth perceives, and from her bosom pours
Unbidden herbs and voluntary flowers:

Thick, new-born violets a soft carpet spread,
And clust'ring lotos swelled the rising bed;
And sudden hyacinths the earth bestrow,
And flamy crocus made the mountain glow."

According to a very early custom the Grecian bride was required to eat a quince, and the hawthorn was the flower which formed her wreath, which at the present day is still worn at Greek nuptials, the altar being decked with its blossoms. Among the Romans the hazel held a significant position, torches having been burnt on the wedding evening to insure prosperity to the newly-married couple, and both in Greece and Rome young married couples were crowned with marjoram. At Roman weddings, too, oaken boughs were carried during the ceremony as symbols of fecundity; and the bridal wreath was of verbena, plucked by the bride herself. Holly wreaths were sent as tokens of congratulation, and wreaths of parsley and rue were given under a belief that they were effectual preservatives against evil spirits. In Germany, nowadays, a wreath of vervain is presented to the newly-married bride; a plant which, on account of its mystic virtues, was formerly much used for love-philtres and charms. The bride herself wears a myrtle wreath, as also does the Jewish maiden, but this wreath was never given either to a widow or a divorced woman. Occasionally, too, it is customary in Germany to present the bride and bridegroom with an almond at the wedding banquet, and in the nuptial ceremonies of the Czechs this plant is distributed among the guests. In Switzerland so much importance was in years past attached to flowers and their symbolical significance that, "a very strict law was in force prohibiting brides from wearing chaplets or garlands in the church, or at any time during the wedding feast, if they had previously in any way forfeited their rights to the privileges of maidenhood."[5] With the Swiss maiden the edelweiss is almost a sacred flower, being regarded as a proof of the devotion of her lover, by whom it is often gathered with much risk from growing in inaccessible spots. In Italy, as in days of old, nuts are scattered at the marriage festival, and corn is in many cases thrown over the bridal couple, a survival of the old Roman custom of making offerings of corn to the bride. A similar usage prevails at an Indian wedding, where, "after the first night, the mother of the husband, with all the female relatives, comes to the young bride and places on her head a measure of corn--emblem of fertility. The husband then comes forward and takes from his bride's head some handfuls of the grain, which he scatters over himself." As a further illustration we may quote the old Polish custom, which consisted of visitors throwing wheat, rye, oats, barley, rice, and beans at the door of the bride's house, as a symbol that she never would want any of these grains so long as she did her duty. In the Tyrol is a fine grove of pine-trees--the result of a long-established custom for every newly united couple to plant a marriage tree, which is generally of the pine kind. Garlands of wild asparagus are used by the Boeotians, while with the Chinese the peach-blossom is the popular emblem of a bride.

In England, flowers have always been largely employed in the wedding ceremony, although they have varied at different periods, influenced by the caprice of fashion. Thus, it appears that flowers were once worn by the betrothed as tokens of their engagement, and Quarles in his "Sheapheard's Oracles," 1646, tells us how,

> "*Love-sick swains*
> *Compose rush-rings and myrtle-berry chains,*
> *And stuck with glorious kingcups, and their bonnets*
> *Adorn'd with laurell slips, chaunt their love sonnets.*"

Spenser, too, in his "Shepherd's Calendar" for April, speaks of "Coronations and sops in wine worn of paramours"--sops in wine having been a nickname for pinks (Dianthus plumarius), although Dr. Prior assigns the name to Dianthus caryophyllus. Similarly willow was worn by a discarded lover. In the bridal crown, the rosemary often had a distinguished place, besides figuring at the ceremony itself, when it was, it would seem, dipped in scented water, an allusion to which we find in Beaumont and Fletcher's "Scornful Lady," where it is asked, "Were the rosemary branches dipped?" Another flower which was entwined in the bridal garland was the lily, to which Ben Jonson refers in speaking of the marriage of his friend Mr. Weston with the Lady Frances Stuart:--

> "*See how with roses and with lilies shine,*
> *Lilies and roses (flowers of either sex),*
> *The bright bride's paths.*"

It was also customary to plant a rose-bush at the head of the grave of a deceased lover, should either of them die before the wedding. Sprigs of bay were also introduced into the bridal wreath, besides ears of corn, emblematical of the plenty which might always crown the bridal couple. Nowadays the bridal wreath is almost entirely composed of orange-blossom, on a background of maiden-hair fern, with a sprig of stephanotis interspersed here and there. Much uncertainty exists as to why this plant was selected, the popular reason being that it was adopted as an emblem of fruitfulness. According to a correspondent of Notes and Queries, the practice may be traced to the Saracens, by whom the orange-blossom was regarded as a symbol of a prosperous marriage — a circumstance which is partly to be accounted for by the fact that in the East the orange-tree bears ripe fruit and blossom at the same time.

Then there is the bridal bouquet, which is a very different thing from what it was in years gone by. Instead of being composed of the scarcest and most costly flowers arranged in the most elaborate manner, it was a homely nosegay of mere country flowers--some of the favourite ones, says Herrick, being pansy, rose, lady-smock, prick-madam, gentle-heart, and maiden-blush. A spray of gorse was generally inserted, in allusion, no doubt, to the time-honoured proverb, "When the furze is out of bloom, kissing is out of fashion." In spring-time again, violets and primroses were much in demand, probably from being in abundance at the season; although they have generally been associated with early death.

Among the many floral customs associated with the wedding ceremony may be mentioned the bridal-strewings, which were very prevalent in past years, a survival of which is still kept up at Knutsford, in Cheshire. On such an occasion, the flowers used were emblematical, and if the bride happened to be unpopular, she often encountered on her way to the church flowers of a not very complimentary meaning. The practice was not confined to this country, and we are told how in Holland the threshold of the newly-married couple was strewn with flowers, the laurel being as a rule most conspicuous among the festoons. Lastly, the use of flowers in paying honours to the dead has been from time immemorial most widespread. Instances are so numerous that it is impossible to do more than quote some of the most important, as recorded in our own and other countries. For detailed accounts of these funereal floral rites it would be necessary to consult the literature of the past from a very early period, and the result of such inquiries would form material enough for a goodly-sized volume. Therespect for the dead among the early Greeks was very great, and Miss Lambert[6] quotes the complaint of Petala to Simmalion, in the Epistles of Alciphron, to show how special was the dedication of flowers to the dead:--"I have a lover who is a mourner, not a lover; he sends me garlands and roses as if to deck a premature grave, and he says he weeps through the live-long night."

The chief flowers used by them for strewing over graves were the polyanthus, myrtle, and amaranth; the rose, it would appear from Anacreon, having been thought to possess a special virtue for the dead:--

"*When pain afflicts and sickness grieves,*
Its juice the drooping heart relieves;
And after death its odours shed
A pleasing fragrance o'er the dead."

And Electra is represented as complaining that the tomb of her father, Agamemnon, had not been duly adorned with myrtle--

"With no libations, nor with myrtle boughs,
Were my dear father's manes gratified."

The Greeks also planted asphodel and mallow round their graves, as the seeds of these plants were supposed to nourish the dead. Mourners, too, wore flowers at the funeral rites, and Homer relates how the Thessalians used crowns of amaranth at the burial of Achilles. The Romans were equally observant, and Ovid, when writing from the land of exile, prayed his wife--"But do you perform the funeral rites for me when dead, and offer chaplets wet with your tears. Although the fire shall have changed my body into ashes, yet the sad dust will be sensible of your pious affection." Like the Greeks, the Romans set a special value on the rose as a funeral flower, and actually left directions that their graves should be planted with this favourite flower, a custom said to have been introduced by them into this country. Both Camden and Aubrey allude to it, and at the present day in Wales white roses denote the graves of young unmarried girls.

Coming down to modern times, we find the periwinkle, nicknamed "death's flower," scattered over the graves of children in Italy—notably Tuscany--and in some parts of Germany the pink is in request for this purpose. In Persia we read of:--

"The basil-tuft that waves
Its fragrant blossoms over graves;"

And among the Chinese, roses, the anemone, and a species of lycoris are planted over graves. The Malays use a kind of basil, and in Tripoli tombs are adorned with such sweet and fragrant flowers as the orange, jessamine, myrtle, and rose. In Mexico the Indian carnation is popularly known as the "flower of the dead," and the people of Tahiti cover their dead with choice flowers. In America the Freemasons place twigs of acacia on the coffins of brethren. The Buddhists use flowers largely for funeral purposes, and an Indian name for the tamarisk is the "messenger of Yama," the Indian God of Death. The people of Madagascar have a species of mimosa, which is frequently found growing on the tombs, and in Norway the funeral plants are juniper and fir. In France the custom very largely nourishes, roses and orange-blossoms in the southern provinces being placed in the coffins of the young. Indeed, so general is the practice in France that, "sceptics and believers uphold it, and statesmen, and soldiers, and princes, and scholars equally with children and maidens are the objects of it."

Again, in Oldenburg, it is said that cornstalks must be scattered about a house in which death has entered, as a charm against further misfortune, and in the Tyrol an elder bush is often planted on a newly-made grave.

In our own country the practice of crowning the dead and of strewing their graves with flowers has prevailed from a very early period, a custom which has been most pathetically and with much grace described by Shakespeare in "Cymbeline" (Act iv. sc. 2):--

> "With fairest flowers,
> Whilst summer lasts, and I live here, Fidele,
> I'll sweeten thy sad grave: thou shalt not lack
> The flower that's like thy face, pale primrose; nor
> The azured harebell, like thy veins; no, nor
> The leaf of eglantine, whom not to slander,
> Out-sweeten'd not thy breath: the ruddock would,
> With charitable bill, O bill, sore-shaming
> Those rich-left heirs that let their fathers lie
> Without a monument! bring thee all this;
> Yea, and furr'd moss besides, when flowers are none,
> To winter-ground thy corse."

Allusions to the custom are frequently to be met with in our old writers, many of which have been collected together by Brand.[7] In former years it was customary to carry sprigs of rosemary at a funeral, probably because this plant was considered emblematical of remembrance:--

> "To show their love, the neighbours far and near,
> Follow'd with wistful look the damsel's bier;
> Spring'd rosemary the lads and lasses bore,
> While dismally the parson walked before."

Gay speaks of the flowers scattered on graves as "rosemary, daisy, butter'd flower, and endive blue," and Pepys mentions a churchyard near Southampton where the graves were sown with sage. Another plant which has from a remote period been associated with death is the cypress, having been planted by the ancients round their graves. In our own country it was employed as a funeral flower, and Coles thus refers to it, together with the rosemary and bay:--

*"Cypresse garlands are of great account at funerals amongst the
gentler sort, but rosemary and bayes are used by the
commons both at funerals and weddings. They are
all plants which fade not a good while after they are
gathered, and used (as I conceive) to intimate unto us
that the remembrance of the present solemnity might
not die presently (at once), but be kept in mind for
many years."*

The yew has from time immemorial been planted in churchyards
besides being used at funerals. Paris, in "Romeo and Juliet", (Act v. sc. 3),
says:--

*"Under yon yew trees lay thee all along,
Holding thine ear close to the hollow ground;
So shall no foot upon the churchyard tread,
Being loose, unfirm, with digging up of graves,
But thou shall hear it."*

Shakespeare also refers to the custom of sticking yew in the shroud in
the following song in "Twelfth Night" (Act ii. sc. 4):--

*"My shroud of white, stuck all with yew,
  Oh, prepare it;
My part of death, no one so true
  Did share it."*

Unhappy lovers had garlands of willow, yew, and rosemary laid on
their biers, an allusion to which occurs in the "Maid's Tragedy":--

*"Lay a garland on my hearse
  Of the dismal yew;
Maidens, willow branches bear--
  Say I died true.
My love was false, but I was firm
  From my hour of birth;
Upon my buried body lie
  Lightly, gentle earth."*

Among further funeral customs may be mentioned that of carrying a
garland of flowers and sweet herbs before a maiden's coffin, and
afterwards suspending it in the church. Nichols, in his "History of
Lancashire" (vol. ii. pt. i. 382), speaking of Waltham in Framland
Hundred, says: "In this church under every arch a garland is suspended,

one of which is customarily placed there whenever any young unmarried woman dies." It is to this custom Gay feelingly alludes:--

"To her sweet mem'ry flowing garlands strung,
On her now empty seat aloft were hung."

Indeed, in all the ceremonial observances of life, from the cradle to the grave, flowers have formed a prominent feature, the symbolical meaning long attached to them explaining their selection on different occasions.

Footnotes:

1. See "Flower-lore," p. 147.
2. "The Ceremonial Use of Flowers."
3. Fraser's Magazine, 1870, p. 711.
4. "Flower-lore," pp. 149-50.
5. Miss Lambert, Nineteenth Century, May 1880, p. 821.
6. Nineteenth
Century, September 1878, p. 473.
7. "Popular Antiquities," 1870, ii. 24, &c.

CHAPTER XIII

PLANT NAMES

The origin and history of plant names is a subject of some magnitude, and is one that has long engaged the attention of philologists. Of the many works published on plant names, that of the "English Dialect Society"[1] is by far the most complete, and forms a valuable addition to this class of literature.

Some idea of the wide area covered by the nomenclature of plants, as seen in the gradual evolution and descent of vernacular names, may be gathered even from a cursory survey of those most widely known in our own and other countries. Apart, too, from their etymological associations, it is interesting to trace the variety of sources from whence plant names have sprung, a few illustrations of which are given in the present chapter.

At the outset, it is noteworthy that our English plant names can boast of a very extensive parentage, being, "derived from many languages-- Latin, Greek, ancient British, Anglo-Saxon, Norman, Low German, Swedish, Danish, Arabic, Persian."[2] It is not surprising, therefore, that in many cases much confusion has arisen in unraveling their meaning, which in the course of years would naturally become more or less modified by a succession of influences such as the intercommunication and change of ideas between one country and another. On the other hand, numerous plant names clearly display their origin, the lapse of years having left these unaffected, a circumstance which is especially true in the case of Greek and Latin names. Names of French origin are frequently equally distinct, a familiar instance being dandelion, from the French dent-de-lion, "lion's tooth," although the reason for its being so called is by no means evident. At the same time, it is noticeable that in nearly every European language the plant bears a similar name; whereas Professor De Gubernatis connects the name with the sun (Helios), and adds that a lion was the animal symbol of the sun, and that all plants named after him are essentially plants of the sun.[3] One of the popular names of the St. John's wort is tutsan, a corruption of the French toute saine, so called from its healing properties, and the mignonette is another familiar instance. The flower-de-luce, one of the names probably of the iris, is derived from fleur de Louis, from its having been assumed as his device by Louis VII. of France. It has undergone various changes, having been in all probability contracted into fleur-de-luce, and finally into fleur-de-lys or fleur-de-lis. An immense deal of discussion has been devoted to the history of this name, and a great many curious theories proposed in explanation of it, some being of opinion that the lily and not the iris is referred to. But the weight of evidence seem to favour the iris theory, this plant having been undoubtedly famous in French history. Once more, by some,[4] the name fleur-de-lys has been derived from Löys, in which manner the twelve first Louis signed their names, and which was easily contracted into Lys. Some consider it means the flower that grows on the banks of the river Lis, which separated France and Artois from Flanders. Turning to the literature of the past, Shakespeare has several allusions to the plant, as in "I Henry VI," where a messenger enters and exclaims:--

"Awake, awake, English nobility!
Let not sloth dim your honours new begot;
Cropp'd are the flower-de-luces in your arms;
Of England's coat one half is cut away."

Spenser mentions the plant, and distinguishes it from the lily:--

"Show mee the grounde with daifadown-dillies,
And cowslips, and kingcups, and loved lillies;
The pretty pawnee,
And the cherisaunce,
Shall march with the fayre flowre delice."

Another instance is the mignonette of our French neighbours, known also as the "love-flower." One of the names of the deadly nightshade is belladonna which reminds us of its Italian appellation, and "several of our commonest plant names are obtained from the Low German or Dutch, as, for instance, buckwheat (Polygonum fagopyrum), from the Dutch bockweit." The rowan-tree (Pyrus aucuparia) comes from the Danish röun, Swedish rünn, which, as Dr. Prior remarks, is traceable to the "old Norse runa, a charm, from its being supposed to have power to avert evil." Similarly, the adder's tongue (Ophioglossum vulgatum) is said to be from the Dutch adder-stong, and the word hawthorn is found in the various German dialects.

As the authors of "English Plant Names" remark (Intr. xv.), many north-country names are derived from Swedish and Danish sources, an interesting example occurring in the word kemps, a name applied to the black heads of the ribwort plantain (Plantago lanceolata). The origin of this name is to be found in the Danish kaempe, a warrior, and the reason for its being so called is to be found in the game which children in most parts of the kingdom play with the flower-stalks of the plantain, by endeavouring to knock off the heads of each other's mimic weapons. Again, as Mr. Friend points out, the birch would take us back to the primeval forests of India, and among the multitudinous instances of names traceable to far-off countries may be mentioned the lilac and tulip from Persia, the latter being derived from thoulyban, the word used in Persia for a turban. Lilac is equivalent to lilag, a Persian word signifying flower, having been introduced into Europe from that country early in the sixteenth century by Busbeck, a German traveller. But illustrations of this land are sufficient to show from how many countries our plant names have been brought, and how by degrees they have become interwoven into our own language, their pronunciation being Anglicised by English speakers.

Many plants, again, have been called in memory of leading characters in days gone by, and after those who discovered their whereabouts and introduced them into European countries. Thus the fuchsia, a native of Chili, was named after Leonard Fuchs, a well-known German botanist, and the magnolia was so called in honour of Pierre Magnol, an eminent writer on botanical subjects. The stately dahlia after Andrew Dahl, the Swedish botanist. But, without enumerating further instances, for they are familiar to most readers, it may be noticed that plants which embody the names of animals are very numerous indeed. In many cases this has resulted from some fancied resemblance to some part of the animal named; thus from their long tongued-like leaves, the hart's-tongue, lamb's-tongue, and ox-tongue were so called, while some plants have derived their names from the snouts of certain animals, such as the swine's-snout (Lentodon taraxacum), and calf's-snout, or, as it is more commonly termed, snapdragon (Antirrhinum majus). The gaping corollas of various blossoms have suggested such names as dog's-mouth, rabbit's-mouth, and lion's-snap, and plants with peculiarly-shaped leaves have given rise to names like these--mouse-ear (Stachys Zanaia), cat's-ears, and bear's-ears. Numerous names have been suggested by their fancied resemblance to the feet, hoofs, and tails of animals and birds; as, for instance, colt's-foot, crow-foot, bird's-foot trefoil, horse-shoe vetch, bull-foot, and the vervain, nicknamed frog's-foot. Then there is the larkspur, also termed lark's-claw, and lark's-heel, the lamb's-toe being so called from its downy heads of flowers, and the horse-hoof from the shape of the leaf. Among various similar names may be noticed the crane's-bill and stork's-bill, from their long beak-like seed-vessels, and the valerian, popularly designated capon's-tail, from its spreading flowers.

Many plant names have animal prefixes, these indeed forming a very extensive list. But in some instances, "the name of an animal prefixed has a totally different signification, denoting size, coarseness, and frequently worthlessness or spuriousness." Thus the horse-parsley was so called from its coarseness as compared with smallage or celery, and the horse-mushroom from its size in distinction to a species more commonly eaten.

The particular uses to which certain plants have been applied have originated their names: the horse-bean, from being grown as a food for horses; and the horse-chestnut, because used in Turkey for horses that are broken or touched in the wind. Parkinson, too, adds how, "horse-chestnuts are given in the East, and so through all Turkey, unto horses to cure them of the cough, shortness of wind, and such other diseases." The germander is known as horse-chere, from its growing after horse-droppings; and the horse-bane, because supposed in Sweden to cause a kind of palsy in horses--an effect which has been ascribed by Linnaeus not so much to the noxious qualities of the plant itself, as to an insect (Curculio paraplecticus) that breeds in its stem.

The dog has suggested sundry plant names, this prefix frequently suggesting the idea of worthlessness, as in the case of the dog-violet, which lacks the sweet fragrance of the true violet, and the dog-parsley, which, whilst resembling the true plant of this name, is poisonous and worthless. In like manner there is the dog-elder, dog's-mercury, dog's-chamomile, and the dog-rose, each a spurious form of a plant quite distinct; while on the other hand we have the dog's-tooth grass, from the sharp-pointed shoots of its underground stem, and the dog-grass (Triticum caninu), because given to dogs as an aperient. The cat has come in for its due share of plant names, as for instance the sun-spurge, which has been nicknamed cat's-milk, from its milky juice oozing in drops, as milk from the small teats of a cat; and the blossoms of the talix, designated cats-and-kittens, or kittings, probably in allusion to their soft, fur-like appearance. Further names are, cat's-faces (Viola tricolor), cat's-eyes (Veronica chamcaedrys), cat's-tail, the catkin of the hazel or willow, and cat's-ear (Hypochaeris maculata).

The bear is another common prefix. Thus there is the bear's-foot, from its digital leaf, the bear-berry, or bear's-bilberry, from its fruit being a favourite food of bears, and the bear's-garlick. There is the bear's-breech, from its roughness, a name transferred by some mistake from the Acanthus to the cow-parsnip, and the bear's-wort, which it has been suggested "is rather to be derived from its use in uterine complaints than from the animal."

Among names in which the word cow figures may be mentioned the cow-bane, water-hemlock, from its supposed baneful effects upon cows, because, writes Withering, "early in the spring, when it grows in the water, cows often eat it, and are killed by it." Cockayne would derive cowslip from cu, cow, and slyppe, lip, and cow-wheat is so nicknamed from its seed resembling wheat, but being worthless as food for man. The flowers of the Arum maculatum are "bulls and cows;" and in Yorkshire the fruit of Crataegus oxyacantha is bull-horns;--an old name for the horse-leek being bullock's-eye.

Many curious names have resulted from the prefix pig, as in Sussex, where the bird's-foot trefoil is known as pig's-pettitoes; and in Devonshire the fruit of the dog-rose is pig's-noses. A Northamptonshire term for goose-grass (Galium aparine) is pig-tail, and the pig-nut (Brunium flexuosum) derived this name from its tubers being a favourite food of pigs, and resembling nuts in size and flavour. The common cyclamen is sow-head, and a popular name for the Sonchus oleraceus is sow-thistle. Among further names also associated with the sow may be included the sow-fennel, sow-grass, and sow-foot, while the sow-bane (Chenopodium rubrum), is so termed from being, as Parkinson tells us, "found certain to kill swine."

Among further animal prefixes may be noticed the wolfs-bane (Aconitum napellus), wolf's-claws (Lycopodium clavatum), wolf's-milk (Euphorbia helioscopia), and wolfs-thistle (Carlina acaulis). The mouse has given us numerous names, such as mouse-ear (Hieracium pilosella), mouse-grass (Aira caryophyllea), mouse-ear scorpion-grass (Myosotis palustris), mouse-tail (Myosurus minimus), and mouse-pea. The term rat-tail has been applied to several plants having a tail-like inflorescence, such as the Plantago lanceolata (ribwort plantain).

The term toad as a prefix, like that of dog, frequently means spurious, as in the toad-flax, a plant which, before it comes into flower, bears a tolerably close resemblance to a plant of the true flax. The frog, again, supplies names, such as frog's-lettuce, frog's-foot, frog-grass, and frog-cheese; while hedgehog gives us such names as hedgehog-parsley and hedgehog-grass.

Connected with the dragon we have the name dragon applied to the snake-weed (Polygonum bistorta), and dragon's-blood is one of the popular names of the Herb-Robert. The water-dragon is a nickname of the Caltha palustris, and dragon's-mouth of the Digitalis purpurea.

Once more, there is scorpion-grass and scorpion-wort, both of which refer to various species of Myosotis; snakes and vipers also adding to the list. Thus there is viper's-bugloss, and snake-weed. In Gloucestershire the fruit of the Arum maculatum is snake's-victuals, and snake's-head is a common name for thefritillary. There is the snake-skin willow and snake's-girdles;--snake's-tongue being a name given to the bane-wort (Ranunculus flammula).

Names in which the devil figures have been noticed elsewhere, as also those in which the words fairy and witch enter. As the authors, too, of the "Dictionary of Plant Names" have pointed out, a great number of names may be called dedicatory, and embody the names of many of the saints, and even of the Deity. The latter, however, are very few in number, owing perhaps to a sense of reverence, and "God Almighty's bread and cheese," "God's eye," "God's grace," "God's meat," "Our Lord's, or Our Saviour's flannel," "Christ's hair," "Christ's herb," "Christ's ladder," "Christ's thorn," "Holy Ghost," and "Herb-Trinity," make up almost the whole list. On the other hand, the Virgin Mary has suggested numerous names, some of which we have noticed in the chapter on sacred plants. Certain of the saints, again, have perpetuated their names in our plant nomenclature, instances of which are scattered throughout the present volume.

Some plants, such as flea-bane and wolf's-bane, refer to the reputed property of the plant to keep off or injure the animal named,[5] and there is a long list of plants which derived their names from their real or imaginary medicinal virtues, many of which illustrate the old doctrine of signatures.

Birds, again, like animals, have suggested various names, and among some of the best-known ones may be mentioned the goose-foot, goose-grass, goose-tongue. Shakespeare speaks of cuckoo-buds, and there is cuckoo's-head, cuckoo-flower, and cuckoo-fruit, besides the stork's-bill and crane's-bill. Bees are not without their contingent of names; a popular name of the Delphinium grandiflorum being the bee-larkspur, "from the resemblance of the petals, which are studded with yellow hairs, to the humble-bee whose head is buried in the recesses of the flower." There is the bee-flower (Ophrys apifera), because the, "lip is in form and colour so like a bee, that any one unacquainted therewith would take it for a living bee sucking of the flower."

In addition to the various classes of names already mentioned, there are a rich and very varied assortment found in most counties throughout the country, many of which have originated in the most amusing and eccentric way. Thus "butter and eggs" and "eggs and bacon" are applied to several plants, from the two shades of yellow in the flower, and butter-churn to the Nuphar luteum, from the shape of the fruit. A popular term for Nepeta glechoma is "hen and chickens," and "cocks and hens" for the Plantago lanceolata. A Gloucestershire nickname for the Plantago media is fire-leaves, and the hearts'-ease has been honoured with all sorts of romantic names, such as "kiss me behind the garden gate;" and "none so pretty" is one of the popular names of the saxifrage. Among the names of the Arum may be noticed "parson in the pulpit," "cows and calves," "lords and ladies," and "wake-robin." The potato has a variety of names, such as leather-jackets, blue-eyes, and red-eyes.

A pretty name in Devonshire for the Veronica chamcaedrys is angel's-eyes:--

"Around her hat a wreath was twined
Of blossoms, blue as southern skies;
I asked their name, and she replied,
We call them angel's-eyes." [6]

In the northern counties the poplar, on account of its bitter bark, was termed the bitter-weed.[7]

"Oak, ash, and elm-tree,
The laird can hang for a' the three;
But fir, saugh, and bitter-weed,
The laird may flyte, but make naething be' et."

According to the compilers of "English Plant Names," "this name is assigned to no particular species of poplar, nor have we met with it elsewhere." The common Solomon's seal (Polygonatum multiflorum) has been nicknamed "David's harp,"[8] and, "appears to have arisen from the exact similarity of the outline of the bended stalk, with its pendent bill-like blossoms, to the drawings of monkish times in which King David is represented as seated before an instrument shaped like the half of a pointed arch, from which are suspended metal bells, which he strikes with two hammers."

In the neighbourhood of Torquay, fir-cones are designated oysters, and in Sussex the Arabis is called "snow-on-the-mountain," and "snow-in-summer." A Devonshire name for the sweet scabriosis is the mournful-widow, and in some places the red valerian (Centranthus ruber) is known as scarlet-lightning. A common name for Achillaea ptarmica is sneezewort, and the Petasites vulgaris has been designated "son before the father." The general name for Drosera rotundifolia is sun-dew, and in Gloucestershire the Primula auricula is the tanner's-apron. The Viola tricolor is often known as "three faces in a hood," and the Aconitum napellus as "Venus's chariot drawn by two doves." The Stellaria holostea is "lady's white petticoat," and the Scandix pecten is "old wife's darning-needles." One of the names of the Campion is plum-pudding, and "spittle of the stars" has been applied to the Nostoc commune. Without giving further instances of these odd plant names, we would conclude by quoting the following extract from the preface of Mr. Earle's charming little volume on "English Plant Names," a remark which, indeed, most equally applies to other sections of our subject beyond that of the present chapter:--"The fascination of plant names has its foundation in two instincts, love of Nature, and curiosity about Language. Plant names are often of the highest antiquity, and more or less common to the whole stream of related nations. Could we penetrate to the original suggestive idea that called forth the name, it would bring valuable information about the first openings of the human mind towards Nature; and the merest dream of such a discovery invests with a strange charm the words that could tell, if we could understand, so much of the forgotten infancy of the human race."

Footnotes:

1. "Dictionary of English Plant Names," by J. Britten and Robert Holland. 1886.
2. "English Plant Names," Introduction, p. xiii.
3. See Folkard's "Legends," p. 309; Friend's "Flowers and Flowerlore," ii. 401-5.
4. See "Flower-lore," p. 74.
5. Friend's "Flower-lore," ii. 425.
6. Garden, June 29, 1872.
7. Johnston's "Botany of Eastern Borders," 1853, p. 177.
8. Lady Wilkinson's "Weeds and Wild Flowers," p. 269.

CHAPTER XIV

PLANT LANGUAGE

Plant language, as expressive of the various traits of human character, can boast of a world-wide and antique history. It is not surprising that flowers, the varied and lovely productions of nature's dainty handiwork, should have been employed as symbolic emblems, and most aptly indicative oftentimes of what words when even most wisely chosen can ill convey; for as Tennyson remarks:--

> "*Any man that walks the mead*
> *In bud, or blade, or bloom, may find*
> *A meaning suited to his mind.*"

Hence, whether we turn to the pages of the Sacred Volume, or to the early Greek writings, we find the symbolism of flowers most eloquently illustrated, while Persian poetry is rich in allusions of the same kind. Indeed, as Mr. Ingram has remarked in his "Flora Symbolica,"[1] — Every age and every clime has promulgated its own peculiar system of floral signs, and it has been said that the language of flowers is as old as the days of Adam; having, also, thousands of years ago, existed in the Indian, Egyptian, and Chaldean civilisations which have long since passed away. He further adds how the Chinese, whose, "chronicles antedate the historic records of all other nations, seem to have had a simple but complete mode of communicating ideas by means of florigraphic signs;" whereas, "the monuments of the old Assyrian and Egyptian races bear upon their venerable surfaces a code of floral telegraphy whose hieroglyphical meaning is veiled or but dimly guessed at in our day." The subject is an extensive one, and also enters largely into the ceremonial use of flowers, many of which were purposely selected for certain rites from their long-established symbolical character. At the same time, it must be remembered that many plants have had a meaning attached to them by poets and others, who have by a license of their own made them to represent certain sentiments and ideas for which there is no authority save their own fancy.

Hence in numerous instances a meaning, wholly misguiding, has been assigned to various plants, and has given rise to much confusion. This, too, it may be added, is the case in other countries as well as our own.

Furthermore, as M. de Gubernatis observes, "there exist a great number of books which pretend to explain the language of flowers, wherein one may occasionally find a popular or traditional symbol; but, as a rule, these expressions are generally the wild fancies of the author himself." Hence, in dealing with plant language, one is confronted with a host of handbooks, many of which are not only inaccurate, but misleading. But in enumerating the recognised and well-known plants that have acquired a figurative meaning, it will be found that in a variety of cases this may be traced to their connection with some particular event in years past, and not to some chance or caprice, as some would make us believe. The amaranth, for instance, which is the emblem of immortality, received its name, "never-fading," from the Greeks on account of the lasting nature of its blossoms. Accordingly, Milton crowns with amaranth the angelic multitude assembled before the Deity:--

> "To the ground,
> With solemn adoration, down they cast
> Their crowns, inwove with amaranth and gold.
> Immortal amaranth, a flower which once
> In Paradise, fast by the tree of life,
> Began to bloom; but soon, for man's offence,
> To heaven removed, where first it grew, there grows
> And flowers aloft, shading the font of life," &c.

And in some parts of the Continent churches are adorned at Christmas-tide with the amaranth, as a symbol "of that immortality to which their faith bids them look."

Grass, from its many beneficial qualities, has been made the emblem of usefulness; and the ivy, from its persistent habit of clinging to the heaviest support, has been universally adopted as the symbol of confiding love and fidelity. Growing rapidly, it iron clasps:--

> "The fissured stone with its entwining arms,
> And embowers with leaves for ever green,
> And berries dark."

According to a Cornish tradition, the beautiful Iseult, unable to endure the loss of her betrothed--the brave Tristran--died of a broken heart, and was buried in the same church, but, by order of the king, the two graves were placed at a distance from each other. Soon, however, there burst forth from the tomb of Tristran a branch of ivy, and another from the grave of Iseult; these shoots gradually growing upwards, until at last the lovers, represented by the clinging ivy, were again united beneath the vaulted roof of heaven.[2]

Then, again, the cypress, in floral language, denotes mourning; and, as an emblem of woe, may be traced to the familiar classical myth of

Cyparissus, who, sorrow-stricken at having skin his favourite stag, was transformed into a cypress tree. Its ominous and sad character is the subject of constant allusion, Virgil having introduced it into the funeral rites of his heroes. Shelley speaks of the unwept youth whom no mourning maidens decked,

"With weeping flowers, or votive cypress wreath,
The love-couch of his everlasting sleep."

And Byron describes the cypress as,

"Dark tree! still sad when other's grief is fled,
The only constant mourner o'er the dead."

The laurel, used for classic wreaths, has long been regarded emblematical of renown, and Tasso thus addresses a laurel leaf in the hair of his mistress:--

"O glad triumphant bough,
That now adornest conquering chiefs, and now
Clippest the bows of over-ruling kings
From victory to victory.
Thus climbing on through all the heights of story,
From worth to worth, and glory unto glory,
To finish all, O gentle and royal tree,
Thou reignest now upon that flourishing head,
At whose triumphant eyes love and our souls are led."

Like the rose, the myrtle is the emblem of love, having been dedicated by the Greeks and Romans to Venus, in the vicinity of whose temples myrtle-groves were planted; hence, from time immemorial,

"Sacred to Venus is the myrtle shade."

This will explain its frequent use in bridal ceremonies on the Continent, and its employment for the wedding wreath of the Jewish damsel. Herrick, mindful of its associations, thus apostrophises Venus:--

"Goddess, I do love a girl,
Ruby lipp'd and toothed like pearl;
If so be I may but prove
Lucky in this maid I love,
I will promise there shall be
Myrtles offered up to thee."

To the same goddess was dedicated the rose, and its world-wide reputation as "the flower of love," in which character it has been extolled by poets in ancient and modern times, needs no more than reference here.

The olive indicates peace, and as an emblem was given to Judith when she restored peace to the Israelites by the death of Holofernes.[3] Shakespeare, in "Twelfth Night" (Act i. sc. 5), makes Viola say:--"I bring no overture of war, no taxation of homage; I hold the olive in my hand; my words are as full of peace as of matter." Similarly, the palm, which, as the symbol of victory, was carried before the conqueror in triumphal processions, is generally regarded as denoting victory. Thus, palm-branches were scattered in the path of Christ upon His public entry into Jerusalem; and, at the present day, a palm-branch is embroidered on the lappet of the gown of a French professor, to indicate that a University degree has been attained.[4]

Some flowers have become emblematical from their curious characteristics. Thus, the balsam is held to be expressive of impatience, because its seed-pods when ripe curl up at the slightest touch, and dart forth their seeds, with great violence; hence one of its popular names, "touch-me-not." The wild anemone has been considered indicative of brevity, because its fragile blossom is so quickly scattered to the wind and lost:--

"The winds forbid the flowers to flourish long,
Which owe to winds their name in Grecian song."

The poppy, from its somniferous effects, has been made symbolic of sleep and oblivion; hence Virgil calls it the Lethean poppy, whilst our old pastoral poet, William Browne, speaks of it as "sleep-bringing poppy." The heliotrope denotes devoted attachment, from its having been supposed to turn continually towards the sun; hence its name, signifying the sun and to turn. The classic heliotrope must not be confounded with the well-known Peruvian heliotrope or "cherry-pie," a plant with small lilac-blue blossoms of a delicious fragrance. It would seem that many of the flowers which had the reputation of opening and shutting at the sun's bidding were known as heliotropes, or sunflowers, or turnesol. Shakespeare alludes to the,

"Marigold, that goes to bed with the sun,
And with him rises weeping."

And Moore, describing its faithful constancy, says:--

"The sunflower turns on her god when he sets
The same look which she did when he rose."

Such a flower, writes Mr. Ellacombe, was to old writers "the emblem of constancy in affection and sympathy in joy and sorrow," though it was also the emblem of the fawning courtier, who can only shine when everything is right. Anyhow, the so-called heliotrope was the subject of constant symbolic allusion:--

"The flower, enamoured of the sun,
At his departure hangs her head and weeps,
And shrouds her sweetness up, and keeps
Sad vigils, like a cloistered nun,
Till his reviving ray appears,
Waking her beauty as he dries her tears." [5]

The aspen, from its tremulous motion, has been made symbolical of fear. The restless movement of its leaves is "produced by the peculiar form of the foot-stalks, and, indeed, in some degree, the whole tribe of poplars are subject to have their leaves agitated by the slightest breeze."[6] Another meaning assigned to the aspen in floral language is scandal, from an old saying which affirmed that its tears were made from women's tongues--an allusion to which is made in the subjoined rhyme by P. Hannay in the year 1622:--

"The quaking aspen, light and thin,
To the air quick passage gives;
* Resembling still*
* The trembling ill*
Of tongues of womankind,
* Which never rest,*
* But still are prest*
To wave with every wind."

The almond, again, is regarded as expressive of haste, in reference to its hasty growth and early maturity; while the evening primrose, from the time of its blossoms expanding, indicates silent love — refraining from unclosing "her cup of paly gold until her lowly sisters are rocked into a balmy slumber." The bramble, from its manner of growth, has been chosen as the type of lowliness; and "from the fierceness with which it grasps the passer-by with its straggling prickly stems, as an emblem of remorse."

Fennel was in olden times generally considered an inflammatory herb, and hence to eat "conger and fennel" was to eat two high and hot things together, which was an act of libertinism. Thus in "2 Henry IV." (Act ii. sc. 4), Falstaff says of Poins, "He eats conger and fennel."

Rosemary formerly had the reputation of strengthening the memory, and on this account was regarded as a symbol of remembrance. Thus, according to an old ballad:--

"Rosemary is for remembrance
Between us day and night,
Wishing that I may always have
You present in my sight."

And in "Hamlet," where Ophelia seems to be addressing Laertes, she says (Act iv. sc. 5):--

"There's rosemary, that's for remembrance."

Vervain, from time immemorial, has been the floral symbol of enchantment, owing to its having been in ancient times much in request for all kinds of divinations and incantations. Virgil, it may be remembered, alludes to this plant as one of the charms used by an enchantress:--

"Bring running water, bind those altars round
With fillets, with vervain strew the ground."

Parsley, according to floral language, has a double signification, denoting feasting and death. On festive occasions the Greeks wore wreaths of parsley, and on many other occasions it was employed, such as at the Isthmian games. On the other hand, this plant was strewn over the bodies of the dead, and decked their graves.

"The weeping willow," as Mr. Ingram remarks, "is one of those natural emblems which bear their florigraphical meaning so palpably impressed that their signification is clear at first sight." This tree has always been regarded as the symbol of sorrow, and also of forsaken love. In China it is employed in several rites, having from a remote period been regarded as a token of immortality. As a symbol of bitterness the aloe has long been in repute, and "as bitter as aloes" is a proverbial expression, doubtless derived from the acid taste of its juice. Eastern poets frequently speak of this plant as the emblem of bitterness; a meaning which most fitly coincides with its properties. The lily of the valley has had several emblems conferred upon it, each of which is equally apposite. Thus in reference to the bright hopeful season of spring, in which it blossoms, it has been regarded as symbolical of the return of happiness, whilst its delicate perfume has long been indicative of sweetness, a characteristic thus beautifully described by Keats:--

"No flower amid the garden fairer grows
Than the sweet lily of the lowly vale,
The queen of flowers."

Its perfect snow-white flower is the emblem of purity, allusions to which we find numerously scattered in the literature of the past. One of the emblems of the white poplar in floral language is time, because its leaves appear always in motion, and "being of a dead blackish-green above, and white below," writes Mr. Ingram, "they were deemed by the ancients to indicate the alternation of night and day." Again, the plane-tree has been from early times made the symbol of genius and magnificence; for in olden times philosophers taught beneath its branches, which acquired for it a reputation as one of the seats of learning. From its beauty and size it obtained a figurative meaning; and the arbutus or strawberry-tree (Arbutus unedo) is the symbol of inseparable love, and the narcissus denotes self-love, from the story of Narcissus, who, enamoured of his own beauty, became spell-bound to the spot, where he pined to death. Shelley describes it as one of the flowers growing with the sensitive plant in that garden where:--

"The pied wind flowers and the tulip tall,
And narcissi, the fairest among them all,
Who gaze on their eyes in the stream's recess,
Till they die at their own dear loveliness."

The sycamore implies curiosity, from Zacchaeus, who climbed up into this tree to witness the triumphal entry of Christ into Jerusalem; and from time immemorial the violet has been the emblem of constancy:--

"Violet is for faithfulness,
Which in me shall abide,
Hoping likewise that from your heart
You will not let it hide."

In some cases flowers seem to have derived their symbolism from certain events associated with them. Thus the periwinkle signifies "early recollections, or pleasures of memory," in connection with which Rousseau tells us how, as Madame Warens and himself were proceeding to Charmattes, she was struck by the appearance of some of these blue flowers in the hedge, and exclaimed, "Here is the periwinkle still in flower."

Thirty years afterwards the sight of the periwinkle in flower carried his memory back to this occasion, and he inadvertently cried, "Ah, there is the periwinkle." Incidents of the kind have originated many of the symbols found in plant language, and at the same time invested them with a peculiar historic interest.

Once more, plant language, it has been remarked, is one of those binding links which connects the sentiments and feelings of one country with another; although it may be, in other respects, these communities have little in common. Thus, as Mr. Ingram remarks in the introduction to his "Flora Symbolica" (p. 12), "from the unlettered North American Indian to the highly polished Parisian; from the days of dawning among the mighty Asiatic races, whose very names are buried in oblivion, down to the present times, the symbolism of flowers is everywhere and in all ages discovered permeating all strata of society. It has been, and still is, the habit of many peoples to name the different portions of the year after the most prominent changes of the vegetable kingdom."

In the United States, the language of flowers is said to have more votaries than in any other part of the world, many works relative to which have been published in recent years. Indeed, the subject will always be a popular one; for further details illustrative of which the reader would do well to consult Mr. H.G. Adams's useful work on the "Moral Language and Poetry of Flowers," not to mention the constant allusions scattered throughout the works of our old poets, such as Shakespeare, Chaucer, and Drayton.

Footnotes:
1. Introduction, p. 12.
2. Folkard's "Plant Legends," p. 389.
 3. See Judith xv. 13.
4. "Flower-lore," pp. 197-198.
5. "Plant-lore of Shakespeare."
6. "Flower-lore," p. 168.

CHAPTER XV

FABULOUS PLANTS

The curious traditions of imaginary plants found amongst most nations have partly a purely mythological origin. Frequently, too, they may be attributed to the exaggerated accounts given by old travellers, who, "influenced by a desire to make themselves famous, have gone so far as to pretend that they saw these fancied objects." Anyhow, from whatever source sprung, these productions of ignorance and superstition have from a very early period been firmly credited. But, like the accounts given us of fabulous animals, they have long ago been acknowledged as survivals of popular errors, which owed their existence to the absence of botanical knowledge.

We have elsewhere referred to the great world tree, and of the primitive idea of a human descent from trees. Indeed, according to the early and uncultured belief of certain communities, there were various kinds of animal-producing trees, accounts of which are very curious. Among these may be mentioned the vegetable lamb, concerning which olden writers have given the most marvellous description. Thus Sir John Maundeville, who in his "Voyage and Travel" has recorded many marvellous sights which either came under his notice, or were reported to him during his travels, has not omitted to speak of this remarkable tree. Thus, to quote his words:--"There groweth a manner of fruit as though it were gourdes; and when they be ripe men cut them in two, and men find within a little beast, in flesh, in bone, and blood--as though it were a little lamb withouten wolle--and men eat both the fruit and the beast, and that is a great marvel; of that fruit I have eaten although it were wonderful; but that I know well that God is marvellous in His works." Various accounts have been given of this wondrous plant, and in Parkinson's "Paradisus" it is represented as one of the plants which grew in the Garden of Eden. Its local name is the Scythian or Tartarian Lamb; and, as it grows, it might at a short distance be taken for an animal rather than a vegetable production. It is one of the genus Polypodium; root decumbent, thickly clothed with a very soft close hoal, of a deep yellow colour. It is also called by the Tartars "Barometz," and a Chinese nickname is "Rufous dog." Mr. Bell, in his "Journey to Ispahan," thus describes a specimen which he saw:--"It seemed to be made by art to imitate a lamb. It is said to eat up and devour all the grass and weeds within its reach. Though it may be thought that an opinion so very absurd could never find credit with people of the meanest understanding, yet I have conversed with some who were much inclined to believe it; so very prevalent is the prodigious and absurd with some part of mankind. Among the more sensible and experienced Tartars, I found they laughed at it as a ridiculous fable." Blood was said to flow from it when cut or injured, a superstition which probably originated in the fact that the fresh root when cut yields a tenacious gum like the blood of animals. Dr. Darwin, in his "Loves of the Plants," adopts the fable thus:--

"E'en round the pole the flames of love aspire,
And icy bosoms feel the sacred fire,
Cradled in snow, and fanned by arctic air,
Shines, gentle Barometz, the golden hair;
Rested in earth, each cloven hoof descends,
And round and round her flexile neck she bends.
Crops of the grey coral moss, and hoary thyme,
Or laps with rosy tongue the melting rime,
Eyes with mute tenderness her distant dam,
Or seems to bleat a vegetable lamb."

Another curious fiction prevalent in olden times was that of the barnacle-tree, to which Sir John Maundeville also alludes:--"In our country were trees that bear a fruit that becomes flying birds; those that fell in the water lived, and those that fell on the earth died, and these be right good for man's meat." As early as the twelfth century this idea was promulgated by Giraldus Cambrensis in his "Topographia Hiberniae;" and Gerarde in his "Herball, or General History of Plants," published in the year 1597, narrates the following:--"There are found in the north parts of Scotland, and the isles adjacent, called Orcades, certain trees, whereon do grow small fishes, of a white colour, tending to russet, wherein are contained little living creatures; which shells, in time of maturity, do open, and out of them grow those little living things which, falling into the water, do become fowls, whom we call barnacles, in the north of England brant-geese, and in Lancashire tree-geese; but the others that do fall upon the land perish, and do come to nothing." But, like many other popular fictions, this notion was founded on truth, and probably originated in mistaking the fleshy peduncle of the barnacle (Lepas analifera) for the neck of a goose, the shell for its head, and the tentacula for a tuft of feather. There were many versions of this eccentric myth, and according to one modification given by Boëce, the oldest Scottish historian, these barnacle-geese are first produced in the form of worms in old trees, and further adds that such a tree was cast on shore in the year 1480, when there appeared, on its being sawn asunder, a multitude of worms, "throwing themselves out of sundry holes and pores of the tree; some of them were nude, as they were new shapen; some had both head, feet, and wings, but they had no feathers; some of them were perfect shapen fowls. At last, the people having this tree each day in more admiration, brought it to the kirk of St. Andrew's, beside the town of Tyre, where it yet remains to our day."

Du Bartas thus describes the various transformations of this bird:--

"So, slowe Boôtes underneath him sees,
In th' ycie iles, those goslings hatcht of trees;
Whose fruitful leaves, falling into the water,
Are turn'd, they say, to living fowls soon after.

So, rotten sides of broken ships do change
To barnacles; O transformation change,
'Twas first a green tree, then a gallant hull,
Lately a mushroom, now a flying gull."

Meyer wrote a treatise on this strange "bird without father or mother," and Sir Robert Murray, in the "Philosophical Transactions," says that, "these shells are hung at the tree by a neck, longer than the shell, of a filmy substance, round and hollow and creased, not unlike the windpipe of a chicken, spreading out broadest where it is fastened to the tree, from which it seems to draw and convey the matter which serves for the growth and vegetation of the shell and the little bird within it. In every shell that I opened," he adds, "I found a perfect sea-fowl; the little bill like that of a goose, the eyes marked; the head, neck, breast, wing, tail, and feet formed; the feathers everywhere perfectly shaped, and the feet like those of other water-fowl." The Chinese have a tradition of certain trees, the leaves of which were finally changed into birds.

With this story may be compared that of the oyster-bearing tree, which Bishop Fleetwood describes in his "Curiosities of Agriculture and Gardening," written in the year 1707. The oysters as seen, he says, by the Dominican Du Tertre, at Guadaloupe, grew on the branches of trees, and, "are not larger than the little English oysters, that is to say, about the size of a crown-piece. They stick to the branches that hang in the water of a tree called Paretuvier. No doubt the seed of the oysters, which is shed in the tree when they spawn, cleaves to those branches, so that the oysters form themselves there, and grow bigger in process of time, and by their weight bend down the branches into the sea, and then are refreshed twice a day by the flux and reflux of it." Kircher speaks of a tree in Chili, the leaves of which brought forth a certain kind of worm, which eventually became changed into serpents; and describes a plant which grew in the Molucca Islands, nicknamed "catopa," on account of its leaves when falling off being transformed into butterflies.

Among some of the many other equally wonderful plants may be mentioned the "stony wood," which is thus described by Gerarde:-- "Being at Rugby, about such time as our fantastic people did with great concourse and multitudes repair and run headlong unto the sacred wells of Newnam Regis, in the edge of Warwickshire, as unto the Waters of Life, which could cure all diseases." He visited these healing-wells, where he, "found growing over the same a fair ash-tree, whose boughs did hang over the spring of water, whereof some that were seare and rotten, and some that of purpose were broken off, fell into the water and were all turned into stone. Of these, boughs, or parts of the tree, I brought into London, which, when I had broken into pieces, therein might be seen that the pith and all the rest was turned into stones, still remaining the same shape and fashion that they were of before they were in the water." Similarly, Sir John Maundeville notices the "Dead Sea fruit"—fruit found on the apple-trees near the Dead Sea. To quote his own words:-- "There be full fair apples, and fair of colour to behold; but whoso breaketh them or cutteth them in two, he shall find within them coals and cinders, in token that by the wrath of God, the city and the land were burnt and sunken into hell." Speaking of the many legendary tales connected with the apple, may be mentioned the golden apples which Hera received at her marriage with Zeus, and placed under the guardianship of the dragon Ladon, in the garden of the Hesperides. The northern Iduna kept guarded the sacred apples which, by a touch, restored the aged gods to youth; and according to Sir J. Maundeville, the apples of Pyban fed the pigmies with their smell only. This reminds us of the singing apple in the fairy romance, which would persuade by its smell alone, and enable the possessor to write poetry or prose, and to display the most accomplished wit; and of the singing tree in the "Arabian Nights," each leaf of which was musical, all the leaves joining together in a delightful harmony.

But peculiarities of this kind are very varied, and form an extensive section in "Plant-lore;"--very many curious examples being found in old travels, and related with every semblance of truth. In some instances trees have obtained a fabulous character from being connected with certain events. Thus there was the "bleeding tree."[1] It appears that one of the indictments laid to the charge of the Marquis of Argyll was this:-- "That a tree on which thirty-six of his enemies were hanged was immediately blasted, and when hewn down, a copious stream of blood ran from it, saturating the earth, and that blood for several years was emitted from the roots." Then there is the "poet's tree," which grows over the tomb of Tan-Sein, a musician at the court of Mohammed Akbar. Whoever chews a leaf of this tree was long said to be inspired with sweet melody of voice, an allusion to which is made by Moore, in "Lalla Kookh:"--"His voice was sweet, as if he had chewed the leaves of that

enchanted tree which grows over the tomb of the musician Tan-Sein."
The rare but occasional occurrence of vegetation in certain trees and
shrubs, happening to take place at the period of Christ's birth, gave rise
to the belief that such trees threw out their leaves with a holy joy to
commemorate that anniversary. An oak of the early budding species for
two centuries enjoyed such a notoriety, having been said to shoot forth
its leaves on old Christmas Day, no leaf being seen either before or after
that day during winter. There was the famous Glastonbury thorn, and in
the same locality a walnut tree was reported never to put forth its leaves
before the feast of St. Barnabas, the 11th June. The monkish legend runs
thus: Joseph of Arimathaea, after landing at no great distance from
Glastonbury, walked to a hill about a mile from the town. Being weary
he sat down here with his companions, the hill henceforth being
nicknamed "Weary-All-Hill," locally abbreviated into "Werral." Whilst
resting Joseph struck his staff into the ground, which took root, grew,
and blossomed every Christmas Day. Previous to the time of Charles I a
branch of this famous tree was carried in procession, with much
ceremony, at Christmas time, but during the Civil War the tree was cut
down. Many plants, again, as the "Sesame" of the "Arabian Nights," had
the power of opening doors and procuring an entrance into caverns and
mountain sides--a survival of which we find in the primrose or key-
flower of German legend. Similarly, other plants, such as the golden-rod,
have been renowned for pointing to hidden springs of water, and
revealing treasures of gold and silver. Such fabulous properties have
been also assigned to the hazel-branch, popularly designated the
divining-rod:--

"Some sorcerers do boast they have a rod,
Gather'd with vows and sacrifice,
And, borne aloft, will strangely nod
The hidden treasure where it lies."

With plants of the kind we may compare the wonder-working
moonwort (Botrychium lunaria), which was said to open locks and to
unshoe horses that trod on it, a notion which Du Bartas thus mentions in
his "Divine Weekes"--

"Horses that, feeding on the grassy hills,
Tread upon moonwort with their hollow heels,
Though lately shod, at night go barefoot home,
Their maister musing where their shoes become.
O moonwort! tell me where thou bid'st the smith,
Hammer and pinchers, thou unshodd'st them with.

Alas! what lock or iron engine is't,
That can thy subtle secret strength resist,
Still the best farrier cannot set a shoe
So sure, but thou (so shortly) canst undo."

The blasting-root, known in Germany as spring-wurzel, and by us as spring-wort, possesses similar virtues, for whatever lock is touched by it must yield. It is no easy matter to find this magic plant, but, according to a piece of popular folklore, it is obtained by means of the woodpecker. When this bird visits its nest, it must have been previously plugged up with wood, to remove which it goes in search of the spring-wort. On holding this before the nest the wood shoots out from the tree as if driven by the most violent force. Meanwhile, a red cloth must be placed near the nest, which will so scare the woodpecker that it will let the fabulous root drop. There are several versions of this tradition. According to Pliny the bird is the raven; in Swabia it is the hoopoe, and in Switzerland the swallow. In Russia, there is a plant growing in marshy land, known as the rasir-trava, which when applied to locks causes them to open instantly. In Iceland similar properties are ascribed to the herb-paris, there known as lasa-grass.

According to a piece of Breton lore, the selago, or "cloth of gold," cannot be cut with steel without the sky darkening and some disaster taking place:--

"The herb of gold is cut; a cloud
Across the sky hath spread its shroud
To war."

On the other hand, if properly gathered with due ceremony, it conferred the power of understanding the language of beast or bird.[2] As far back as the time of Pliny, we have directions for the gathering of this magic plant. The person plucking it was to go barefoot, with feet washed, clad in white, after having offered a sacrifice of bread and wine. Another plant which had to be gathered with special formalities was the magic mandragora. It was commonly reported to shriek in such a hideous manner when pulled out of the earth that,

"Living mortals hearing them run mad."

Hence, various precautions were adopted. According to Pliny, "When they intended to take up the root of this plant, they took the wind thereof, and with a sword describing three circles about it, they digged it up, looking towards the west." Another old authority informs us that he "Who would take it up, in common prudence should tie a dog to it to

accomplish his purpose, as if he did it himself, he would shortly die."
Moore gives this warning:--

"The phantom shapes--oh, touch them not
That appal the maiden's sight,
Look in the fleshy mandrake's stem,
That shrieks when plucked at night."

To quote one or two more illustrations, we may mention the famous
lily at Lauenberg, which is said to have sprung up when a poor and
beautiful girl was spirited away out of the clutches of a dissolute baron.
It made its appearance annually, an event which was awaited with much
interest by the inhabitants of the Hartz, many of whom made a
pilgrimage to behold it. "They returned to their homes," it is said,
"overpowered by its dazzling beauty, and asserting that its splendour
was so great that it shed beams of light on the valley below." Similarly,
we are told how the common break-fern flowers but once a year, at
midnight, on Michaelmas Eve, when it displays a small blue flower,
which vanishes at the approach of dawn. According to a piece of folklore
current in Bohemia and the Tyrol, the fern-seed shines like glittering
gold at the season, so that there is no chance of missing its appearance,
especially as it has its sundry mystic properties which are described
elsewhere.

Professor Mannhardt relates a strange legend current in Mecklenburg
to the effect that in a certain secluded and barren spot, where a murder
had been committed, there grows up every day at noon a peculiarly-
shaped thistle, unlike any other of its kind. On inspection there are to be
seen human arms, hands, and heads, and as soon as twelve heads have
appeared, the weird plant vanishes. It is further added that on one
occasion a shepherd happened to pass the mysterious spot where the
thistle was growing, when instantly his arms were paralysed and his
staff became tinder. Accounts of these fabulous trees and plants have in
years gone been very numerous, and have not yet wholly died out,
surviving in the legendary tales of most countries. In some instances, too,
it would seem that certain trees like animals have gained a notoriety,
purely fabulous, through trickery and credulity. About the middle of the
last century, for instance, there was the groaning-tree at Badesly, which
created considerable sensation. It appears that a cottager, who lived in
the village of Badesly, two miles from Lymington, frequently heard a
strange noise behind his house, like a person in extreme agony. For
about twenty months this tree was an object of astonishment, and at last
the owner of the tree, in order to discover the cause of its supposed
sufferings, bored a hole in the trunk. After this operation it ceased to
groan, it was rooted up, but nothing appeared to account for its strange

peculiarity. Stories of this kind remind us of similar wonders recorded by Sir John Maundeville, as having been seen by him in the course of his Eastern travels. Thus he describes a certain table of ebony or blackwood, "that once used to turn into flesh on certain occasions, but whence now drops only oil, which, if kept above a year, becomes good flesh and bone."

Footnotes:

1. Laing's "History of Scotland," 1800, ii. p. II.
2. "Flower-lore," p. 46.

CHAPTER XVI

DOCTRINE OF SIGNATURES

The old medical theory, which supposed that plants by their external character indicated the particular diseases for which Nature had intended them as remedies, was simply a development of the much older notion of a real connection between object and image. Thus, on this principle, it was asserted that the properties of substances were frequently denoted by their colour; hence, white was regarded as refrigerant, and red as hot. In the same way, for disorders of the blood, burnt purple, pomegranate seeds, mulberries, and other red ingredients were dissolved in the patient's drink; and for liver omplaints yellow substances were recommended. But this fanciful and erroneous notion "led to serious errors in practice," [1] and was occasionally productive of the most fatal results. Although, indeed, Pliny spoke of the folly of the magicians in using the catanance (Greek: katanhankae, compulsion) for love-potions, on account of its shrinking "in drying into the shape of the claws of a dead kite," [2] and so holding the patient fast; yet this primitive idea, after the lapse of centuries, was as fully credited as in the early days when it was originally started. Throughout the sixteenth and seventeenth centuries, for instance, it is noticed in most medical works, and in many cases treated with a seriousness characteristic of the backward state of medical science even at a period so comparatively recent. Crollius wrote a work on the subject; and Langham, in his "Garden of Health," published in the year 1578, accepted the doctrine. Coles, in his "Art of Simpling" (1656), thus describes it:--

"Though sin and Satan have plunged mankind into an ocean of infirmities, yet the mercy of God, which is over all His workes, maketh grasse to growe upon the mountains and herbes for the use of men, and hath not only stamped upon them a distinct forme, but also given them particular signatures, whereby a man may read even in legible characters the use of them."

John Ray, in his treatise on "The Wisdom of God in Creation," was among the first to express his disbelief of this idea, and writes:--"As for the signatures of plants, or the notes impressed upon them as notices of their virtues, some lay great stress upon them, accounting them strong arguments to prove that some understanding principle is the highest original of the work of Nature, as indeed they were could it be certainly made to appear that there were such marks designedly set upon them, because all that I find mentioned by authors seem to be rather fancied by men than designed by Nature to signify, or point out, any such virtues, or qualities, as they would make us believe." His views, however, are somewhat contradictory, inasmuch as he goes on to say that, "the noxious and malignant plants do, many of them, discover something of their nature by the sad and melancholick visage of their leaves, flowers, or fruit. And that I may not leave that head wholly untouched, one observation I shall add relating to the virtues of plants, in which I think there is something of truth--that is, that there are of the wise dispensation of Providence such species of plants produced in every country as are made proper and convenient for the meat and medicine of the men and animals that are bred and inhabit therein." Indeed, however much many of the botanists of bygone centuries might try to discredit this popular delusion, they do not seem to have been wholly free from its influence themselves. Some estimate, also, of the prominence which the doctrine of signatures obtained may be gathered from the frequent allusions to it in the literature of the period. Thus, to take one illustration, the euphrasia or eye-bright (Euphrasia officinalis), which was, and is, supposed to be good for the eye, owing to a black pupil-like spot in its corolla, is noticed by Milton, who, it may be remembered, represents the archangel as clearing the vision of our first parents by its means:--

"Then purged with euphrasy and rue
His visual orbs, for he had much to see."

Spenser speaks of it in the same strain:--

"Yet euphrasie may not be left unsung,
That gives dim eyes to wander leagues around."

And Thomson says:--

"If she, whom I implore, Urania, deign
With euphrasy to purge away the mists,
Which, humid, dim the mirror of the mind."

With reference to its use in modern times, Anne Pratt[3] tells us how, "on going into a small shop in Dover, she saw a quantity of the plant suspended from the ceiling, and was informed that it was gathered and dried as being good for weak eyes;" and in many of our rural districts I learn that the same value is still attached to it by the peasantry.

Again, it is interesting to observe how, under a variety of forms, this piece of superstition has prevailed in different parts of the world. By virtue of a similar association of ideas, for instance, the gin-seng [4] was said by the Chinese and North American Indians to possess certain virtues which were deduced from the shape of the root, supposed to resemble the human body [5]--a plant with which may be compared our mandrake. The Romans of old had their rock-breaking plant called "saxifraga" or sassafras; [6] and we know in later times how the granulated roots of our white meadow saxifrage (Saxifraga granulata), resembling small stones, were supposed to indicate its efficacy in the cure of calculous complaints. Hence one of its names, stonebreak. The stony seeds of the gromwell were, also, used in cases of stone--a plant formerly known as lichwale, or, as in a MS. of the fifteenth century, lythewale, stone-switch. [7]

In accordance, also, with the same principle it was once generally believed that the seeds of ferns were of an invisible sort, and hence, by a transference of properties, it came to be admitted that the possessor of fern-seed could likewise be invisible--a notion which obtained an extensive currency on the Continent. As special good-luck was said to attend the individual who succeeded in obtaining this mystic seed, it was eagerly sought for--Midsummer Eve being one of the occasions when it could be most easily procured. Thus Grimm, in his "Teutonic Mythology," [8] relates how a man in Westphalia was looking on Midsummer night for a foal he had lost, and happened to pass through a meadow just as the fern-seed was ripening, so that it fell into his shoes. In the morning he went home, walked into the sitting-room and sat down, but thought it strange that neither his wife nor any of the family took the least notice of him. "I have not found the foal," said he. Thereupon everybody in the room started and looked alarmed, for they heard his voice but saw him not. His wife then called him, thinking he must have hid himself, but he only replied, "Why do you call me? Here I am right before you." At last he became aware that he was invisible, and, remembering how he had walked in the meadow on the preceding evening, it struck him that he might possibly have fern-seed in his shoes. So he took them off, and as he shook them the fern-seed dropped out, and he was no longer invisible. There are numerous stories of this kind; and, according to Dr. Kuhn, one method for obtaining the fern-seed was, at the summer solstice, to shoot at the sun when it had attained its midday height. If this were done, three drops of blood would fall, which were to be gathered up and preserved--this being the fern-seed. In Bohemia, [9] on old St. John's Night (July 8), one must lay a communion chalice-cloth under the fern, and collect the seed which will fall before sunrise. Among some of the scattered allusions to this piece of folklore in the literature of our own country, may be mentioned one by Shakespeare in "I Henry IV." (ii. 1):--

"Gadshill. *We have the receipt of fern-seed, we walk invisible-* ---[10]

"Chamberlain. *Nay, by my faith, I think you are more beholding to the night than to fern-seed for your walking invisible.*"

In Ben Jonson's "New Inn" (i. 1), it is thus noticed:--

"*I had*
No medicine, sir, to go invisible,
No fern-seed in my pocket."

Brand [11] was told by an inhabitant of Heston, in Middlesex, that when he was a young man he was often present at the ceremony of catching the fern-seed at midnight, on the eve of St. John Baptist. The attempt was frequently unsuccessful, for the seed was to fall into a plate of its own accord, and that too without shaking the plate. It is unnecessary to add further illustrations on this point, as we have had occasion to speak elsewhere of the sundry other magical properties ascribed to the fern-seed, whereby it has been prominently classed amongst the mystic plants. But, apart from the doctrine of signatures, it would seem that the fern-seed was also supposed to derive its power of making invisible from the cloud, says Mr. Kelly, [12] "that contained the heavenly fire from which the plant is sprung." Whilst speaking, too, of the fern-seed's property of making people invisible, it is of interest to note that in the Icelandic and Pomeranian myths the schamir or "raven-stone" renders its possessor invisible; and according to a North German tradition the luck-flower is enbued with the same wonderful qualities. It is essential, however, that the flower be found by accident, for he who seeks it never finds it. In Sweden hazel-nuts are reputed to have the power of making invisible, and from their reputed magical properties have been, from time immemorial, in great demand for divination. All those plants whose leaves bore a fancied resemblance to the moon were, in days of old, regarded with superstitious reverence.The moon-daisy, the type of a class of plants resembling the pictures of a full moon, were exhibited, says Dr. Prior, "in uterine complaints, and dedicated in pagan times to the goddess of the moon." The moonwort (Botrychium lunaria), often confounded with the common "honesty" (Lunaria biennis) of our gardens, so called from the semi-lunar shape of the segments of its frond, was credited with the most curious properties, the old alchemists affirming that it was good among other things for converting quicksilver into pure silver, and unshoeing such horses as trod upon it. A similar virtue was ascribed to the horse-shoe vetch (Hippocrepis comosa), so called from the shape of the legumes, hence another of its mystic nicknames was "unshoe the horse."

But referring to the doctrine of signatures in folk-medicine, a favourite garden flower is Solomon's seal (Polygonatum multiflorum). On cutting the roots transversely, some marks are apparent not unlike the characters of a seal, which to the old herbalists indicated its use as a seal for wounds. [13] Gerarde, describing it, tells us how, "the root of Solomon's seal stamped, while it is fresh and greene, and applied, taketh away in one night, or two at the most, any bruise, black or blue spots, gotten by falls, or women's wilfulness in stumbling upon their hasty husbands' fists." For the same reason it was called by the French herbalists "l'herbe de la rupture." The specific name of the tutsan [14] (Hypericum androsoemum), derived from the two Greek words signifying man and blood, in reference to the dark red juice which exudes from the capsules when bruised, was once applied to external wounds, and hence it was called "balm of the warrior's wound," or "all-heal." Gerarde says, "The leaves laid upon broken skins and scabbed legs heal them, and many other hurts and griefs, whereof it took its name 'toute-saine' of healing all things." The pretty plant, herb-robert (Geranium robertianum), was supposed to possess similar virtues, its power to arrest bleeding being indicated by the beautiful red hue assumed by the fading leaves, on account of which property it was styled "a stauncher of blood." The garden Jerusalem cowslip (Pulmonaria offinalis) owes its English name, lungwort, to the spotting of the leaves, which were said to indicate that they would be efficacious in healing diseases of the lungs. Then there is the water-soldier (Stratiotes aloides), which from its sword-shaped leaves was reckoned among the appliances for gun-shot wounds. Another familiar plant which has long had a reputation as a vulnerary is the self-heal, or carpenter's herb (Prunella vulgaris), on account of its corolla being shaped like a bill-hook.

Again, presumably on the doctrine of signatures, the connection between roses and blood is very curious. Thus in France, Germany, and Italy it is a popular notion that if one is desirous of having ruddy cheeks, he must bury a drop of his blood under a rose-bush. [15] As a charm against haemorrhage of every kind, the rose has long been a favourite remedy in Germany, and in Westphalia the following formula is employed: "Abek, Wabek, Fabek; in Christ's garden stand three red roses--one for the good God, the other for God's blood, the third for the angel Gabriel: blood, I pray you, cease to flow." Another version of this charm is the following [16]:--"On the head of our Lord God there bloom three roses: the first is His virtue, the second is His youth, the third is His will. Blood, stand thou in the wound still, so that thou neither sore nor abscess givest."

Turning to some of the numerous plants which on the doctrine of signatures were formerly used as specifics from a fancied resemblance, in the shape of the root, leaf, or fruit, to any particular part of the human body, we are confronted with a list adapted for most of the ills to which the flesh is heir. [17] Thus, the walnut was regarded as clearly good for mental cases from its bearing the signature of the whole head; the outward green cortex answering to the pericranium, the harder shell within representing the skull, and the kernel in its figure resembling the cover of the brain. On this account the outside shell was considered good for wounds of the head, whilst the bark of the tree was regarded as a sovereign remedy for the ringworm. [18] Its leaves, too, when bruised and moistened with vinegar were used for ear-ache. For scrofulous glands, the knotty tubers attached to the kernel-wort (Scrophularia nodosa) have been considered efficacious. The pith of the elder, when pressed with the fingers, "doth pit and receive the impress of them thereon, as the legs and feet of dropsical persons do," Therefore the juice of this tree was reckoned a cure for dropsy. Our Lady's thistle (Cardmis Marianus), from its numerous prickles, was recommended for stitches of the side; and nettle-tea is still a common remedy with many of our peasantry for nettle-rash. The leaves of the wood-sorrel (Oxalis acetosella) were believed to preserve the heart from many diseases, from their being "broad at the ends, cut in the middle, and sharp towards the stalk." Similarly the heart-trefoil, or clover (Medicago maculata), was so called, because, says Coles in his "Art of Simpling," "not only is the leaf triangular like the heart of a man, but also because each leaf contains the perfect image of an heart, and that in its proper colour--a flesh colour. It defendeth the heart against the noisome vapour of the spleen." Another plant which, on the same principle, was reckoned as a curative for heart-disease, is the heart's-ease, a term meaning a cordial, as in Sir Walter Scott's "Antiquary" (chap, xi.), "try a dram to be eilding and claise, and a supper and heart's-ease into the bargain." The knot-grass (Polygonum aviculare), with its reddish-white flowers and trailing pointed stems, was probably so called "from some unrecorded character by the doctrine of signatures," Suggests Mr. Ellacombe, [19] that it would stop the growth of children. Thus Shakespeare, in his "Midsummer Night's Dream" (Act iii. sc. 2), alludes to it as the "hindering knot-grass," and in Beaumont and Fletcher's "Coxcomb" (Act ii. sc. 2) it is further mentioned:--

"We want a boy extremely for this function,
Kept under for a year with milk and knot-grass."

According to Crollius, the woody scales of which the cones of the pine-tree are composed "resemble the fore-teeth;" hence pine-leaves boiled in vinegar were used as a garlic for the relief of toothache. White-coral, from its resemblance to the teeth, was also in requisition, because "it keepeth children to heed their teeth, their gums being rubbed therewith." For improving the complexion, an ointment made of cowslip-flowers was once recommended, because, as an old writer observes, it "taketh away the spots and wrinkles of the skin, and adds beauty exceedingly." Mr. Burgess, in his handy little volume on "English Wild Flowers" (1868, 47), referring to the cowslip, says, "the village damsels use it as a cosmetic, and we know it adds to the beauty of the complexion of the town-immured lassie when she searches for and gathers it herself in the early spring morning." Some of the old herbalists speak of moss gathered from a skull as useful for disorders of the head, and hence it was gathered and preserved.

The rupture-wort (Herniaria glabra) was so called from its fancied remedial powers, and the scabious in allusion to the scaly pappus of its seeds, which led to its use in leprous diseases. The well-known fern, spleen-wort (Asplenium), had this name applied to it from the lobular form of the leaf, which suggested it as a remedy for diseases of the spleen. Another of its nicknames is miltwaste, because:--

"The finger-ferne, which being given to swine,
It makes their milt to melt away in fine--"

A superstition which seems to have originated in a curious statement made by Vitruvius, that in certain localities in the island of Crete the flocks and herds were found without spleen from their browsing on this plant, whereas in those districts in which it did not grow the reverse was the case. [20]

The yellow bark of the berberry-tree (Berberis vulgaris), [21] when taken as a decoction in ale, or white wine, is said to be a purgative, and to have proved highly efficacious in the case of jaundice, hence in some parts of the country it is known as the "jaundice-berry." Turmeric, too, was formerly prescribed--a plant used for making a yellow dye; [22] and celandine, with its yellow juice, was once equally in repute. Similar remedies we find recommended on the Continent, and in Westphalia an apple mixed with saffron is a popular curative against jaundice. [23] Rhubarb, too, we are told, by the doctrine of signatures, was the "life, soul, heart, and treacle of the liver." Mr. Folkard [24] mentions a curious superstition which exists in the neighbourhood of Orleans, where a seventh son without a daughter intervening is called a Marcon. It is believed that, "the Marcon's body is marked somewhere with a Fleur-de-Lis, and that if a patient suffering under king's-evil touch this Fleur-de-Lis, or if the Marcon breathe upon him, the malady will be sure to disappear."

As shaking is one of the chief characteristics of that tedious and obstinate complaint ague, so there was a prevalent notion that the quaking-grass (Briza media), when dried and kept in the house, acted as a most powerful deterrent. For the same reason, the aspen, from its constant trembling, has been held a specific for this disease. The lesser celandine (Ranunculus ficaria) is known in many country places as the pilewort, because its peculiar tuberous root was long thought to be efficacious as a remedial agent. And Coles, in his "Art of Simpling," speaks of the purple marsh-wort (Comarum palustre) as "an excellent remedy against the purples." The common tormentil (Tormentilla officinalis), from the red colour of its root, was nicknamed the "blood-root," and was said to be efficacious in dysentery; while the bullock's-lungwort derives its name from the resemblance of its leaf to a dewlap, and was on this account held as a remedy for the pneumonia of bullocks.[25] Such is the curious old folklore doctrine of signatures, which in olden times was regarded with so much favour, and for a very long time was recognised, without any questioning, as worthy of men's acceptation. It is one of those popular delusions which scientific research has scattered to the winds, having in its place discovered the true medicinal properties of plants, by the aid of chemical analysis.

Footnotes:

1. Pettigrew's "Medical Superstitions," 1844, p. 18.
2. Tylor's "Researches into the Early History of Mankind," 1865, p. 123; Chapiel's "La Doctrine des Signatures," Paris, 1866.
3. "Flowering Plants of Great Britain," iv. 109; see Dr. Prior's "Popular Names of British Plants," 1870-72.
4. Tylor's "Researches into the Early History of Mankind," p. 123.
5. See Porter Smith's "Chinese Materia Medica," p. 103; Lockhart, "Medical Missionary in China," 2nd edition, p. 107; "Reports on Trade at the Treaty Ports of China," 1868, p. 63.
6. Fiske, "Myths and Mythmakers," 1873, p. 43.
7. Dr. Prior's "Popular Names of British Plants," p. 134.
8. See Kelly's "Indo-European Tradition Folklore," 1863, pp. 193-198; Ralston's "Russian Folk-Songs," 1872, p. 98.
9. "Mystic Trees and Flowers," Mr. D. Conway, Frasers Magazine, Nov. 1870, p. 608.
10. The "receipt," so called, was the formula of magic words to be employed during the process. See Grindon's "Shakspere Flora," 1883, p. 242.
11. "Popular Antiquities," 1849, i. 315.
12. "Indo-European Tradition and Folklore," p. 197.
13. See Dr. Prior's "Popular Names of British Plants," p. 130; Phillips' "Flora Historica," i. 163.
14. See Sowerby's "English Botany," 1864, i., p. 144.

15. See "Folklore of British Plants," Dublin University Magazine, September 1873, p. 318.

16. See Thorpe's "Northern Mythology," 1852, iii. 168.

17. "Sketches of Imposture, Deception, and Credulity," 1837, p. 300.

18. See Phillips' "Pomarium Britannicum," 1821, p. 351.

19. "Plant-lore of Shakespeare," 1878, p. 101.

20. See Dr. Prior's "Popular Names of British Plants," p. 154.

21. Hogg's "Vegetable Kingdom," p. 34.

22. See Friend's "Flowers and Flower-lore," ii. 355.

23. "Mystic Trees and Flowers," Fraser's Magazine, November 1870, p. 591.

24. "Plant Lore Legends and Lyrics," p. 341.

25. Ibid., pp, 150-160.

CHAPTER XVII

PLANTS AND THE CALENDAR

A goodly array of plants have cast their attractions round the festivals of the year, giving an outward beauty to the ceremonies and observances celebrated in their honour. These vary in different countries, although we frequently find the same flower almost universally adopted to commemorate a particular festival. Many plants, again, have had a superstitious connection, having in this respect exercised a powerful influence among the credulous of all ages, numerous survivals of which exist at the present day. Thus, in Westphalia, it is said that if the sun makes its appearance on New Year's Day, the flax will be straight; and there is a belief current in Hessia, that an apple must not be eaten on New Year's Day, as it will produce an abscess.

According to an old adage, the laurestinus, dedicated to St. Faine (January 1), an Irish abbess in the sixth century, may be seen in bloom:--

"Whether the weather be snow or rain,
We are sure to see the flower of St. Faine;
Rain comes but seldom and often snow,
And yet the viburnum is sure to blow."

And James Montgomery notices this cheerful plant, speaking of it as the,

"Fair tree of winter, fresh and flowering,
When all around is dead and dry,
Whose ruby buds, though storms are lowering,
Spread their white blossoms to the sky."

Then there is the dead nettle, which in Italy is assigned to St. Vincent; and the Christmas rose (Helleboris niger), dedicated to St. Agnes (21st January), is known in Germany as the flower of St. Agnes, and yet this flower has generally been regarded a plant of evil omen, being coupled by Campbell with the hemlock, as growing "by the witches' tower," where it seems to weave,

"Round its dark vaults a melancholy bower,
For spirits of the dead at night's enchanted hour."

At Candlemas it was customary, writes Herrick, to replace the Christmas evergreens with sprigs of box, which were kept up till Easter Eve:--

"Down with the rosemary and bays,
Down with the mistletoe,
Instead of holly now upraise
The greener box for show."

The snowdrop has been nicknamed the "Fair Maid of February," from its blossoming about this period, when it was customary for young women dressed in white to walk in procession at the Feast of the Purification, and, according to the old adage:--

"The snowdrop in purest white array,
First rears her head on Candlemas Day."

The dainty crocus is said to blow "before the shrine at vernal dawn of St. Valentine." And we may note here how county traditions affirm that in some mysterious way the vegetable world is affected by leap-year influences. A piece of agricultural folklore current throughout the country tells us how all the peas and beans grow the wrong way in their pods, the seeds being set in quite the contrary to what they are in other years. The reason assigned for this strange freak of nature is that, "it is the ladies' year, and they (the peas and beans) always lay the wrong way in leap year."

The leek is associated with St. David's Day, the adoption of this plant as the national device of Wales having been explained in various ways. According to Shakespeare it dates from the battle of Cressy, while some have maintained it originated in a victory obtained by Cadwallo over the Saxons, 640, when the Welsh, to distinguish themselves, wore leeks in their hats. It has also beeen suggested that Welshmen "beautify their hats with verdant leek," from the custom of every farmer, in years gone by, contributing his leek to the common repast when they met at the Cymortha or Association, and mutually helped one another in ploughing their land.

In Ireland the shamrock is worn on St. Patrick's Day. Old women, with plenteous supplies of trefoil, may be heard in every direction crying, "Buy my shamrock, green shamrocks," while little children have "Patrick's crosses" pinned to their sleeves, a custom which is said to have originated in the circumstance that when St. Patrick was preaching the doctrine of the Trinity he made use of the trefoil as a symbol of the great mystery. Several plants have been identified as the shamrock; and in "Contributions towards a Cybele Hibernica," [1] is the following extensive note:--"Trifolium repens, Dutch clover, shamrock.--This is the plant still worn as shamrock on St. Patrick's Day, though Medicago lupulina is also sold in Dublin as the shamrock. Edward Lhwyd, the celebrated antiquary, writing in 1699 to Tancred Robinson, says, after a recent visit to Ireland: 'Their shamrug is our common clover' (Phil. Trans., No. 335). Threkeld, the earliest writer on the wild plants of Ireland, gives Seamar-oge (young trefoil) as the Gaelic name for Trifolium pratense album, and expressly says this is the plant worn by the people in their hats on St. Patrick's Day." Some, again, have advocated the claims of the wood-sorrel, and others those of the speedwell, whereas a correspondent of Notes and Queries (4th Ser. iii. 235) says the Trifolium filiforme is generally worn in Cork, the Trifolium minus also being in demand. It has been urged that the watercress was the plant gathered by the saint, but this plant has been objected to on the ground that its leaf is not trifoliate, and could not have been used by St. Patrick to illustrate the doctrine of the Trinity. On the other hand, it has been argued that the story is of modern date, and not to be found in any of the lives of that saint. St. Patrick's cabbage also is a name for "London Pride," from its growing in the West of Ireland, where the Saint lived.

Few flowers have been more popular than the daffodil or lent-lily, or, as it is sometimes called, the lent-rose. There are various corruptions of this name to be found in the West of England, such as lentils, lent-a-lily, lents, and lent-cocks; the last name doubtless referring to the custom of cock-throwing, which was allowed in Lent, boys, in the absence of live cocks, having thrown sticks at the flower. According also to the old rhyme:--

"Then comes the daffodil beside
Our Lady's smock at our Lady's tide."

In Catholic countries Lent cakes were flavoured with the herb-tansy, a plant dedicated to St. Athanasius.

In Silesia, on Mid-Lent Sunday, pine boughs, bound with variegated paper and spangles, are carried about by children singing songs, and are hung over the stable doors to keep the animals from evil influences.

Palm Sunday receives its English and the greater part of its foreign names from the old practice of bearing palm-branches, in place of which the early catkins of the willow or yew have been substituted, sprigs of box being used in Brittany.

Stow, in his "Survey of London," tells us that:--"In the weeke before Easter had ye great shows made for the fetching in of a twisted tree or with, as they termed it, out of the wodes into the king's house, and the like into every man's house of honour of worship." This anniversary has also been nicknamed "Fig Sunday," from the old custom of eating figs;

while in Wales it is popularly known as "Flowering Sunday," because persons assemble in the churchyard and spread fresh flowers upon the graves of their friends and relatives.

In Germany, on Palm Sunday, the palm is credited with mystic virtues; and if as many twigs, as there are women of a family, be thrown on a fire--each with a name inscribed on it--the person whose leaf burns soonest will be the first to die.

On Good Friday, in the North of England, an herb pudding was formerly eaten, in which the leaves of the passion-dock (Polygonum bistorta) formed the principal ingredient. In Lancashire fig-sue is made, a mixture consisting of sliced figs, nutmeg, ale, and bread.

Wreaths of elder are hung up in Germany after sunset on Good Friday, as charms against lightning; and in Swabia a twig of hazel cut on this day enables the possessor to strike an absent person. In the Tyrol, too, the hazel must be cut on Good Friday to be effectual as a divining-rod. A Bohemian charm against fleas is curious. During Holy Week a leaf of palm must be placed behind a picture of the Virgin, and on Easter morning taken down with this formula: "Depart, all animals without bones." If this rite is observed there will be no more fleas in the house for the remainder of the year.

Of the flowers associated with Eastertide may be mentioned the garden daffodil and the purple pasque flower, another name for the anemone (Anemone pulsatilla), in allusion to the Passover and Paschal ceremonies. White broom is also in request, and indeed all white flowers are dedicated to this festival. On Easter Day the Bavarian peasants make garlands of coltsfoot and throw them into the fire; and in the district of Lechrain every household brings to the sacred fire which is lighted at Easter a walnut branch, which, when partially burned, is laid on the hearth-fire during tempests as a charm against lightning. In Slavonian regions the palm is supposed to specially protect the locality where it grows from inclement weather and its hurtful effects; while, in Pomerania, the apple is eaten against fevers.

In Bareuth young girls go at midnight on Easter Day to a fountain silently, and taking care to escape notice, throw into the water little willow rings with their friends' names inscribed thereon, the person whose ring sinks the quickest being the first to die.

In years past the milkwort (Polygala vulgaris), from being carried in procession during Rogation Week, was known by such names as the rogation-flower, gang-flower, procession-flower, and cross-flower, a custom noticed by Gerarde, who tells us how, "the maidens which use in the countries to walke the procession do make themselves garlands and nosegaies of the milkwort."

On Ascension Day the Swiss make wreaths of the edelweisse, hanging them over their doors and windows; another plant selected for this purpose being the amaranth, which, like the former, is considered an emblem of immortality.

In our own country may be mentioned the well-dressing of Tissington, near Dovedale, in Derbyshire, the wells in the village having for years past been most artistically decorated with the choicest flowers. [2]

Formerly, on St. George's Day (April 23), blue coats were worn by people of fashion. Hence, the harebell being in bloom, was assigned to the saint:--

"On St. George's Day, when blue is worn,
The blue harebells the fields adorn."

Flowers have always entered largely into the May Day festival; and many a graphic account has been bequeathed us of the enthusiasm with which both old and young went "a-Maying" soon after midnight, breaking down branches from the trees, which, decorated with nosegays and garlands of flowers, were brought home soon after sunrise and placed at the doors and windows. Shakespeare ("Henry VIII.," v. 4), alluding to the custom, says:--

"'Tis as much impossible,
Unless we sweep them from the doors with cannons,
To scatter 'em, as 'tis to make 'em sleep
On May Day morning."

Accordingly, flowers were much in demand, many being named from the month itself, as the hawthorn, known in many places as May-bloom and May-tree, whereas the lily of the valley is nicknamed May-lily. Again, in Cornwall lilac is termed May-flower, and the narrow-leaved elm, which is worn by the peasant in his hat or button-hole, is called May. Similarly, in Germany, we find the term May-bloom applied to such plants as the king-cup and lily of the valley. In North America, says the author of "Flower-lore," the podophyllum is called "May-apple," and the fruit of the Passiflora incarnata "May-hops." The chief uses of these May-flowers were for the garlands, the decoration of the Maypole, and the adornment of the home:--

"To get sweet setywall (red valerian),
The honeysuckle, the harlock,
The lily, and the lady-smock,
To deck their summer hall."

But one plant was carefully avoided--the cuckoo flower.[3] As in other floral rites, the selection of plants varies on the Continent, branches of the elder being carried about in Savoy, and in Austrian Silesia the Maypole is generally made of fir. According to an Italian proverb, the universal lover is "one who hangs every door with May."

Various plants are associated with Whitsuntide, and according to Chaucer, in his "Romaunt of the Rose":--

"Have hatte of floures fresh as May,
Chapelett of roses of Whitsunday,
For sich array be costeth but lite."

In Italy the festival is designated "Pasqua Rosata," from falling at a time when roses are in bloom, while in Germany the peony is the Pentecost rose.

Herrick tells us it was formerly the practice to use birch and spring-flowers for decorative purposes at Whitsuntide:--

"When yew is out then birch comes in,
And May-flowers beside,
Both of a fresh and fragrant kinne,
To honour Whitsontide."

At this season, too, box-boughs were gathered to deck the large open fire-places then in fashion, and the guelder rose was dedicated to the festival. Certain flower-sermons have been preached in the city at Whitsuntide, as, for instance, that at St. James's Church, Mitre Court, Aldgate, and another at St. Leonard's Church, Shoreditch, known as the Fairchild Lecture. Turning to the Continent, it is customary in Hanover on Whit-Monday to gather the lily of the valley, and at the close of the day there is scarcely a house without a large bouquet, while in Germany the broom is a favourite plant for decorations. In Russia, at the completion of Whitsuntide, young girls repair to the banks of the Neva and cast in wreaths of flowers in token of their absent friends.

Certain flowers, such as the rose, lavender, woodruff, and box were formerly in request for decking churches on St. Barnabas' Day, the officiating clergy having worn wreaths of roses. Among the allusions to the usage may be mentioned the following entries in the churchwarden's accounts of St. Mary-at-Hill, London, in the reigns of Edward IV. And Henry VII.:--"For rose garlondis and woodrolf garlondis on St. Barnabe Daye, xj'd." "Item, for two doss (dozen?) di bocse (box) garlands for prestes and clerkes on St. Barnabe Day, j's. v'd."

St. Barnabas' thistle (Centaurea solstitialis) derived its name from flowering at the time of the saint's festival, and we are told how:--

"When St. Barnaby bright smiles night and day,
Poor ragged robin blooms in the hay."

To Trinity Sunday belong the pansy, or herb-trinity and trefoil, hence the latter has been used for decorations on this anniversary.

In commemoration of the Restoration of Charles II., oak leaves and gilded oak apples have been worn; oak branches having been in past years placed over doors and windows.

Stowe, in his "Survey of London," speaks of the old custom of hanging up St. John's wort over the doors of houses, along with green birch or pine, white lilies, and other plants. The same practice has existed very largely on the Continent, St. John's wort being still regarded as an effective charm against witchcraft. Indeed, few plants have been in greater request on any anniversary, or been invested with such mystic virtues. Fennel, another of the many plants dedicated to St. John, was hung over doors and windows on his night in England, numerous allusions to which occur in the literature of the past. And in connection with this saint we are told how:--

"The scarlet lychnis, the garden's pride,
Flames at St. John the Baptist's tyde."

Hemp was also in demand, many forms of divination having been practiced by means of its seed.

According to a belief in Iceland, the trijadent (Spiraea ulmaria) will, if put under water on this day, reveal a thief; floating if the thief be a woman, and sinking if a man.

In the Harz, on Midsummer night, branches of the fir-tree are decorated with flowers and coloured eggs, around which the young people dance, singing rhymes. The Bolognese, who regard garlic as the symbol of abundance, buy it at the festival as a charm against poverty during the coming year. The Bohemian, says Mr. Conway, "thinks he can make himself shot-proof for twenty-four hours by finding on St. John's Day pine-cones on the top of a tree, taking them home, and eating a single kernel on each day that he wishes to be invulnerable." In Sicily it is customary, on Midsummer Eve, to fell the highest poplar, and with shouts to drag it through the village, while some beat a drum. Around this poplar, says Mr. Folkard,[4] "symbolising the greatest solar ascension and the decline which follows it, the crowd dance, and sing an appropriate refrain;" and he further mentions that, at the commencement of the Franco-German War, he saw sprigs of pine stuck on the railway carriages bearing the German soldiers into France.

In East Prussia, the sap of dog-wood, absorbed in a handkerchief, will fulfil every wish; and a Brandenburg remedy for fever is to lie naked under a cherry-tree on St. John's Day, and to shake the dew on one's back. Elsewhere we have alluded to the flowering of the fern on this anniversary, and there is the Bohemian idea that its seed shines like glittering gold.

Corpus Christi Day was, in olden times, observed with much ceremony, the churches being decorated with roses and other choice garlands, while the streets through which the procession passed were strewn with flowers. In North Wales, flowers were scattered before the door; and a particular fern, termed Rhedyn Mair, or Mary's fern-- probably the maiden-hair — was specially used for the purpose.

We may mention here that the daisy (Bellis perennis) was formerly known as herb-Margaret or Marguerite, and was erroneously supposed to have been named after the virtuous St. Margaret of Antioch:--

"Maid Margarete, that was so meek and mild;"

Whereas it, in all probability, derives its name from St. Margaret of Cortona. According to an old legend it is stated:--

"There is a double flouret, white and red,
That our lasses call herb-Margaret,
In honour of Cortona's penitent,
Whose contrite soul with red remorse was rent;
While on her penitence kind heaven did throw
The white of purity, surpassing snow;
So white and red in this fair flower entwine,
Which maids are wont to scatter at her shrine."

Again, of the rainy saint, St. Swithin, we are reminded that:--

"Against St. Swithin's hastie showers,
The lily white reigns queen of the flowers"--

A festival around which so much curious lore has clustered.

In former years St. Margaret's Day (July 20) was celebrated with many curious ceremonies, and, according to a well-known couplet in allusion to the emblem of the vanquished dragon, which appears in most pictures of St. Margaret:--

"Poppies a sanguine mantle spread
For the blood of the dragon that Margaret shed."

Archdeacon Hare says the Sweet-William, designated the "painted lady," was dedicated to Saint William (June 25), the term "sweet" being a substitution for "saint." This seems doubtful, and some would corrupt the word "sweet" from the French oeillet, corrupted to Willy, and thence to William. Mr. King, however, considers that the small red pink (Dianthus prolifer), found wild in the neighbourhood of Rochester, "is perhaps the original Saint Sweet-William," for, he adds, the word "saint" has only been dropped since days which saw the demolition of St. William's shrine in the cathedral. This is but a conjecture, it being uncertain whether the masses of bright flowers which form one of the chief attractions of old-fashioned gardens commemorate St. William of Rochester, St. William of York, or, likeliest perhaps of the three, St. William of Aquitaine, the half soldier, half monk, whose fame was so widely spread throughout the south of Europe.

Roses were said to fade on St. Mary Magdalene's Day (July 20), to whom we find numerous flowers dedicated, such as the maudlin, a nickname of the costmary, either in allusion to her love of scented ointment, or to its use in uterine affections, over which she presided as the patroness of unchaste women, and maudlin-wort, another name for the moon-daisy. But, as Dr. Prior remarks, it should, "be observed that the monks in the Middle Ages mixed up with the story of the Magdalene that of another St. Mary, whose early life was passed in a course of debauchery."

A German piece of folklore tells us that it is dangerous to climb a cherry-tree on St. James's Night, as the chance of breaking one's neck will be great, this day being held unlucky. On this day is kept St. Christopher's anniversary, after whom the herb-christopher is named, a species of aconite, according to Gerarde. But, as Dr. Prior adds, the name is applied to many plants which have no qualities in common, some of these being the meadow-sweet, fleabane, osmund-fern, herb-impious, everlasting-flower, and baneberry.

Throughout August, during the ingathering of the harvest, a host of customs have been kept up from time immemorial, which have been duly noticed by Brand, while towards the close of the month we are reminded of St. Bartholomew's Day by the gaudy sunflower, which has been nicknamed St. Bartholomew's star, the term "star" having been often used "as an emblematical representation of brilliant virtues or any sign of admiration." It is, too, suggested by Archdeacon Hare that the filbert may owe its name to St. Philbert, whose festival was on the 22nd August.

The passion-flower has been termed Holy Rood flower, and it is the ecclesiastical emblem of Holy Cross Day, for, according to the familiar couplet:--

" The passion-flower long has blow'd
To betoken us signs of the Holy Rood."

Then there is the Michaelmas Day, which:--

> *"Among dead weeds,*
> *Bloom for St. Michael's valorous deeds,"*

and the golden star lily, termed St. Jerome's lily. On St. Luke's Day, certain flowers, as we have already noticed, have been in request for love divinations; and on the Continent the chestnut is eaten on the festival of St. Simon, in Piedmont on All Souls' Day, and in France on St. Martin's, when old women assemble beneath the windows and sing a long ballad. Hallowe'en has its use among divinations, at which time various plants are in request, and among the observance of All Souls' Day was blessing the beans. It would appear, too, that in days gone by, on the eve of All Saints' Day, heath was specially burnt by way of a bonfire:--

> *"On All Saints' Day bare is the place where the heath is burnt;*
> *The plough is in the furrow, the ox at work."*

From the shape of its flower, the trumpet-flowered wood-sorrel has been called St. Cecilia's flower, whose festival is kept on November 22. The Nigella damascena, popularly known as love-in-a-mist, was designated St. Catherine's flower, "from its persistent styles," writes Dr. Prior,[5] "resembling the spokes of her wheel." There was also the Catherine-pear, to which Gay alludes in his "Pastorals," where Sparabella, on comparing herself with her rival, says:--

> *"Her wan complexion's like the withered leek,*
> *While Catherine-pears adorn my ruddy cheek."*

Herb-Barbara, or St. Barbara's cress (Barbarea vulgaris), was so called from growing and being eaten about the time of her festival (December 4).

Coming to Christmas, some of the principal evergreens used in this country for decorative purposes are the ivy, laurel, bay, arbor vitae, rosemary, and holly; mistletoe, on account of its connection with Druidic rites, having been excluded from churches. Speaking of the holly, Mr. Conway remarks that, "it was to the ancient races of the north a sign of the life which preserved nature through the desolation of winter, and was gathered into pagan temples to comfort the sylvan spirits during the general death." He further adds that "it is a singular fact that it is used by the wildest Indians of the Pacific coast in their ceremonies of purification. The ashen-faggot was in request for the Christmas fire, the ceremonies relating to which are well known."

Footnotes:

1. By D. Moore and A.G. Moore, 1866.
2. See "Journal of the Arch. Assoc.," 1832, vii. 206.
3. See "British Popular Customs."
4. "Plant Lore Legends and Lyrics," p. 504.
5. "Popular Names of British Plants," 1879, p. 204.

CHAPTER XVIII

CHILDREN'S RHYMES AND GAMES

Children are more or less observers of nature, and frequently far more so than their elders. This, perhaps, is in a great measure to be accounted for from the fact that childhood is naturally inquisitive, and fond of having explained whatever seems in any way mysterious. Such especially is the case in the works of nature, and in a country ramble with children their little voices are generally busy inquiring why this bird does this, or that plant grows in such a way--a variety of questions, indeed, which unmistakably prove that the young mind instinctively seeks after knowledge. Hence, we find that the works of nature enter largely into children's pastimes; a few specimens of their rhymes and games associated with plants we quote below.

In Lincolnshire, the butter-bur (Petasites vulgaris) is nicknamed bog-horns, because the children use the hollow stalks as horns or trumpets, and the young leaves and shoots of the common hawthorn (Cratoegus oxyacantha), from being commonly eaten by children in spring, are known as "bread and cheese;" while the ladies-smock (Cardamine pratensis) is termed "bread and milk," from the custom, it has been suggested, of country people having bread and milk for breakfast about the season when the flower first comes in. In the North of England this plant is known as cuckoo-spit, because almost every flower stem has deposited upon it a frothy patch not unlike human saliva, in which is enveloped a pale green insect. Few north-country children will gather these flowers, believing that it is unlucky to do so, adding that the cuckoo has spit upon it when flying over. [1]

The fruits of the mallow are popularly termed by children cheeses, in allusion to which Clare writes:--

"The sitting down when school was o'er,
Upon the threshold of the door,
Picking from mallows, sport to please,
The crumpled seed we call a cheese."

A Buckinghamshire name with children for the deadly nightshade (Atropa belladonna) is the naughty-man's cherry, an illustration of which we may quote from Curtis's "Flora Londinensis":--"On Keep Hill, near High Wycombe, where we observed it, there chanced to be a little boy. I asked him if he knew the plant. He answered 'Yes; it was naughty-man's cherries.'" In the North of England the broad-dock (Rumex obtusifolius), when in seed, is known by children as curly-cows, who milk it by drawing the stalks through their fingers. Again, in the same locality, children speaking of the dead-man's thumb, one of the popular names of the Orchis mascula, tell one another with mysterious awe that the root was once the thumb of some unburied murderer. In one of the "Roxburghe Ballads" the phrase is referred to:--

> "Then round the meadows did she walke,
> Catching each flower by the stalke,
> Suche as within the meadows grew,
> As dead-man's thumbs and harebell blue."

It is to this plant that Shakespeare doubtless alludes in "Hamlet" (Act iv. sc. 7), where:--

> "Long purples
> That liberal shepherds give a grosser name,
> But our cold maids do dead-men's fingers call them."

In the south of Scotland, the name "doudle," says Jamieson, is applied to the root of the common reed-grass (Phragmites communis), which is found, partially decayed, in morasses, and of "which the children in the south of Scotland make a sort of musical instrument, similar to the oaten pipes of the ancients." In Yorkshire, the water-scrophularia (Scrophularia aquatica), is in children's language known as "fiddle-wood," so called because the stems are by children stripped of their leaves, and scraped across each other fiddler-fashion, when they produce a squeaking sound. This juvenile music is the source of infinite amusement among children, and is carried on by them with much enthusiasm in their games. Likewise, the spear-thistle (Carduus lanceolatus) is designated Marian in Scotland, while children blow the pappus from the receptacle, saying:--

> "Marian, Marian, what's the time of day,
> One o'clock, two o'clock--it's time we were away."

In Cheshire, when children first see the heads of the ribwort plantain (Plantago lanceolata) in spring, they repeat the following rhyme:--

> "Chimney sweeper all in black,
> Go to the brook and wash your back,
> Wash it clean, or wash it none;
> Chimney sweeper, have you done?":--

Being in all probability a mode of divination for insuring good luck. Another name for the same plant is "cocks," from children fighting the flower-stems one against another.

The common hazel-nut (Corylus avellana) is frequently nicknamed the "cob-nut," and was so called from being used in an old game played by children. An old name for the devil's-bit (Scabiosa succisa), in the northern counties, and in Scotland, is "curl-doddy," from the resemblance of the head of flowers to the curly pate of a boy, this nickname being often used by children who thus address the plant:--

"Curly-doddy, do my biddin',
Soop my house, and shoal my widden'."

In Ireland, children twist the stalk, and as it slowly untwists in the hand, thus address it:--

"Curl-doddy on the midden,
Turn round an' take my biddin'."

In Cumberland, the Primula farinosa, commonly known as bird's-eye, is called by children "bird-een."

"The lockety-gowan and bonny bird-een
Are the fairest flowers that ever were seen."

And in many places the Leontodon taraxacum is designated "blow-ball," because children blow the ripe fruit from the receptacle to tell the time of day and for various purposes of divination. Thus in the "Sad Shepherd," page 8, it is said:--

"Her treading would not bend a blade of grass,
Or shake the downy blow-ball from his stalk."

In Scotland, one of the popular names of the Angelica sylvestris is "aik-skeiters," or "hear-skeiters," because children shoot oats through the hollow stems, as peas are shot through a pea-shooter. Then there is the goose-grass (Galium aparine), variously called goose-bill, beggar's-lice, scratch-weed, and which has been designated blind-tongue, because "children with the leaves practise phlebotomy upon the tongue of those playmates who are simple enough to endure it," a custom once very general in Scotland. [2]

The catkins of the willow are in some counties known as "goslings," or "goslins,"--children, says Halliwell, [3] sometimes playing with them by putting them in the fire and singeing them brown, repeating verses at the same time. One of the names of the heath-pea (Lathyrus macrorrhizus) is liquory-knots, and school-boys in Berwickshire so call them, for when dried their taste is not unlike that of the real liquorice. [4] Again, a children's name of common henbane (Hyoscyamus niger) is "loaves of bread," an allusion to which is made by Clare in his "Shepherd's Calendar":--

> *"Hunting from the stack-yard sod*
> *The stinking henbane's belted pod,*
> *By youth's warm fancies sweetly led*
> *To christen them his loaves of bread."*

A Worcestershire name for a horse-chestnut is the "oblionker tree." According to a correspondent of Notes and Queries (5th Ser. x. 177), in the autumn, when the chestnuts are falling from their trunks, boys thread them on string and play a "cob-nut" game with them. When the striker is taking aim, and preparing for a shot at his adversary's nut, he says:--

> *"Oblionker!*
> *My first conker (conquer)."*

The word oblionker apparently being a meaningless invention to rhyme with the word conquer, which has by degrees become applied to the fruit itself.

The wall peniterry (Parietaria officinalis) is known in Ireland as "peniterry," and is thus described in "Father Connell, by the O'Hara Family" (chap, xii.):--

> *"A weed called, locally at least, peniterry, to which the suddenly terrified [schoolboy] idler might run in his need, grasping it hard and threateningly, and repeating the following 'words of power':--*

> *'Peniterry, peniterry, that grows by the wall,*
> *Save me from a whipping, or I'll pull you roots and all.'"*

Johnston, who has noticed so many odd superstitions, tells us that the tuberous ground-nut (Bunium flexuosum), which has various nicknames, such as "lousy," "loozie," or "lucie arnut," is dug up by children who eat the roots, "but they are hindered from indulging to excess by a cherished belief that the luxury tends to generate vermin in the head." [5]

An old rhyme often in years past used by country children when the daffodils made their annual appearance in early spring, was as follows:--

"Daff-a-down-dill
Has now come to town,
In a yellow petticoat
And a green gown."

A name for the shepherd's purse is "mother's-heart," and in the eastern Border district, says Johnston, children have a sort of game with the seed-pouch. They hold it out to their companions, inviting them to "take a haud o' that." It immediately cracks, and then follows a triumphant shout, "You've broken your mother's heart." In Northamptonshire, children pick the leaves of the herb called pick-folly, one by one, repeating each time the words, "Rich man, poor man, beggar-man, thief," &c., fancying that the one which comes to be named at the last plucking will prove the conditions of their future partners. Variations of this custom exist elsewhere, and a correspondent of "Science Gossip" (1876, xi. 94). writes:--"I remember when at school at Birmingham that my playmates manifested a very great repugnance to this plant. Very few of them would touch it, and it was known to us by the two bad names, "haughty-man's plaything," and "pick your mother's heart out." In Hanover, as well as in the Swiss canton of St. Gall, the same plant is offered to uninitiated persons with a request to pluck one of the pods. Should he do so the others exclaim, "You have stolen a purse of gold from your father and mother."" "It is interesting to find," writes Mr. Britten in the "Folklore Record" (i. 159), "that a common tropical weed, Ageratum conyzoides, is employed by children in Venezuela in a very similar manner."

The compilers of the "Dictionary of Plant Names" consider that the double (garden) form of Saxifraga granulata, designated "pretty maids," may be referred to in the old nursery rhyme:--

"Mary, Mary, quite contrary,
How does your garden grow?
Cockle-shells, and silver bells,
And pretty maids all in a row."

The old-man's-beard (Clematis vitalba) is in many places popularly known as smoke-wood, because "our village-boys smoke pieces of the wood as they do of rattan cane; hence, it is sometimes called smoke-wood, and smoking-cane." [6]

The children of Galloway play at hide-and-seek with a little black-topped flower which is known by them as the Davie-drap, meantime repeating the following rhyme:--

"Within the bounds of this I hap
My black and bonnie Davie-drap:
Wha is he, the cunning ane,
To me my Davie-drap will fin'?"

This plant, it has been suggested, [7] being the cuckoo grass (Luzula campestris), which so often figures in children's games and rhymes.

Once more, there are numerous games played by children in which certain flowers are introduced, as in the following, known as "the three flowers," played in Scotland, and thus described in Chambers's "Popular Rhymes," p. 127:--"A group of lads and lasses being assembled round the fire, two leave the party and consult together as to the names of three others, young men or girls, whom they designate as the red rose, the pink, and the gillyflower. The two young men then return, and having selected a member of the fairer group, they say to her:--

'My mistress sent me unto thine,
Wi' three young flowers baith fair and fine:--
The pink, the rose, and the gillyflower,
  And as they here do stand,
Whilk will ye sink, whilk will ye swim,
  And whilk bring hame to land?'

The maiden must choose one of the flowers named, on which she passes some approving epithet, adding, at the same time, a disapproving rejection of the other two, as in the following terms: 'I will sink the pink, swim the rose, and bring hame the gillyflower to land.' The young men then disclose the names of the parties upon whom they had fixed those appellations respectively, when it may chance she has slighted the person to whom she is most attached, and contrariwise." Games of this kind are very varied, and still afford many an evening's amusement among the young people of our country villages during the winter evenings.

Footnotes:

1. Journal of Horticulture, 1876, p. 355.
2. Johnston's "Botany of Eastern Borders."
3. "Dictionary of Archaic and Provincial Words."
4. Johnston's "Botany of Eastern Borders," p. 57.
5. "Botany of Eastern Borders," p. 85.
6. "English Botany," ed. I, iii. p. 3.
7. "Dictionary of Plant Names" (Britten and Holland), p. 145.

CHAPTER XIX

SACRED PLANTS

Closely allied with plant-worship is the sacred and super-stitious reverence which, from time immemorial, has been paid by various communities to certain trees and plants.

In many cases this sanctity originated in the olden heathen mythology, when "every flower was the emblem of a god; every tree the abode of a nymph." From their association, too, with certain events, plants frequently acquired a sacred character, and occasionally their specific virtues enhanced their veneration. In short, the large number of sacred plants found in different countries must be attributed to a variety of causes, illustrations of which are given in the present chapter.

Thus going back to mythological times, it may be noticed that trees into which persons were metamorphosed became sacred. The laurel was sacred to Apollo in memory of Daphne, into which tree she was changed when escaping from his advances:--

"Because thou canst not be
My mistress, I espouse thee for my tree;
Be thou the prize of honour and renown,
The deathless poet and the poet's crown;
Thou shalt the Roman festivals adorn,
And, after poets, be by victors won."

But it is unnecessary to give further instances of such familiar stories, of which early history is full. At the same time it is noteworthy that many of these plants which acquired a sanctity from heathen mythology still retain their sacred character--a fact which has invested them with various superstitions, in addition to having caused them to be selected for ceremonial usage and homage in modern times. Thus the pine, with its mythical origin and heathen associations, is an important tree on the Continent, being surrounded with a host of legends, most of which, in one shape or another, are relics of early forms of belief. The sacred character of the oak still survives in modern folklore, and a host of flowers which grace our fields and hedges have sacred associations from their connection with the heathen gods of old. Thus the anemone, poppy, and violet were dedicated to Venus; and to Diana "all flowers growing in untrodden dells and shady nooks, uncontaminated by the tread of man, more especially belonged." The narcissus and maidenhair were sacred to Proserpina, and the willow to Ceres. The pink is Jove's flower, and of the flowers assigned to Juno may be mentioned the lily, crocus, and asphodel.

Passing on to other countries, we find among the plants most conspicuous for their sacred character the well-known lotus of the East (Nelunibium speciosum), around which so many traditions and mythological legends have clustered. According to a Hindu legend, from its blossom Brahma came forth:--

"*A form Cerulean fluttered o'er the deep;*
Brightest of beings, greatest of the great,
  Who, not as mortals steep
  Their eyes in dewy sleep,
But heavenly pensive on the lotus lay,
That blossom'd at his touch, and shed a golden ray.
  Hail, primal blossom! hail, empyreal gem,
Kemel, or Pedma, [1] or whate'er high name
Delight thee, say. What four-formed godhead came,
  With graceful stole and beamy diadem,
  Forth from thy verdant stem." [2]

Buddha, too, whose symbol is the lotus, is said to have first appeared floating on this mystic flower, and, indeed, it would seem that many of the Eastern deities were fond of resting on its leaves; while in China, the god Pazza is generally represented as occupying this position. Hence the lotus has long been an object of worship, and as a sacred plant holds a most distinguished place, for it is the flower of the,

"*Old Hindu mythologies, wherein*
The lotus, attribute of Ganga--embling
The world's great reproductive power--was held
In veneration."

We may mention here that the lotus, known also as the sacred bean of Egypt, and the rose-lily of the Nile, as far back as four thousand years ago was held in high sanctity by the Egyptian priests, still retaining its sacred character in China, Japan, and Asiatic Russia.

Another famous sacred plant is the soma or moon-plant of India, the Asclepias acida, a climbing plant with milky juice, which Windischmann has identified with the "tree of life which grew in paradise." Its milk juice was said to confer immortality, the plant itself never decaying; and in a hymn in the Rig Veda the soma sacrifice is thus described:--

"*We've quaffed the soma bright*
 And are immortal grown,
 We've entered into light

And all the gods have known.
What mortal can now harm,
Or foeman vex us more?
Through thee beyond alarm,
Immortal God! we soar."

Then there is the peepul or bo-tree (Ficus religiosa), which is held in high veneration by the followers of Buddha, in the vicinity of whose temples it is generally planted. One of these trees in Ceylon is said to be of very great antiquity, and according to Sir J. E. Tennant, "to it kings have even dedicated their dominions in testimony of their belief that it is a branch of the identical fig-tree under which Gotama Buddha reclined when he underwent his apotheosis."

The peepul-tree is highly venerated in Java, and by the Buddhists of Thibet is known as the bridge of safety, over which mortals pass from the shores of this world to those of the unseen one beyond. Occasionally confounded with this peepul is the banyan (Ficus indica), which is another sacred tree of the Indians. Under its shade Vishnu is said to have been born; and by the Chinese, Buddha is represented as sitting beneath its leaves to receive the homage of the god Brahma. Another sacred tree is the deodar (Cedrus deodara), a species of cedar, being the Devadara, or tree-god of the Shastras, which in so many of the ancient Hindu hymns is depicted as the symbol of power and majesty. [3] The aroka, or Saraca indica, is said to preserve chastity, and is dedicated to Kama, the Indian god of love, while with the negroes of Senegambia the baobab-tree is an object of worship. In Borneo the nipa-palm is held in veneration, and the Mexican Indians have their moriche-palm (Mauritia flexuosa). The Tamarindus Indica is in Ceylon dedicated to Siva, the god of destruction; and in Thibet, the jambu or rose-apple is believed to be the representative of the divine amarita-tree which bears ambrosia.

The pomegranate, with its mystic origin and early sacred associations, was long reverenced by the Persians and Jews, an old tradition having identified it as the forbidden fruit given by Eve to Adam. Again, as a sacred plant the basil has from time immemorial been held in high repute by the Hindus, having been sacred to Vishnu. Indeed it is worshipped as a deity itself, and is invoked as the goddess Tulasî for the protection of the human frame. It is further said that "the heart of Vishnu, the husband of the Tulasî, is agitated and tormented whenever the least sprig is broken of a plant of Tulasî, his wife."

Among further flowers holding a sacred character may be mentioned the henna, the Egyptian privet (Lawsonia alba), the flower of paradise, which was pronounced by Mahomet as "chief of the flowers of this world and the next," the wormwood having been dedicated to the goddess Iris. By the aborigines of the Canary Islands, the dragon-tree

(Dracoena draco) of Orotava was an object of sacred reverence; [4] and in Burmah at the present day the eugenia is held sacred. [5]

It has been remarked that the life of Christ may be said to fling its shadow over the whole vegetable world. [6] "From this time the trees and the flowers which had been associated with heathen rites and deities, began to be connected with holier names, and not unfrequently with the events of the crucifixion itself."

Thus, upon the Virgin Mary a wealth of flowers was lavished, all white ones, having been "considered typical of her purity and holiness, and consecrated to her festivals." [7] Indeed, not only, "were the finer flowers wrested from the classic Juno and Diana, and from the Freyja and Bertha of northern lands given to her, but lovely buds of every hue were laid upon her shrines." [8] One species, for instance, of the maiden-hair fern, known also as "Our Lady's hair," is designated in Iceland "Freyja's hair," and the rose, often styled "Frau rose," or "Mother rose," the favourite flower of Hulda, was transferred to the Virgin. On the other hand, many plants bearing the name of Our Lady, were, writes Mr. Folkard, in Puritan times, "replaced by the name of Venus, thus recurring to the ancient nomenclature; 'Our Lady's comb' becoming 'Venus's comb.'" But the two flowers which were specially connected with the Virgin were the lily and the rose. Accordingly, in Italian art, a vase of lilies stands by the Virgin's side, with three flowers crowning three green stems. The flower is generally the large white lily of our gardens, "the pure white petals signifying her spotless body, and the golden anthers within typifying her soul sparkling with divine light." [9]

The rose, both red and white, appears at an early period as an emblem of the Virgin, "and was specially so recognised by St. Dominic when he instituted the devotion of the rosary, with direct reference to her." [10] Among other flowers connected with the Virgin Mary may be mentioned the flowering-rod, according to which Joseph was chosen for her husband, because his rod budded into flower, and a dove settled upon the top of it. In Tuscany a similar legend is attached to the oleander, and elsewhere the white campanula has been known as the "little staff of St. Joseph," while a German name for the white double daffodill is "Joseph's staff."

Then there is "Our Lady's bed-straw," which filled the manger on which the infant Jesus was laid; while of the plant said to have formed the Virgin's bed may be mentioned the thyme, woodroof, and groundsel. The white-spotted green leaves of "Our Lady's thistle" were caused by some drops of her milk falling upon them, and in Cheshire we find the same idea connected with the pulmonaria or "lady's milk sile," the word "sile" being a provincialism for "soil," or "stain." A German tradition makes the common fern (Polypodium vulgare) to have sprung from the Virgin's milk.

Numerous flowers have been identified with her dress, such as the marigold, termed by Shakespeare "Mary-bud," which she wore in her bosom. The cuckoo-flower of our meadows is "Our Lady's smock," which Shakespeare refers to in those charming lines in "Love's Labour's Lost," where:--

"When daisies pied and violets blue,
And lady's smocks all silver white,
And cuckoo-buds of yellow hue
Do paint the meadows with delight,
The cuckoo then on every tree
Mocks married men, for thus sings he,
Cuckoo."

And one of the finest of our orchids is "Our Lady's slipper." The ribbon grass is "Our Lady's garters," and the dodder supplies her "laces." In the same way many flowers have been associated with the Virgin herself. Thus, there is "Our Lady's tresses," and a popular name for the maiden-hair fern and quaking-grass is "Virgin's hair." The lilies of the valley are her tears, and a German nickname for the lungwort is "Our Lady's milk-wort." The Anthlyllis vulneraria is "Our Lady's fingers," and the kidney-wort has been designated "lady's navel." Certain orchids, from the peculiar form of their hand-shaped roots, have been popularly termed "Our Lady's hands," a name given in France to the dead-nettle.

Of the many other plants dedicated to the Virgin may be mentioned the snowdrop, popularly known as the "fair maid of February," opening its floweret at the time of Candlemas. According to an old monkish tradition it blooms at this time, in memory of the Virgin having taken the child Jesus to the temple, and there presented her offering. A further reason for the snowdrop's association with the Virgin originated in the custom of removing her image from the altar on the day of the Purification, and strewing over the vacant place with these emblems of purity. The bleeding nun (Cyclamen europoeum) was consecrated to the Virgin, and in France the spearmint is termed "Our Lady's mint." In Germany the costmary (Costaminta vulgaris) is "Our Lady's balsam," the white-flowered wormwood the "smock of our Lady," and in olden days the iris or fleur-de-lis was held peculiarly sacred.

The little pink is "lady's cushion," and the campanula is her looking-glass. Then there is "Our Lady's comb," with its long, fragile seed-vessels resembling the teeth of a comb, while the cowslip is "Our Lady's bunch of keys." In France, the digitalis supplies her with gloves, and in days gone by the Convallaria polygonatum was the "Lady's seal." According to some old writers, the black briony went by this name, and Hare gives this explanation:--"'Our Lady's seal' (Sigillum marioe) is among the names of the black briony, owing to the great efficacy of its roots when spread in a plaster and applied as it were to heal up a scar or bruise." Formerly a species of primula was known as "lady's candlestick," and a Wiltshire nickname for the common convolvulus is "lady's nightcap," Canterbury bells in some places supplying this need. The harebell is "lady's thimble," and the plant which affords her a mantle is the Alchemilla vulgaris, with its grey-green leaf covered with a soft silky hair. This is the Maria Stakker of Iceland, which when placed under the pillow produces sleep.

Once more, the strawberry is one of the fruits that has been dedicated to her; and a species of nut, popularly known as the molluka bean, is in many parts called the "Virgin Mary's nut." The cherry-tree, too, has long been consecrated to the Virgin from the following tradition:-- Being desirous one day of refreshing herself with some cherries which she saw hanging upon a tree, she requested Joseph to gather some for her. But he hesitated, and mockingly said, "Let the father of thy child present them to you." But these words had been no sooner uttered than the branch of the cherry-tree inclined itself of its own accord to the Virgin's hand. There are many other plants associated in one way or another with the Virgin, but the instances already given are representative of this wide subject. In connection, too, with her various festivals, we find numerous plants; and as the author of "Flower-lore" remarks, "to the Madonna were assigned the white iris, blossoming almond-tree, narcissus, and white lily, all appropriate to the Annunciation." The flowers appropriate to the "Visitation of Our Lady" were, in addition to the lily, roses red and white, while to the "Feast of Assumption" is assigned the "Virgin's bower," "worthy to be so called," writes Gerarde, "by reason of the goodly shadow which the branches make with their thick bushing and climbing, as also for the beauty of the flowers, and the pleasant scent and savour of the same."

Many plants have been associated with St. John the Baptist, from his having been the forerunner of Christ. Thus, the common plant which bears his name, St. John's wort, is marked with blood-like spots, known as the "blood of St. John," making their appearance on the day he was beheaded. The scarlet lychnis, popularly nicknamed the "great candlestick," was commonly said to be lighted up for his day. The carob tree has been designated "St. John's bread," from a tradition that it supplied him with food in the wilderness; and currants, from beginning to ripen at this time, have been nicknamed "berries of St. John." The artemisia was in Germany "St. John's girdle," and in Sicily was applied to his beard.

In connection with Christ's birth it may be noted that the early painters represent the Angel Gabriel with either a sceptre or spray of the olive tree, while in the later period of Italian art he has in his hand a branch of white lilies.[11] The star which pointed out the place of His birth has long been immortalised by the Ornithogalum umbellatum, or Star of Bethlehem, which has been thought to resemble the pictures descriptive of it; in France there is a pretty legend of the rose-coloured sainfoin. When the infant Jesus was lying in the manger the plant was found among the grass and herbs which composed his bed. But suddenly it opened its pretty blossom, that it might form a wreath around His head. On this account it has been held in high repute. Hence the practice in Italy of decking mangers at Christmas time with moss, sow-thistle, cypress, and holly. [12]

Near the city of *On* there was shown for many centuries the sacred fig-tree, under which the Holy Family rested during their "Flight into Egypt," and a Bavarian tradition makes the tree under which they found shelter a hazel. A German legend, on the other hand, informs us that as they took their flight they came into a thickly-wooded forest, when, on their approach, all the trees, with the exception of the aspen, paid reverential homage. The disrespectful arrogance of the aspen, however, did not escape the notice of the Holy Child, who thereupon pronounced a curse against it, whereupon its leaves began to tremble, and have done so ever since:--

"Once as our Saviour walked with men below,
His path of mercy through a forest lay;
And mark how all the drooping branches show
What homage best a silent tree may pay.

Only the aspen stood erect and free,
Scorning to join the voiceless worship pure,
But see! He cast one look upon the tree,
Struck to the heart she trembles evermore."

The "rose of Jericho" has long been regarded with special reverence, having first blossomed at Christ's birth, closed at His crucifixion, and opened again at the resurrection. At the flight into Egypt it is reported to have sprung up to mark the footsteps of the sacred family, and was consequently designated Mary's rose. The pine protected them from Herod's soldiers, while the juniper opened its branches and offered a welcome shelter, although it afterwards, says an old legend, furnished the wood for the cross.

But some trees were not so thoughtful, for "the brooms and the chick-peas rustled and crackled, and the flax bristled up." According to another old legend we are informed that by the fountain where the Virgin Mary washed the swaddling-clothes of her sacred infant, beautiful bushes sprang up in memory of the event. Among the many further legends connected with the Virgin may be mentioned the following connected with her death:--The story runs that she was extremely anxious to see her Son again, and that whilst weeping, an angel appeared, and said, "Hail, O Mary! I bring thee here a branch of palm, gathered in paradise; command that it be carried before thy bier in the day of thy death, for in three days thy soul shall leave thy body, and thou shalt enter into paradise, where thy Son awaits thy coming." The angel then departed, but the palm-branch shed a light from every leaf, and the apostles, although scattered in different parts of the world, were miraculously caught up and set down at the Virgin's door. The sacred palm-branch she then assigned to the care of St. John, who carried it before her bier at the time of her burial. [13]

The trees and flowers associated with the crucifixion are widely represented, and have given rise to many a pretty legend. Several plants are said to owe their dark-stained blossoms to the blood-drops which trickled from the cross; amongst these being the wood-sorrel, the spotted persicaria, the arum, the purple orchis, which is known in Cheshire as "Gethsemane," and the red anemone, which has been termed the "blood-drops of Christ." A Flemish legend, too, accounts in the same way for the crimson-spotted leaves of the rood-selken. The plant which has gained the unenviable notoriety of supplying the crown of thorns has been variously stated as the boxthorn, the bramble, the buckthorns, [14] and barberry, while Mr. Conway quotes an old tradition, which tells how the drops of blood that fell from the crown of thorns, composed of the rose-briar, fell to the ground and blossomed to roses. [15] Some again maintain that the wild hyssop was employed, and one plant which was specially signalled out in olden times is the auberpine or white-thorn. In Germany holly is Christ-thorn, and according to an Eastern tradition it was the prickly rush, but as Mr. King [16] remarks, "the belief of the East has been tolerably constant to what was possibly the real plant employed, the nabk (Zizyphus spina-Christi), a species of buckthorn." The negroes of the West Indies say that, "a branch of the cashew tree was used, and that in consequence one of the bright golden petals of the flower became black and blood-stained."

Then again, according to a Swedish legend, the dwarf birch tree afforded the rod with which Christ was scourged, which accounts for its stunted appearance; while another legend tells us it was the willow with its drooping branches. Rubens, together with the earlier Italian painters, depict the reed-mace [17] or bulrush (Typha latifolia) as the rod given to Him to carry; a plant still put by Catholics into the hands of statues of Christ. But in Poland, where the plant is difficult to procure, "the flower-stalk of the leek is substituted."

The mournful tree which formed the wood of the cross has always been a disputed question, and given rise to a host of curious legends.

According to Sir John Maundeville, it was composed of cedar, cypress, palm, and olive, while some have instituted in the place of the two latter the pine and the box; the notion being that those four woods represented the four quarters of the globe. Foremost amongst the other trees to which this distinction has been assigned, are the aspen, poplar, oak, elder, and mistletoe. Hence is explained the gloomy shivering of the aspen leaf, the trembling of the poplar, and the popular antipathy to utilising elder twigs for fagots. But it is probable that the respect paid to the elder "has its roots in the old heathenism of the north," and to this day, in Denmark, it is said to be protected by "a being called the elder-mother," so that it is not safe to damage it in any way. [18] The mistletoe, which exists now as a mere parasite, was before the crucifixion a fine forest tree; its present condition being a lasting monument of the disgrace it incurred through its ignominious use. [19] A further legend informs us that when the Jews were in search of wood for the cross, every tree, with the exception of the oak, split itself to avoid being desecrated. On this account, Grecian woodcutters avoid the oak, regarding it as an accursed tree.

The bright blue blossoms of the speedwell, which enliven our wayside hedges in spring-time, are said to display in their markings a representation of the kerchief of St Veronica, imprinted with the features of Christ. [20] According to an old tradition, when our Lord was on His way to Calvary, bearing His Cross, He happened to pass by the door of Veronica, who, beholding the drops of agony on His brow, wiped His face with a kerchief or napkin. The sacred features, however, remained impressed upon the linen, and from the fancied resemblance of the blossom of the speedwell to this hallowed relic, the plant was named Veronica.

A plant closely connected by tradition with the crucifixion is the passion-flower. As soon as the early Spanish settlers in South America first glanced on it, they fancied they had discovered not only a marvellous symbol of Christ's passion, but received an assurance of the ultimate triumph of Christianity. Jacomo Bosio, who obtained his knowledge of it from certain Mexican Jesuits, speaks of it as "the flower of the five wounds," and has given a very minute description of it, showing how exactly every part is a picture of the mysteries of the Passion. "It would seem," he adds, "as if the Creator of the world had chosen it to represent the principal emblems of His Son's Passion; so that in due season it might assist, when its marvels should be explained to them, in the condition of the heathen people, in whose country it grew." In Brittany, vervain is popularly termed the "herb of the cross," and when gathered with a certain formula is efficacious in curing wounds. [21]

In legendary lore, much uncertainty exists as to the tree on which Judas hanged himself. According to Sir John Maundeville, there it stood in the vicinity of Mount Sion, "the tree of eldre, that Judas henge himself upon, for despeyr," a legend which has been popularly received. Shakespeare, in his "Love's Labour's Lost," says "Judas was hanged on an elder," and the story is further alluded to in Piers Plowman's vision:--

"Judas, he japed
With Jewen silver,
And sithen on an eller,
Hanged himselve."

Gerarde makes it the wild carob, a tree which, as already stated, was formerly known as "St. John's bread," from a popular belief that the Baptist fed upon it while in the wilderness. A Sicilian tradition identifies the tree as a tamarisk, and a Russian proverb, in allusion to the aspen, tells us "there is an accursed tree which trembles without even a breath of wind." The fig, also, has been mentioned as the ill-fated tree, and some traditions have gone so far as to say that it was the very same one as was cursed by our Lord.

As might be expected, numerous plants have become interwoven with the lives of the saints, a subject on which many works have been written. Hence it is unnecessary to do more than briefly note some of the more important items of sacred lore which have been embodied in many of the early Christian legends. The yellow rattle has been assigned to St. Peter, and the Primula veris, from its resemblance to a bunch of keys, is St. Peter's wort. Many flowers, too, from the time of their blossoming, have been dedicated to certain saints, as the square St. John's wort (Hypericum quadrangulare), which is also known as St. Peter's wort; while in Germany wall-barley is termed Peter's corn. Of the many legends connected with the cherry we are reminded that on one occasion Christ gave one to St. Peter, at the same time reminding him not to despise little things.

St. James is associated with several plants--the St. James' wort (Senecio Jacoboea), either from its having been much used for the diseases of horses, of which the saint was the patron, or owing to its blossoming on his festival. The same name was applied to the shepherd's purse and the rag-weed. Incidentally, too, in our chapter on the calendar we have alluded to many flowers associated with the saints, and spoken of the customs observed in their honour.

Similarly the later saints had particular flowers dedicated to their memory; and, indeed, a complete catalogue of flowers has been compiled--one for each day in the year--the flower in many cases having been selected because it flowered on the festival of that saint. Thus the common bean was dedicated to St. Ignatius, and the blue hyacinth to St. Dorothy, while to St. Hilary the barren strawberry has been assigned. St. Anne is associated with the camomile, and St. Margaret with the

Virginian dragon's head. Then there is St. Anthony's turnips and St. Barbara's cress--the "Saints' Floral Directory," in "Hone's Every-Day Book," giving a fuller and more extensive list. But the illustrations we have already given are sufficient to show how fully the names of the saints have been perpetuated by so many of our well-known plants not only being dedicated to, but named after them, a fact which is perhaps more abundantly the case on the Continent. Then, as it has been remarked, flowers have virtually become the timepieces of our religious calendar, reminding us of the various festivals, as in succession they return, in addition to immortalising the history and events which such festivals commemorate. In many cases, too, it should be remembered, the choice of flowers for dedication to certain saints originated either in their medical virtues or in some old tradition which was supposed to have specially singled them out for this honour.

Footnotes:

1. Sanscrit for lotus.
2. Hindu poem, translated by Sir William Jones.
3. "Flower-lore," p. 118.
4. Folkard's "Plant Legends," p. 245.
5. "Flower-lore," p. 120.
6. Quarterly Review, cxiv. 231.
7. "Flower-lore," p. 2.
8. Ibid.
9. Quarterly Review, cxiv. 235.
10. Ibid., p. 239.
11. "Flower-lore."
12. Folkard's "Plant Legends," p. 44.
13. Folkard's "Plant Legends," p. 395.
14. "Flower-lore," p. 13.
15. Fraser's Magazine, 1870, p. 714.
16. "Flower-lore," p. 14.
17. "Flower-lore," p. 14.
18. Quarterly Review, cxiv. 233; "Flower-lore," p. 15.
19. See Baring-Gould's "Myths of the Middle Ages."
20. "Flower-lore," p. 12. 21. See chapter on Folk-Medicine.

CHAPTER XX

PLANT SUPERSTITIONS

The superstitious notions which, under one form or another, have clustered round the vegetable kingdom, hold a prominent place in the field of folklore. To give a full and detailed account of these survivals of bygone beliefs, would occupy a volume of no mean size, so thickly scattered are they among the traditions and legendary lore of almost every country. Only too frequently, also, we find the same superstition assuming a very different appearance as it travels from one country to another, until at last it is almost completely divested of its original dress. Repeated changes of this kind, whilst not escaping the notice of the student of comparative folklore, are apt to mislead the casual observer who, it may be, assigns to them a particular home in his own country, whereas probably they have travelled, before arriving at their modern destination, thousands of miles in the course of years.

There is said to be a certain mysterious connection between certain plants and animals. Thus, swine when affected with the spleen are supposed to resort to the spleen-wort, and according to Coles, in his "Art of Simpling," the ass does likewise, for he tells us that, "if the asse be oppressed with melancholy, he eates of the herbe asplemon or mill-waste, and eases himself of the swelling of the spleen." One of the popular names of the common sow-thistle (Sonchus oleraceus) is hare's-palace, from the shelter it is supposed to afford the hare. According to the "Grete Herbale," "if the hare come under it, he is sure that no beast can touch hym." Topsell also, in his "Natural History," alludes to this superstition:--"When hares are overcome with heat, they eat of an herb called Latuca leporina, that is, hare's-lettuce, hare's-house, hare's-palace; and there is no disease in this beast the cure whereof she does not seek for in this herb."

The hound's-tongue (cynoglossum) has been reputed to have the magical property of preventing dogs barking at a person, if laid beneath the feet; and Gerarde says that wild goats or deer, "when they be wounded with arrows, do shake them out by eating of this plant, and heal their wounds." Bacon in his "Natural History" alludes to another curious idea connected with goats, and says, "There are some tears of trees, which are combed from the beards of goats; for when the goats bite and crop them, especially in the morning, the dew being on, the tear cometh forth, and hangeth upon their beards; of this sort is some kind of laudanum." The columbine was once known as Herba leonis, from a belief that it was the lion's favourite plant, and it is said that when bears were half-starved by hybernating--having remained for days without food--they were suddenly restored by eating the arum. There is a curious tradition in Piedmont, that if a hare be sprinkled with the juice of henbane, all the hares in the neighbourhood will run away as if scared by some invisible power.

Gerarde also alludes to an old belief that cats, "Are much delighted with catmint, for the smell of it is so pleasant unto them, that they rub themselves upon it, and swallow or tumble in it, and also feed on the branches very greedily." And according to an old proverb they have a liking for the plant maram:--

"If you set it, the cats will eat it;
If you sow it, the cats won't know it."

Equally fond, too, are cats of valerian, being said to dig up the roots and gnaw them to pieces, an allusion to which occurs in Topsell's "Four-footed Beasts" (1658-81):--"The root of the herb valerian (commonly called Phu) is very like to the eye of a cat, and wheresoever it groweth, if cats come thereunto they instantly dig it up for the love thereof, as I myself have seen in mine own garden, for it smelleth moreover like a cat."

Then there is the moonwort, famous for drawing the nails out of horses' shoes, and hence known by the rustic name of "unshoe the horse;" while the mouse-ear was credited with preventing the horses being hurt when shod.

We have already alluded to the superstitions relating to birds and plants, but may mention another relating to the celandine. One of the well-known names of this plant is swallow-wort, so termed, says Gerarde, not, "because it first springeth at the coming in of the swallows, or dieth when they go away, for it may be found all the year, but because some hold opinion that with this herbe the darns restore eyesight to their young ones, when their eye be put out." Coles strengthens the evidence in favour of this odd notion by adding: "It is known to such as have skill of nature, what wonderful care she hath of the smallest creatures, giving to them a knowledge of medicine to help themselves, if haply diseases annoy them. The swallow cureth her dim eyes with celandine; the wesell knoweth well the virtue of herb-grace; the dove the verven; the dogge dischargeth his mawe with a kind of grasse," &c.

In Italy cumin is given to pigeons for the purpose of taming them, and a curious superstition is that of the "divining-rod," with "its versatile sensibility to water, ore, treasure and thieves," and one whose history is apparently as remote as it is widespread. Francis Lenormant, in his "Chaldean Magic," mentions the divining-rods used by the Magi, wherewith they foretold the future by throwing little sticks of tamarisk-wood, and adds that divination by wands was known and practised in Babylon, "and that this was even the most ancient mode of divination used in the time of the Accadians." Among the Hindus, even in the Vedic period, magic wands were in use, and the practice still survives in China, where the peach-tree is in demand. Tracing its antecedent history in this country, it appears that the Druids were in the habit of cutting their divining-rods from the apple-tree; and various notices of this once popular fallacy occur from time to time, in the literature of bygone years.

The hazel was formerly famous for its powers of discernment, and it is still held in repute by the Italians. Occasionally, too, as already noticed, the divining-rod was employed for the purpose of detecting the locality of water, as is still the case in Wiltshire. An interesting case was quoted some years ago in the Quarterly Review (xxii. 273). A certain Lady N----is here stated to have convinced Dr. Hutton of her possession of this remarkable gift, and by means of it to have indicated to him the existence of a spring of water in one of his fields adjoining the Woolwich College, which, in consequence of the discovery, he was enabled to sell to the college at a higher price. This power Lady N----repeatedly exhibited before credible witnesses, and the Quarterly Review of that day considered the fact indisputable. The divining-rod has long been in repute among Cornish miners, and Pryce, in his "Mineralogia Cornubiensis," says that many mines have been discovered by this means; but, after giving a minute account of cutting, tying, and using it, he rejects it, because, "Cornwall is so plentifully stored with tin and copper lodes, that some accident every week discovers to us a fresh vein."

Billingsley, in his "Agricultural Survey of the County of Cornwall," published in the year 1797, speaks of the belief of the Mendip miners in the efficacy of the mystic rod:--"The general method of discovering the situation and direction of those seams of ore (which lie at various depths, from five to twenty fathoms, in a chasm between two inches of solid rock) is by the help of the divining-rod, vulgarly called josing; and a variety of strong testimonies are adduced in supporting this doctrine. So confident are the common miners of the efficacy, that they scarcely ever sink a shaft but by its direction; and those who are dexterous in the use of it, will mark on the surface the course and breadth of the vein; and after that, with the assistance of the rod, will follow the same course twenty times following blindfolded." Anecdotes of the kind are very numerous, for there are few subjects in folklore concerning which more has been written than on the divining-rod, one of the most exhaustive being that of Mr. Baring-Gould in his "Curious Myths of the Middle Ages." The literature, too, of the past is rich in allusions to this piece of superstition, and Swift in his "Virtues of Sid Hamet the Magician's Rod" (1710) thus refers to it:--

"They tell us something strange and odd
About a certain magic rod
That, bending down its top, divines
Whene'er the soil has golden mines;
Where there are none, it stands erect,
Scorning to show the least respect.
As ready was the wand of Sid
To bend where golden mines were hid.
In Scottish hills found precious ore,
Where none e'er looked for it before;
And by a gentle bow divined,
How well a Cully's purse was lined;
To a forlorn and broken rake,
Stood without motion like a stake."

De Quincey has several amusing allusions to this fallacy, affirming that he had actually seen on more than one occasion the process applied with success, and declared that, in spite of all science or scepticism might say, most of the tea-kettles in the Vale of Wrington, North Somersetshire, are filled by rhabdomancy. But it must be admitted that the phenomena of the divining-rod and table-turning are of precisely the same character, both being referable to an involuntary muscular action resulting from a fixedness of idea. Moreover, it should be remembered that experiments with the divining-rod are generally made in a district known to be metalliferous, and therefore the chances are greatly in favour of its bending over or near a mineral lode. On the other hand, it is surprising how many people of culture have, at different times, in this and other countries, displayed a lamentable weakness in partially accepting this piece of superstition. Of the many anecdotes related respecting it, we may quote an amusing one in connection with the celebrated botanist, Linnaeus:--"When he was on one of his voyages, hearing his secretary highly extol the virtues of his divining-wand, he was willing to convince him of its insufficiency, and for that purpose concealed a purse of one hundred ducats under a ranunculus, which grew up by itself in a meadow, and bid the secretary find it if he could. The wand discovered nothing, and Linnaeus' mark was soon trampled down by the company who were present, so that when he went to finish the experiment by fetching the gold himself, he was utterly at a loss where to find it. The man with the wand assisted him, and informed him that it could not lie in the way they were going, but quite the contrary, so pursued the direction of the wand, and actually dug out the gold. Linnaeus thereupon added that such another experiment would be sufficient to make a proselyte of him." [1]

In 1659, the Jesuit, Gaspard Schott, tells us that this magic rod was at this period used in every town in Germany, and that he had frequently had opportunities of seeing it used in the discovery of hidden treasure. He further adds:--"I searched with the greatest care into the question whether the hazel rod had any sympathy with gold and silver, and whether any natural property set it in motion. In like manner, I tried whether a ring of metal, held suspended by a thread in the midst of a tumbler, and which strikes the hours, is moved by any similar force." But many of the mysterious effects of these so-called divining-rods were no doubt due to clever imposture. In the year 1790, Plunet, a native of Dauphiné, claimed a power over the divining-rod which attracted considerable attention in Italy. But when carefully tested by scientific men in Padua, his attempts to discover buried metals completely failed; and at Florence he was detected trying to find out by night what he had secreted to test his powers on the morrow. The astrologer Lilly made sundry experiments with the divining-rod, but was not always successful; and the Jesuit, Kircher, tried the powers of certain rods which were said to have sympathetic influences for particular metals, but they never turned on the approach of these. Once more, in the "Shepherd's Calendar," we find a receipt to make the "Mosaic wand to find hidden treasure" without the intervention of a human operator:--"Cut a hazel wand forked at the upper end like a Y. Peel off the rind, and dry it in a moderate heat, then steep it in the juice of wake-robin or nightshade, and cut the single lower end sharp; and where you suppose any rich mine or hidden treasure is near, place a piece of the same metal you conceive is hid, or in the earth, to the top of one of the forks by a hair, and do the like to the other end; pitch the sharp single end lightly to the ground at the going down of the sun, the moon being in the increase, and in the morning at sunrise, by a natural sympathy, you will find the metal inclining, as it were pointing, to the places where the other is hid."

According to a Tuscany belief, the almond will discover treasures; and the golden rod has long had the reputation in England of pointing to hidden springs of water, as well as to treasures of gold and silver. Similarly, the spring-wort and primrose--the key-flower--revealed the hidden recesses in mountains where treasures were concealed, and the mystic fern-seed, termed "wish-seed," was supposed in the Tyrol to make known hidden gold; and, according to a Lithuanian form of this superstition, one who secures treasures by this means will be pursued by adders, the guardians of the gold. Plants of this kind remind us of the magic "sesame" which, at the command of Ali Baba, in the story of the "Forty Thieves," gave him immediate admission to the secret treasure-cave. Once more, among further plants possessing the same mystic property may be mentioned the sow-thistle, which, when invoked, discloses hidden treasures. In Sicily a branch of the pomegranate tree is considered to be a most effectual means of ascertaining the whereabouts of concealed wealth. Hence it has been invested with an almost reverential awe, and has been generally employed when search has been made for some valuable lost property. In Silesia, Thuringia, and Bohemia the mandrake is, in addition to its many mystic properties, connected with the idea of hidden treasures.

Numerous plants are said to be either lucky or the reverse, and hence have given rise to all kinds of odd beliefs, some of which still survive in our midst, having come down from a remote period.

There is in many places a curious antipathy to uprooting the house-leek, some persons even disliking to let it blossom, and a similar prejudice seems to have existed against the cuckoo-flower, for, if found accidentally inverted in a May garland, it was at once destroyed. In Prussia it is regarded as ominous for a bride to plant myrtle, although in this country it has the reputation of being a lucky plant. According to a Somersetshire saying, "The flowering myrtle is the luckiest plant to have in your window, water it every morning, and be proud of it." We may note here that there are many odd beliefs connected with the myrtle. "Speaking to a lady," says a correspondent of the Athenaeum (Feb. 5, 1848), "of the difficulty which I had always found in getting a slip of myrtle to grow, she directly accounted for my failure by observing that perhaps I had not spread the tail or skirt of my dress, and looked proud during the time I was planting it. It is a popular belief in Somersetshire that unless a slip of myrtle is so planted, it will never take root." The deadly nightshade is a plant of ill omen, and Gerarde describing it says, "if you will follow my counsel, deal not with the same in any case, and banish it from your gardens, and the use of it also, being a plant so furious and deadly; for it bringeth such as have eaten thereof into a dead sleep, wherein many have died." There is a strong prejudice to sowing parsley, and equally a great dislike to transplanting it, the latter notion being found in South America. Likewise, according to a Devonshire belief, it is highly unlucky to plant a bed of lilies of the valley, as the person doing so will probably die in the course of the next twelve months.

The withering of plants has long been regarded ominous, and, according to a Welsh superstition, if there are faded leaves in a room where a baby is christened it will soon die. Of the many omens afforded by the oak, we are told that the change of its leaves from their usual colour gave more than once "fatal premonition" of coming misfortunes during the great civil wars; and Bacon mentions a tradition that "if the oak-apple, broken, be full of worms, it is a sign of a pestilent year." In olden times the decay of the bay-tree was considered an omen of disaster, and it is stated that, previous to the death of Nero, though the winter was very mild, all these trees withered to the roots, and that a great pestilence in Padua was preceded by the same phenomenon. [2] Shakespeare speaks of this superstition:--

> *"'Tis thought the king is dead; we will not stay,*
> *The bay-trees in our county are all withered."*

Lupton, in his "Notable Things," tells us that,

> *"If a fir-tree be touched, withered, or burned with lightning, it*
> *signifies that the master or mistress thereof shall shortly die."*

It is difficult, as we have already noted in a previous chapter, to discover why some of our sweetest and fairest spring-flowers should be associated with ill-luck. In the western counties, for instance, one should never take less than a handful of primroses or violets into a farmer's house, as neglect of this rule is said to affect the success of the ducklings and chickens. A correspondent of Notes and Queries (I. Ser. vii. 201) writes:--"My gravity was sorely tried by being called on to settle a quarrel between two old women, arising from one of them having given one primrose to her neighbour's child, for the purpose of making her hens hatch but one egg out of each set of eggs, and it was seriously maintained that the charm had been successful." In the same way it is held unlucky to introduce the first snowdrop of the year into a house, for, as a Sussex woman once remarked, "It looks for all the world like a corpse in its shroud." We may repeat, too, again the familiar adage:--

> *"If you sweep the house with blossomed broom in May,*
> *You are sure to sweep the head of the house away."*

And there is the common superstition that where roses and violets bloom in autumn, it is indicative of some epidemic in the following year; whereas, if a white rose put forth unexpectedly, it is believed in Germany to be a sign of death in the nearest house; and in some parts of Essex there is a current belief that sickness or death will inevitably ensue if blossoms of the whitethorn be brought into a house; the idea in Norfolk being that no one will be married from the house during the year. Another ominous sign is that of plants shedding their leaves, or of their blossoms falling to pieces. Thus the peasantry in some places affirm that the dropping of the leaves of a peach-tree betokens a murrain; and in Italy it is held unlucky for a rose to do so. A well-known illustration of this superstition occurred many years ago in the case of the unfortunate Miss Bay, who was murdered at the piazza entrance of Covent Garden by Hackman (April 1779), the following account of which we quote from the "Life and Correspondence of M. G. Lewis":-- "When the carriage was announced, and she was adjusting her dress, Mr. Lewis happened to make some remark on a beautiful rose which Miss Kay wore in her bosom. Just as the words were uttered the flower fell to the ground. She immediately stooped to regain it, but as she picked it up, the red leaves scattered themselves on the carpet, and the stalk alone remained in her hand. The poor girl, who had been depressed in spirits before, was evidently affected by this incident, and said, in a slightly faltering voice, 'I trust I am not to consider this as an evil omen!' But soon rallying, she expressed to Mr. Lewis, in a cheerful tone, her hope that they would meet again after the theatre--a hope, alas! Which it was decreed should not be realised." According to a German belief, one who throws a rose into a grave will waste away.

There is a notion prevalent in Dorsetshire that a house wherein the plant "bergamot" is kept will never be free from sickness; and in Norfolk it is said to be unlucky to take into a house a bunch of the grass called "maiden-hair," or, as it is also termed, "dudder-grass." Among further plants of ill omen may be mentioned the bluebell (Campanula rotundifolia), which in certain parts of Scotland was called "The aul' man's bell," and was regarded with a sort of dread, and commonly left unpulled. In Cumberland, about Cockermouth, the red campion (Lychnis diurna) is called "mother-die," and young people believe that if plucked some misfortune will happen to their parents. A similar belief attaches to the herb-robert (Geranium robertianum) in West Cumberland, where it is nicknamed "Death come quickly;" and in certain parts of Yorkshire there is a notion that if a child gather the germander speedwell (Veronica chamoedrys), its mother will die during the year. Herrick has a pretty allusion to the daffodil:--

"When a daffodil I see
Hanging down her head t'wards me,
Guess I may what I must be:
First, I shall decline my head;
Secondly, I shall be dead;
Lastly, safely buried."

In Germany, the marigold is with the greatest care excluded from the flowers with which young women test their love-affairs; and in Austria it is held unlucky to pluck the crocus, as it draws away the strength.

An ash leaf is still frequently employed for invoking good luck, and in Cornwall we find the old popular formula still in use:--

"Even ash, I do thee pluck,
Hoping thus to meet good luck;
If no good luck I get from thee,
I shall wish thee on the tree."

And there is the following well-known couplet:--

"With a four-leaved clover, a double-leaved ash, and a green-topped leave,
You may go before the queen's daughter without asking leave."

But, on the other hand, the finder of the five-leaved clover, it is said, will have bad luck.

In Scotland [3] it was formerly customary to carry on the person a piece of torch-fir for good luck--a superstition which, Mr. Conway remarks, is found in the gold-mines of California, where the men tip a cone with the first gold they discover, and keep it as a charm to ensure good luck in future.

Nuts, again, have generally been credited with propitious qualities, and have accordingly been extensively used for divination. In some mysterious way, too, they are supposed to influence the population, for when plentiful, there is said to be a corresponding increase of babies. In Russia the peasantry frequently carry a nut in their purses, from a belief that it will act as a charm in their efforts to make money. Sternberg, in his "Northamptonshire Glossary" (163), says that the discovery of a double nut, "presages well for the finder, and unless he mars his good fortune by swallowing both kernels, is considered an infallible sign of approaching 'luck.' The orthodox way in such cases consists in eating one, and throwing the other over the shoulder."

The Icelanders have a curious idea respecting the mountain-ash, affirming that it is an enemy of the juniper, and that if one is planted on one side of a tree, and the other on the other, they will split it. It is also asserted that if both are kept in the same house it will be burnt down; but, on the other hand, there is a belief among some sailors that if rowan-tree be used in a ship, it will sink the vessel unless juniper be found on board. In the Tyrol, the Osmunda regalis, called "the blooming fern," is placed over the door for good teeth; and Mr. Conway, too, in his valuable papers, to which we have been often indebted in the previous chapters, says that there are circumstances under which all flowers are injurious. "They must not be laid on the bed of a sick person, according to a Silesian superstition; and in Westphalia and Thuringia, no child under a year old must be permitted to wreathe itself with flowers, or it will soon die. Flowers, says a common German saying, must in no case be laid on the mouth of a corpse, since the dead man may chew them, which would make him a 'Nachzehrer,' or one who draws his relatives to the grave after him."

In Hungary, the burnet saxifrage (Pimpinella saxifraga) is a mystic plant, where it is popularly nicknamed Chaba's salve, there being an old tradition that it was discovered by King Chaba, who cured the wounds of fifteen thousand of his men after a bloody battle fought against his brother. In Hesse, it is said that with knots tied in willow one may slay a distant enemy; and the Bohemians have a belief that seven-year-old children will become beautiful by dancing in the flax. But many superstitions have clustered round the latter plant, it having in years gone by been a popular notion that it will only flower at the time of day on which it was originally sown. To spin on Saturday is said in Germany to bring ill fortune, and as a warning the following legend is among the household tales of the peasantry:--"Two old women, good friends, were the most industrious spinners in their village, Saturday finding them as engrossed in their work as on the other days of the week. At length one of them died, but on the Saturday evening following she appeared to the other, who, as usual, was busy at her wheel, and showing her burning hand, said:--

'See what I in hell have won,
Because on Saturday eve I spun.' "

Flax, nevertheless, is a lucky plant, for in Thuringia, when a young woman gets married, she places flax in her shoes as a charm against poverty. It is supposed, also, to have health-giving virtues; for in Germany, when an infant seems weakly and thrives slowly, it is placed naked upon the turf on Midsummer day, and flax-seed is sprinkled over it; the idea being that as the flax-seed grows so the infant will gradually grow stronger. Of the many beliefs attached to the ash-tree, we are told in the North of England that if the first parings of a child's nails be buried beneath its roots, it will eventually turn out, to use the local phrase, a "top-singer," and there is a popular superstition that wherever the purple honesty (Lunaria biennis) flourishes, the cultivators of the garden are noted for their honesty. The snapdragon, which in years gone by was much cultivated for its showy blossoms, was said to have a supernatural influence, and amongst other qualities to possess the power of destroying charms. Many further illustrations of this class of superstition might easily be added, so thickly interwoven are they with the history of most of our familiar wild-flowers. One further superstition may be noticed, an allusion to which occurs in "Henry V." (Act i. sc. i):--

"The strawberry grows underneath the nettle,
And wholesome berries thrive and ripen best
Neighbour'd by fruit of baser quality;"

It having been the common notion that plants were affected by the neighbourhood of other plants to such an extent that they imbibed each other's virtues and faults. Accordingly sweet flowers were planted near fruit-trees, with the idea of improving the flavour of the fruit; and, on the other hand, evil-smelling trees, like the elder, were carefully cleaned away from fruit-trees, lest they should become tainted. [4] Further superstitions have been incidentally alluded to throughout the present volume, necessarily associated as they are with most sections of plant folklore. It should also be noticed that in the various folk-tales which have been collected together in recent years, many curious plant superstitions are introduced, although, to suit the surroundings of the story, they have only too frequently been modified, or the reverse. At the same time, embellishments of the kind are interesting, as showing how familiar these traditionary beliefs were in olden times to the story-teller, and how ready he was to avail himself of them.

———————————————

Footnotes:

1. See Baring-Gerald's "Curious Myths of the Middle Ages."
2. Ingram's "Florica Symbolica," p. 326.
3. Stewart's "Popular Superstitions of the Highlanders."
4. See Ellacombe's "Plant-lore of Shakespeare," p. 319.

CHAPTER XXI

PLANTS IN FOLK-MEDICINE

From the earliest times plants have been most extensively used in the cure of disease, although in days of old it was not so much their inherent medicinal properties which brought them into repute as their supposed magical virtues. Oftentimes, in truth, the only merit of a plant lay in the charm formula attached to it, the due utterance of which ensured relief to the patient. Originally there can be no doubt that such verbal forms were prayers, "since dwindled into mystic sentences." [1] Again, before a plant could work its healing powers, due regard had to be paid to the planet under whose influence it was supposed to be; [2] for Aubrey mentions an old belief that if a plant "be not gathered according to the rules of astrology, it hath little or no virtue in it." Hence, in accordance with this notion, we find numerous directions for the cutting and preparing of certain plants for medicinal purposes, a curious list of which occurs in Culpepper's "British Herbal and Family Physician." This old herbalist, who was a strong believer in astrology, tells us that such as are of this way of thinking, and none else, are fit to be physicians. But he was not the only one who had strict views on this matter, as the literature of his day proves--astrology, too, having held a prominent place in most of the gardening books of the same period. Michael Drayton, who has chronicled so many of the credulities of his time, referring to the longevity of antediluvian men, writes:--

"Besides, in medicine, simples had the power that none need then the planetary hour to help their workinge, they so juiceful were."

The adder's-tongue, if plucked during the wane of the moon, was a cure for tumours, and there is a Swabian belief that one, "who on Friday of the full moon pulls up the amaranth by the root, and folding it in a white cloth, wears it against his naked breast, will be made bullet-proof." [3] Consumptive patients, in olden times, were three times passed, "Through a circular wreath of woodbine, cut during the increase of the March moon, and let down over the body from head to foot." [4] In France, too, at the present day, the vervain is gathered under the different changes of the moon, with secret incantations, after which it is said to possess remarkable curative properties.

In Cornwall, the club-moss, if properly gathered, is considered "good against all diseases of the eye." The mode of procedure is this:--"On the third day of the moon, when the thin crescent is seen for the first time, show it the knife with which the moss is to be cut, and repeat this formula:--

'As Christ healed the issue of blood,
Do thou cut what thou cuttest for good.'

At sundown, the operator, after carefully washing his hands, is to cut the club-moss kneeling. It is then to be wrapped in a white cloth, and subsequently boiled in water taken from the spring nearest to its place of growth. This may be used as a fomentation, or the club-moss may be made into an ointment with the butter from the milk of a new cow." [5]

Some plants have, from time immemorial, been much in request from the season or period of their blooming, beyond which fact it is difficult to account for the virtues ascribed to them. Thus, among the Romans, the first anemone of the year, when gathered with this form of incantation, "I gather thee for a remedy against disease," was regarded as a preservative from fever; a survival of which belief still prevails in our own country:--

"The first spring-blown anemone she in his doublet wove,
To keep him safe from pestilence wherever he should rove."

On the other hand, in some countries there is a very strong prejudice against the wild anemone, the air being said "to be so tainted by them, that they who inhale it often incur severe sickness." [6] Similarly we may compare the notion that flowers blooming out of season have a fatal significance, as we have noted elsewhere.

The sacred associations attached to many plants have invested them, at all times, with a scientific repute in the healing art, instances of which may be traced up to a very early period. Thus, the peony, which, from its mythical divine origin, was an important flower in the primitive pharmacopoeia, has even in modern times retained its reputation; and to this day Sussex mothers put necklaces of beads turned from the peony root around their children's necks, to prevent convulsions and to assist them in their teething. When worn on the person, it was long considered, too, a most effectual remedy for insanity, and Culpepper speaks of its virtues in the cure of the falling sickness. [7] The thistle, sacred to Thor, is another plant of this kind, and indeed instances are very numerous. On the other hand, some plants, from their great virtues as "all-heals," it would seem, had such names as "Angelica" and "Archangel" bestowed on them. [8]

In later times many plants became connected with the name of Christ, and with the events of the crucifixion itself--facts which occasionally explain their mysterious virtues. Thus the vervain, known as the "holy herb," and which was one of the sacred plants of the Druids, has long been held in repute, the subjoined rhyme assigning as the reason:--

"All hail, thou holy herb, vervin,
  Growing on the ground;
On the Mount of Calvary
  There wast thou found;
Thou helpest many a grief,
  And staunchest many a wound.
In the name of sweet Jesu,
  I lift thee from the ground."

To quote one or two further instances, a popular recipe for preventing the prick of a thorn from festering is to repeat this formula:--

"Christ was of a virgin born,
And he was pricked with a thorn,
And it did neither bell nor swell,
And I trust in Jesus this never will."

In Cornwall, some years ago, the following charm was much used, forms of which may occasionally be heard at the present day:--

"Happy man that Christ was born,
He was crowned with a thorn;
He was pierced through the skin,
For to let the poison in.
But His five wounds, so they say,
Closed before He passed away.
In with healing, out with thorn,
Happy man that Christ was born."

Another version used in the North of England is this:--

"Unto the Virgin Mary our Saviour was horn,
And on his head he wore a crown of thorn;
If you believe this true, and mind it well,
This hurt will never fester nor swell."

The Angelica sylvestris was popularly known as "Holy Ghost," from the angel-like properties therein having been considered good "against poisons, pestilent agues, or the pestilence."

Cockayne, in his "Saxon Leechdoms," mentions an old poem descriptive of the virtues of the mugwort:--

"Thou hast might for three,
And against thirty,
For venom availest
For plying vile things."

So, too, certain plants of the saints acquired a notoriety for specific virtues; and hence St. John's wort, with its leaves marked with blood-like spots, which appear, according to tradition, on the anniversary of his decollation, is still "the wonderful herb" that cures all sorts of wounds. Herb-bennet, popularly designated "Star of the earth," a name applied to the avens, hemlock, and valerian, should properly be, says Dr. Prior, "St. Benedict's herb, a name assigned to such plants as were supposed to be antidotes, in allusion to a legend of this saint, which represents that upon his blessing a cup of poisoned wine which a monk had given to destroy him, the glass was shivered to pieces." In the same way, herb-gerard was called from St. Gerard, who was formerly invoked against gout, a complaint for which this plant was once in high repute. St. James's wort was so called from its being used for the diseases of horses, of which this great pilgrim-saint was the patron. It is curious in how many unexpected ways these odd items of folklore in their association with the saints meet us, showing that in numerous instances it is entirely their association with certain saints that has made them of medical repute.

Some trees and plants have gained a medical notoriety from the fact of their having a mystical history, and from the supernatural qualities ascribed to them. But, as Bulwer-Lytton has suggested in his "Strange Story," the wood of certain trees to which magical properties are ascribed may in truth possess virtues little understood, and deserving of careful investigation. Thus, among these, the rowan would take its place, as would the common hazel, from which the miner's divining-rod is always cut. [9] An old-fashioned charm to cure the bite of an adder was to lay a cross formed of two pieces of hazel-wood on the ground, repeating three times this formula [10]:--

"Underneath this hazelin mote,
There's a braggotty worm with a speckled throat,
Nine double is he;
Now from nine double to eight double
And from eight double to seven double-ell."

The mystical history of the apple accounts for its popularity as a medical agent, although, of course, we must not attribute all the lingering rustic cures to this source. Thus, according to an old Devonshire rhyme,

"Eat an apple going to bed,
Make the doctor beg his bread."

Its juice has long been deemed potent against warts, and a Lincolnshire cure for eyes affected by rheumatism or weakness is a poultice made of rotten apples.

The oak, long famous for its supernatural strength and power, has been much employed in folk-medicine. A German cure for ague is to walk round an oak and say:--

"Good evening, thou good one old;
I bring thee the warm and the cold."

Similarly, in our own country, oak-trees planted at the junction of cross-roads were much resorted to by persons suffering from ague, for the purpose of transferring to them their complaint, [11] and elsewhere allusion has already been made to the practice of curing sickly children by passing through a split piece of oak. A German remedy for gout is to take hold of an oak, or of a young shoot already felled, and to repeat these words:--

"Oak-shoot, I to thee complain,
All the torturing gout plagues me;
I cannot go for it,
Thou canst stand it.
The first bird that flies above thee,
To him give it in his flight,
Let him take it with him in the air."

Another plant, which from its mystic character has been used for various complaints, is the elder. In Bohemia, three spoonsful of the water which has been used to bathe an invalid are poured under an elder-tree; and a Danish cure for toothache consists in placing an elder-twig in the mouth, and then sticking it in a wall, saying, "Depart, thou evil spirit." The mysterious origin and surroundings of the mistletoe have invested it with a widespread importance in old folklore remedies, many of which are, even now-a-days, firmly credited; a reputation, too, bestowed upon it by the Druids, who styled it "all-heal," as being an antidote for all diseases. Culpepper speaks of it as "good for the grief of the sinew, itch, sores, and toothache, the biting of mad dogs and venomous beasts;" while Sir Thomas Browne alludes to its virtues in cases of epilepsy. In France, amulets formed of mistletoe were much worn; and in Sweden, a finger-ring made of its wood is an antidote against sickness. The mandrake, as a mystic plant, was extensively sold for medicinal purposes, and in Kent may be occasionally found kept to cure barrenness; [12] and it may be remembered that La Fontaine's fable, La Mandragore, turns upon its supposed power of producing children. How potent its effects were formerly held may be gathered from the very many allusions to its mystic properties in the literature of bygone years. Columella, in his well-known lines, says:--

"Whose roots show half a man, whose juice
With madness strikes."

Shakespeare speaks of it as an opiate, and on the Continent it was much used for amulets.

Again, certain plants seem to have been specially in high repute in olden times from the marvellous influence they were credited with exercising over the human frame; consequently they were much valued by both old and young; for who would not retain the vigour of his youth, and what woman would not desire to preserve the freshness of her beauty?

One of the special virtues of rosemary, for instance, was its ability to make old folks young again. A story is told of a gouty and crooked old queen, who sighed with longing regret to think that her young dancing-days were gone, so:--

"Of rosmaryn she took six pownde,
And grounde it well in a stownde,"

And then mixed it with water, in which she bathed three times a day, taking care to anoint her head with "gode balm" afterwards. In a very short time her old flesh fell away, and she became so young, tender, and fresh, that she began to look out for a husband. [13]

The common fennel (Foeniculum vulgare) was supposed to give strength to the constitution, and was regarded as highly restorative. Longfellow, in his "Goblet of Life," apparently alludes to our fennel:--

"Above the lowly plant it towers,
The fennel, with its yellow flowers;
And in an earlier age than ours
Was gifted with the wondrous powers
  Lost vision to restore.

It gave new strength and fearless mood,
And gladiators, fierce and rude,
Mingled it in their daily food,
And he who battled and subdued,
  The wreath of fennel wore."

The lady's-mantle, too (Alchemilla vulgaris), was once in great request, for, according to Hoffman, it had the power of "restoring feminine beauty, however faded, to its early freshness;" and the wild tansy (Tanacetum vulgare), laid to soak in buttermilk for nine days, had the reputation of "making the complexion very fair." [14] Similarly, also, the great burnet saxifrage was said to remove freckles; and according to the old herbalists, an infusion of the common centaury (Erythroea centaurium) possessed the same property. [15] The hawthorn, too, was in repute among the fair sex, for, according to an old piece of proverbial lore:--

"The fair maid who, the first of May,
Goes to the fields at break of day,
And washes in dew from the hawthorn tree,
Will ever after handsome be;"

And the common fumitory, "was used when gathered in wedding hours, and boiled in water, milk, and whey, as a wash for the complexion of rustic maids." [16] In some parts of France the water-hemlock (Œnanthe crocata), known with us as the "dead-tongue," from its paralyzing effects on the organs of voice, was used to destroy moles; and the yellow toad-flax (Linaria vulgaris) is described as "cleansing the skin wonderfully of all sorts of deformity." Another plant of popular renown was the knotted figwort (Scrophularia nodosa), for Gerarde censures "divers who doe rashly teach that if it be hanged about the necke, or else carried about one, it keepeth a man in health." Coles, speaking of the mugwort (Artemisia vulgaris), says that, "if a footman take mugwort and put it in his shoes in the morning, he may go forty miles before noon and not be weary;" but as far back as the time of Pliny its remarkable properties were known, for he says, "The wayfaring man that hath the herb tied about him feeleth no weariness at all, and he can never be hurt by any poisonous medicine, by any wild beast, neither yet by the sun itself." The far-famed betony was long credited with marvellous medicinal properties, and hence the old saying which recommends a person when ill "to sell his coat and buy betony." A species of thistle was once believed to have the curious virtue of driving away melancholy, and was hence termed the "melancholy thistle." According to Dioscorides, "the root borne about one doth expel melancholy and remove all diseases connected therewith," but it was to be taken in wine.

On the other hand, certain plants have been credited at most periods with hurtful and injurious properties. Thus, there is a popular idea that during the flowering of the bean more cases of lunacy occur than at any other season. [17] It is curious to find the apple--such a widespread curative--regarded as a bane, an illustration of which is given by Mr. Conway. [18] In Swabia it is said that an apple plucked from a graft on the whitethorn will, if eaten by a pregnant woman, increase her pains. On the Continent, the elder, when used as a birch, is said to check boys' growth, a property ascribed to the knot-grass, as in Beaumont and Fletcher's "Coxcomb" (Act ii. sc. 2):--

"We want a boy extremely for this function,   Kept under for a year with milk and knot-grass."

The cat-mint, when chewed, created quarrelsomeness, a property said by the Italians to belong to the rampion.

Occasionally much attention in folk-medicine has been paid to lucky numbers; a remedy, in order to prove efficacious, having to be performed in accordance with certain numerical rules. In Devonshire, poultices must be made of seven different kinds of herbs, and a cure for thrush is this:--"Three rushes are taken from any running stream, passed separately through the mouth of the infant, and then thrown back into the water. As the current bears them away, so, it is believed, will the thrush leave the child."

Similarly, in Brandenburg, if a person is afflicted with dizziness, he is recommended to run after sunset, naked, three times through a field of flax; after doing so, the flax will at once "take the dizziness to itself." A Sussex cure for ague is to eat sage leaves, fasting, nine mornings in succession; while Flemish folklore enjoins any one who has the ague to go early in the morning to an old willow, make three knots in one of its branches, and say "Good morrow, old one; I give thee the cold; good morrow, old one." A very common cure for warts is to tie as many knots on a hair as there are warts, and to throw the hair away; while an Irish charm is to give the patient nine leaves of dandelion, three leaves being eaten on three successive mornings. Indeed, the efficacy of numbers is not confined to any one locality; and Mr. Folkard [19] mentions an instance in Cuba where, "thirteen cloves of garlic at the end of a cord, worn round the neck for thirteen days, are considered a safeguard against jaundice." It is necessary, however, that the wearer, in the middle of the night of the thirteenth day, should proceed to the corner of two streets, take off his garlic necklet, and, flinging it behind him, run home without turning round to see what has become of it. Similarly, six knots of elderwood are employed "in a Yorkshire incantation to ascertain if beasts are dying from witchcraft." [20] In Thuringia, on the extraction of a tooth, the person must eat three daisies to be henceforth free from toothache. In Cornwall [21] bramble leaves are made use of in cases of scalds and inflammatory diseases. Nine leaves are moistened with spring-water, and "these are applied to the burned or diseased parts." While this is being done, for every bramble leaf the following charm is repeated three times:--

"There came three angels out of the east,
One brought fire and two brought frost;
Out fire and in frost,
In the name of the Father, Son, and Holy Ghost."

Of the thousand and one plants used in popular folk-medicine we can but give a few illustrations, so numerous are these old cures for the ills to which flesh is heir. Thus, for deafness, the juice of onion has been long recommended, and for chilblains, a Derbyshire cure is to thrash them with holly, while in some places the juice of the leek mixed with cream is held in repute. To exterminate warts a host of plants have been recommended; the juice of the dandelion being in favour in the Midland counties, whereas in the North, one has but to hang a snail on a thorn, and as the poor creature wastes away the warts will disappear. In Leicestershire the ash is employed, and in many places the elder is considered efficacious. Another old remedy is to prick the wart with a gooseberry thorn passed through a wedding-ring; and according to a Cornish belief, the first blackberry seen will banish warts. Watercress laid against warts was formerly said to drive them away. A rustic specific for whooping-cough in Hampshire is to drink new milk out of a cup made of the variegated holly; while in Sussex the excrescence found on the briar, and popularly known as "robin red-breast's cushion," is in demand. In consumption and diseases of the lungs, St. Fabian's nettle, the crocus, the betony, and horehound, have long been in request, and sea-southern-wood or mugwort, occasionally corrupted into "muggons," was once a favourite prescription in Scotland. A charming girl, whom consumption had brought to the brink of the grave, was lamented by her lover, whereupon a good-natured mermaid sang to him:--

"Wad ye let the bonnie May die in your hand,
And the mugwort flowering i' the land?"

Thereupon, tradition says, he administered the juice of this life-giving plant to his fair lady-love, who "arose and blessed the bestower for the return of health." Water in which peas have been boiled is given for measles, and a Lincolnshire recipe for cramp is cork worn on the person. A popular cure for ringworm in Scotland is a decoction of sun-spurge (Euphorbia helioscopia), or, as it is locally termed, "mare's milk." In the West of England to bite the first fern seen in spring is an antidote for toothache, and in certain parts of Scotland the root of the yellow iris chopped up and chewed is said to afford relief. Some, again, recommend a double hazel-nut to be carried in the pocket, [22] and the elder, as a Danish cure, has already been noticed.

Various plants were, in days gone by, used for the bites of mad dogs and to cure hydrophobia. Angelica, madworts, and several forms of lichens were favourite remedies. The root of balaustrium, with storax, cypress-nuts, soot, olive-oil, and wine was the receipt, according to Bonaventura, of Cardinal Richelieu. Among other popular remedies were beetroot, box leaves, cabbage, cucumbers, black currants, digitalis, and euphorbia. [23] A Russian remedy was Genista sentoria, and in Greece rose-leaves were used internally and externally as a poultice. Horse-radish, crane's-bill, strawberry, and herb-gerard are old remedies for gout, and in Westphalia apple-juice mixed with saffron is administered for jaundice; while an old remedy for boils is dock-tea. For ague, cinquefoil and yarrow were recommended, and tansy leaves are worn in the shoe by the Sussex peasantry; and in some places common groundsel has been much used as a charm. Angelica was in olden times used as an antidote for poisons. The juice of the arum was considered good for the plague, and Gerarde tells us that Henry VIII. was, "wont to drink the distilled water of broom-flowers against surfeits and diseases thereof arising." An Irish recipe for sore-throat is a cabbage leaf tied round the throat, and the juice of cabbage taken with honey was formerly given as a cure for hoarseness or loss of voice. [24] Agrimony, too, was once in repute for sore throats, cancers, and ulcers; and as far back as the time of Pliny the almond was given as a remedy for inebriety. For rheumatism the burdock was in request, and many of our peasantry keep a potato in their pocket as charms, some, again, carrying a chestnut, either begged or stolen. As an antidote for fevers the carnation was prescribed, and the cowslip, and the hop, have the reputation of inducing sleep. The dittany and plantain, like the golden-rod, nicknamed "wound-weed," have been used for the healing of wounds, and the application of a dock-leaf for the sting of a nettle is a well-known cure among our peasantry, having been embodied in the old familiar adage:--

"Nettle out, dock in--
Dock remove the nettle-sting,"

Of which there are several versions; as in Wiltshire, where the child uses this formula:--

"Out 'ettle
In dock.
Dock shall ha' a a new smock,
'Ettle zbant
Ha' nanun."

The young tops of the common nettle are still made by the peasantry into nettle-broth, and, amongst other directions enjoined in an old Scotch rhyme, it is to be cut in the month of June, "ere it's in the blume":--

"Cou' it by the auld wa's,
  Cou' it where the sun ne'er fa'
Stoo it when the day daws,
  Cou' the nettle early."

The juice of fumitory is said to clear the sight, and the kennel-wort was once a popular specific for the king's-evil. As disinfectants, wormwood and rue were much in demand; and hence Tusser says:--

"What savour is better, if physicke be true,
For places infected, than wormwood and rue?"

For depression, thyme was recommended, and a Manx preservative against all kinds of infectious diseases is ragwort. The illustrations we have given above show in how many ways plants have been in demand as popular curatives. And although an immense amount of superstition has been interwoven with folk-medicine, there is a certain amount of truth in the many remedies which for centuries have been, with more or less success, employed by the peasantry, both at home and abroad.

Footnotes:

1. See Tylor's "Primitive Culture," ii.
2. See Folkard's "Plant-lore Legends and Lyrics," p. 164.
3. "Mystic Trees and Shrubs," p. 717.
4. Folkard's "Plant-lore," p. 379.
5. Hunt's "Popular Romances of the West of England," 1871, p. 415
6. Folkard's "Plant-lore Legends and Lyrics," p. 216.
7. See Black's "Folk-medicine," 1883, p.195.
8. Quarterly Review, cxiv. 245.
9. "Sacred Trees and Flowers," Quarterly Review, cxiv. 244.
10. Folkard's "Plant Legends," 364.
11. Fraser's Magazine, 1870, p. 591.
12. "Mystic Trees and Plants;" Fraser's Magazine, 1870, p. 708.
13. "Reliquiae Antiquse," Wright and Halliwell, i. 195; Quarterly Review, 1863, cxiv. 241.
14. Coles, "The Art of Simpling," 1656.

15. Anne Pratt's "Flowering Plants of Great Britain," iv. 9.

16. Black's "Folk-medicine," p. 201.

17. Folkard's "Plant-Lore Legends and Lyrics," p. 248.

18. Fraser's Magazine, 1870, p. 591.

19. "Plant-Lore Legends and Lyrics," p. 349.

20. Black's "Folk-medicine," p. 185.

21. See Hunt's "Popular Romances of the West of England."

22. Black's "Folk-medicine," p. 193.

23. "Rabies or Hydrophobia," T. M. Dolan, 1879, p. 238.

24. Black's "Folk-medicine," p. 193.

CHAPTER XXII

PLANTS AND THEIR LEGENDARY HISTORY

Many of the legends of the plant-world have been incidentally alluded to in the preceding pages. Whether we review their mythological history as embodied in the traditionary stories of primitive times, or turn to the existing legends of our own and other countries in modern times, it is clear that the imagination has at all times bestowed some of its richest and most beautiful fancies on trees and flowers. Even, too, the rude and ignorant savage has clothed with graceful conceptions many of the plants which, either for their grandeur or utility, have attracted his notice. The old idea, again, of metamorphosis, by which persons under certain peculiar cases were changed into plants, finds a place in many of the modern plant-legends. Thus there is the well-known story of the wayside plantain, commonly termed "way-bread," which, on account of its so persistently haunting the track of man, has given rise to the German story that it was formerly a maiden who, whilst watching by the wayside for her lover, was transformed into this plant. But once in seven years it becomes a bird, either the cuckoo, or the cuckoo's servant, the "dinnick," as it is popularly called in Devonshire, the German "wiedhopf" which is said to follow its master everywhere.

This story of the plantain is almost identical with one told in Germany of the endive or succory. A patient girl, after waiting day by day for her betrothed for many a month, at last, worn out with watching, sank exhausted by the wayside and expired. But before many days had passed, a little flower with star-like blossoms sprang up on the spot where the broken-hearted maiden had breathed her final sigh, which was henceforth known as the "Wegewarte," the watcher of the road. Mr. Folkard quotes an ancient ballad of Austrian Silesia which recounts how a young girl mourned for seven years the loss of her lover, who had fallen in war. But when her friends tried to console her, and to procure for her another lover, she replied, "I shall cease to weep only when I become a wild-flower by the wayside." By the North American Indians, the plantain or "way-bread" is "the white man's foot," to which Longfellow, in speaking of the English settlers, alludes in his "Hiawatha":--

"Wheresoe'er they move, before them
Swarms the stinging fly, the Ahmo,
Swarms the bee, the honey-maker;
Wheresoe'er they tread, beneath them

Springs a flower unknown among us,
Springs the white man's foot in blossom."

Between certain birds and plants there exists many curious traditions, as in the case of the nightingale and the rose. According to a piece of Persian folklore, whenever the rose is plucked, the nightingale utters a plaintive cry, because it cannot endure to see the object of its love injured. In a legend told by the Persian poet Attar, we are told how all the birds appeared before Solomon, and complained that they were unable to sleep from the nightly wailings of the nightingale. The bird, when questioned as to the truth of this statement, replied that his love for the rose was the cause of his grief. Hence this supposed love of the nightingale for the rose has been frequently the subject of poetical allusion. Lord Byron speaks of it in the "Giaour":--

"The rose o'er crag or vale,
Sultana of the nightingale,
The maid for whom his melody,
His thousand songs are heard on high,
Blooms blushing to her lover's tale,
His queen, the garden queen, his rose,
Unbent by winds, unchilled by snows."

Thackeray, too, has given a pleasing rendering of this favourite legend:--

"Under the boughs I sat and listened still,
I could not have my fill.
'How comes,' I said, 'such music to his bill?
Tell me for whom he sings so beautiful a trill.'

'Once I was dumb,' then did the bird disclose,
'But looked upon the rose,
And in the garden where the loved one grows,
I straightway did begin sweet music to compose.'"

Mrs. Browning, in her "Lay of the Early Rose," alludes to this legend, and Moore in his "Lalla Rookh" asks:--

"Though rich the spot
With every flower this earth has got,
What is it to the nightingale,
If there his darling rose is not?"

But the rose is not the only plant for which the nightingale is said to have a predilection, there being an old notion that its song is never heard except where cowslips are to be found in profusion. Experience, however, only too often proves the inaccuracy of this assertion. We may also quote the following note from Yarrell's "British Birds" (4th ed., i. 316):--"Walcott, in his 'Synopsis of British Birds' (vol. ii. 228), says that the nightingale has been observed to be met with only where the cowslip grows kindly, and the assertion receives a partial approval from Montagu; but whether the statement be true or false, its converse certainly cannot be maintained, for Mr. Watson gives the cowslip (Primula veris) as found in all the 'provinces' into which he divides Great Britain, as far north as Caithness and Shetland, where we know that the nightingale does not occur." A correspondent of Notes and Queries (5th Ser. ix. 492) says that in East Sussex, on the borders of Kent, "the cowslip is quite unknown, but nightingales are as common as blackberries there."

A similar idea exists in connection with hops; and, according to a tradition current in Yorkshire, the nightingale made its first appearance in the neighbourhood of Doncaster when hops were planted. But this, of course, is purely imaginary, and in Hargrove's "History of Knaresborough" (1832) we read: "In the opposite wood, called Birkans Wood (opposite to the Abbey House), during the summer evenings, the nightingale:--

'Sings darkling, and, in shadiest covert hid,
Tunes her nocturnal lay.' "

Of the numerous stories connected with the origin of the mistletoe, one is noticed by Lord Bacon, to the effect that a certain bird, known as the "missel-bird," fed upon a particular kind of seed, which, through its incapacity to digest, it evacuated whole, whereupon the seed, falling on the boughs of trees, vegetated and produced the mistletoe. The magic springwort, which reveals hidden treasures, has a mysterious connection with the woodpecker, to which we have already referred. Among further birds which are in some way or other connected with plants is the eagle, which plucks the wild lettuce, with the juice of which it smears its eyes to improve its vision; while the hawk was supposed, for the same purpose, to pluck the hawk-bit.

Similarly, writes Mr. Folkard, [1] pigeons and doves made use of vervain, which was termed "pigeon's-grass." Once more, the cuckoo, according to an old proverbial rhyme, must eat three meals of cherries before it ceases its song; and it was formerly said that orchids sprang from the seed of the thrush and the blackbird. Further illustrations might be added, whereas some of the many plants named after well-known birds are noticed elsewhere.

An old Alsatian belief tells us that bats possessed the power of rendering the eggs of storks unfruitful. Accordingly, when once a stork's egg was touched by a bat it became sterile; and in order to preserve it from the injurious influence, the stork placed in its nest some branches of the maple, which frightened away every intruding bat. [2] There is an amusing legend of the origin of the bramble:--The cormorant was once a wool merchant. He entered into partnership with the bramble and the bat, and they freighted a large ship with wool. She was wrecked, and the firm became bankrupt. Since that disaster the bat skulks about till midnight to avoid his creditors, the cormorant is for ever diving into the deep to discover its foundered vessel, while the bramble seizes hold of every passing sheep to make up his loss by stealing the wool.

Returning to the rose, we may quote one or two legendary stories relating to its origin. Thus Sir John Mandeville tells us how when a holy maiden of Bethlehem, "blamed with wrong and slandered," was doomed to death by fire, "she made her prayers to our Lord that He would help her, as she was not guilty of that sin;" whereupon the fire was suddenly quenched, and the burning brands became red "roseres," and the brands that were not kindled became white "roseres" full of roses. "And these were the first roseres and roses, both white and red, that ever any man soughte." Henceforth, says Mr. King,[3] the rose became the flower of martyrs. "It was a basket full of roses that the martyr Saint Dorothea sent to the notary of Theophilus from the garden of Paradise; and roses, says the romance, sprang up all over the field of Ronce-vaux, where Roland and the douze pairs had stained the soil with their blood."

The colour of the rose has been explained by various legends, the Turks attributing its red colour to the blood of Mohammed. Herrick, referring to one of the old classic stories of its divine origin, writes:--

"Tis said, as Cupid danced among the gods, he down the nectar lung,
Which, on the white rose being shed, made it for ever after red."

A pretty origin has been assigned to the moss-rose (Rosa muscosa):-- "The angel who takes care of flowers, and sprinkles upon them the dew in the still night, slumbered on a spring day in the shade of a rosebush, and when she awoke she said, 'Most beautiful of my children, I thank thee for thy refreshing odour and cooling shade; could you now ask any favour, how willingly would I grant it!' 'Adorn me then with a new charm,' said the spirit of the rose-bush; and the angel adorned the loveliest of flowers with the simple moss."

A further Roumanian legend gives another poetic account of the rose's origin. "It is early morning, and a young princess comes down into her garden to bathe in the silver waves of the sea. The transparent whiteness of her complexion is seen through the slight veil which covers it, and shines through the blue waves like the morning star in the azure sky. She springs into the sea, and mingles with the silvery rays of the sun, which sparkle on the dimples of the laughing waves. The sun stands still to gaze upon her; he covers her with kisses, and forgets his duty. Once, twice, thrice has the night advanced to take her sceptre and reign over the world; twice had she found the sun upon her way. Since that day the lord of the universe has changed the princess into a rose; and this is why the rose always hangs her head and blushes when the sun gazes on her." There are a variety of rose-legends of this kind in different countries, the universal popularity of this favourite blossom having from the earliest times made it justly in repute; and according to the Hindoo mythologists, Pagoda Sin, one of the wives of Vishnu, was discovered in a rose--a not inappropriate locality.

Like the rose, many plants have been extensively associated with sacred legendary lore, a circumstance which frequently explains their origin. A pretty legend, for instance, tells us how an angel was sent to console Eve when mourning over the barren earth. Now, no flower grew in Eden, and the driving snow kept falling to form a pall for earth's untimely funeral after the fall of man. But as the angel spoke, he caught a flake of falling snow, breathed on it, and bade it take a form, and bud and blow. Ere it reached the ground it had turned into a beautiful flower, which Eve prized more than all the other fair plants in Paradise; for the angel said to her:--

"This is an earnest, Eve, to thee,
That sun and summer soon shall be."

The angel's mission ended, he departed, but where he had stood a ring of snowdrops formed a lovely posy.

This legend reminds us of one told by the poet Shiraz, respecting the origin of the forget-me-not:--"It was in the golden morning of the early world, when an angel sat weeping outside the closed gates of Eden. He had fallen from his high estate through loving a daughter of earth, nor was he permitted to enter again until she whom he loved had planted the flowers of the forget-me-not in every corner of the world. He returned to earth and assisted her, and they went hand in hand over the world planting the forget-me-not. When their task was ended, they entered Paradise together; for the fair woman, without tasting the bitterness of death, became immortal like the angel, whose love her beauty had won, when she sat by the river twining the forget-me-not in her hair." This is a more poetic legend than the familiar one given in Mill's "History of Chivalry," which tells how the lover, when trying to pick some blossoms of the myosotis for his lady-love, was drowned, his last words as he threw the flowers on the bank being "Forget me not."

Another legend, already noticed, would associate it with the magic spring-wort, which revealed treasure-caves hidden in the mountains. The traveler enters such an opening, but after filling his pockets with gold, pays no heed to the fairy's voice, "Forget not the best," i.e., the spring-wort, and is severed in twain by the mountain clashing together.

In speaking of the various beliefs relative to plant life in a previous chapter, we have enumerated some of the legends which would trace the origin of many plants to the shedding of human blood, a belief which is a distinct survival of a very primitive form of belief, and enters very largely into the stories told in classical mythology. The dwarf elder is said to grow where blood has been shed, and it is nicknamed in Wales "Plant of the blood of man," with which may be compared its English name of "death-wort." It is much associated in this country with the Danes, and tradition says that wherever their blood was shed in battle, this plant afterwards sprang up; hence its names of Dane-wort, Dane-weed, or Dane's-blood. One of the bell-flower tribe, the clustered bell-flower, has a similar legend attached to it; and according to Miss Pratt, "in the village of Bartlow there are four remarkable hills, supposed to have been thrown up by the Danes as monumental memorials of the battle fought in 1006 between Canute and Edmund Ironside. Some years ago the clustered bell-flower was largely scattered about these mounds, the presence of which the cottagers attributed to its having sprung from the Dane's blood," under which name the flower was known in the neighbourhood.

The rose-coloured lotus or melilot is, from the legend, said to have been sprung from the blood of a lion slain by the Emperor Adrian; and, in short, folklore is rich in stories of this kind. Some legends are of a more romantic kind, as that which explains the origin of the wallflower, known in Palestine as the "blood-drops of Christ." In bygone days a castle stood near the river Tweed, in which a fair maiden was kept prisoner, having plighted her troth and given her affection to a young heir of a hostile clan. But blood having been shed between the chiefs on either side, the deadly hatred thus engendered forbade all thoughts of a union. The lover tried various stratagems to obtain his fair one, and at last succeeded in gaining admission attired as a wandering troubadour, and eventually arranged that she should effect her escape, while he awaited her arrival with an armed force. But this plan, as told by Herrick, was unsuccessful:--

"Up she got upon a wall,
Attempted down to slide withal;
But the silken twist untied,
She fell, and, bruised, she died.
Love, in pity to the deed,

And her loving luckless speed,
Twined her to this plant we call
Now the 'flower of the wall.'"

The tea-tree in China, from its marked effect on the human constitution, has long been an agent of superstition, and been associated with the following legend, quoted by Schleiden. It seems that a devout and pious hermit having, much against his will, been overtaken by sleep in the course of his watchings and prayers, so that his eyelids had closed, tore them from his eyes and threw them on the ground in holy wrath. But his act did not escape the notice of a certain god, who caused a tea-shrub to spring out from them, the leaves of which exhibit, "the form of an eyelid bordered with lashes, and possess the gift of hindering sleep." Sir George Temple, in his "Excursions in the Mediterranean," mentions a legend relative to the origin of the geranium. It is said that the prophet Mohammed having one day washed his shirt, threw it upon a mallow plant to dry; but when it was afterwards taken away, its sacred contact with the mallow was found to have changed the plant into a fine geranium, which now for the first time came into existence.

Footnotes:

1. "Plant-Lore Legends and Lyrics."
2. Folkard's "Plant Lore Legends and Lyrics," p. 430.
3. "Sacred Trees and Flowers," Quarterly Review, cxiv. 239.

CHAPTER XXIII

MYSTIC PLANTS

The mystic character and history of certain plants meet us in every age and country. The gradual evolution of these curious plants of belief must, no doubt, partly be ascribed to their mythical origin, and in many cases to their sacred associations; while, in some instances, it is not surprising that, "any plant which produced a marked effect upon the human constitution should become an object of superstition." [1] A further reason why sundry plants acquired a mystic notoriety was their peculiar manner of growth, which, through not being understood by early botanists, caused them to be invested with mystery. Hence a variety of combinations have produced those mystic properties of trees and flowers which have inspired them with such superstitious veneration in our own and other countries. According to Mr. Conway, the apple, of all fruits, seems to have had the widest and most mystical history. Thus, "Aphrodite bears it in her hand as well as Eve; the serpent guards it, the dragon watches it. It is the healing fruit of the Arabian tribes. Azrael, the Angel of Death, accomplishes his mission by holding it to the nostrils, and in the prose Edda it is written, 'Iduna keeps in a box apples which the gods, when they feel old age approaching, have only to taste to become young again.'" Indeed, the legendary mythical lore connected with the apple is most extensive, a circumstance which fully explains its mystic character. Further, as Mr. Folkard points out,[2] in the popular tales of all countries the apple is represented as the principal magical fruit, in support of which he gives several interesting illustrations. Thus, "In the German folk-tale of 'The Man of Iron,' a princess throws a golden apple as a prize, which the hero catches three times, and carries off and wins." And in a French tale, "A singing apple is one of the marvels which Princess Belle-Etoile and her brothers and her cousin bring from the end of the world." The apple figures in many an Italian tale, and holds a prominent place in the Hungarian story of the Iron Ladislas.[3] But many of these so-called mystic trees and plants have been mentioned in the preceding pages in their association with lightning, witchcraft, demonology, and other branches of folklore, although numerous other curious instances are worthy of notice, some of which are collected together in the present chapter. Thus the nettle and milfoil, when carried about the person, were believed to drive away fear, and were, on this account, frequently worn in time of danger. The laurel preserved from misfortune, and in olden times we are told how the superstitious man, to be free from every chance of ill-luck, was wont to carry a bay leaf in his mouth from morning till night. One of the remarkable virtues of the fruit of the balm was its prolonging the lives of those who partook of it to four or five hundred years, and Albertus Magnus, summing up the mystic qualities of the heliotrope, gives this piece of advice:--"Gather it in August, wrap it in a bay leaf with a wolf's tooth, and it will, if placed under the pillow, show a man who has been robbed where are his goods, and who has taken them. Also, if placed in a church, it will keep fixed in their places all the women present who have broken their marriage vow." It was formerly supposed that the cucumber had the power of killing by its great coldness, and the larch was considered impenetrable by fire; Evelyn describing it as "a goodly tree, which is of so strange a composition that 'twill hardly burn."

In addition to guarding the homestead from ill, the hellebore was regarded as a wonderful antidote against madness, and as such is spoken of by Burton, who introduces it among the emblems of his frontispiece, in his "Anatomie of Melancholy:"--

"Borage and hellebore fill two scenes,
Sovereign plants to purge the veins
Of melancholy, and cheer the heart
Of those black fumes which make it smart;
To clear the brain of misty fogs,
Which dull our senses and Soul clogs;
The best medicine that e'er God made
For this malady, if well assay'd."

But, as it has been observed, our forefathers, in strewing their floors with this plant, were introducing a real evil into their houses, instead of an imaginary one, the perfume having been considered highly pernicious to health.

In the many curious tales related of the mystic henbane may be quoted one noticed by Gerarde, who says: "The root boiled with vinegar, and the same holden hot in the mouth, easeth the pain of the teeth. The seed is used by mountebank tooth-drawers, which run about the country, to cause worms to come forth of the teeth, by burning it in a chafing-dish of coles, the party holding his mouth over the fume thereof; but some crafty companions, to gain money, convey small lute-strings into the water, persuading the patient that those small creepers came out of his mouth or other parts which he intended to cure." Shakespeare, it may be remembered, alludes to this superstition in "Much Ado About Nothing" (Act iii. sc. 2), where Leonato reproaches Don Pedro for sighing for the toothache, which he adds "is but a tumour or a worm." The notion is still current in Germany, where the following incantation is employed:--

*"Pear tree, I complain to thee
Three worms sting me."*

The henbane, too, according to a German belief, is said to attract rain, and in olden times was thought to produce sterility. Some critics have suggested that it is the plant referred to in "Macbeth" by Banquo (Act i. sc. 3):--

*"Have we eaten of the insane root
That takes the reason prisoner?"*

Although others think it is the hemlock. Anyhow, the henbane has long been in repute as a plant possessed of mysterious attributes, and Douce quotes the subjoined passage:--"Henbane, called insana, mad, for the use thereof is perillous, for if it be eate or dronke, it breedeth madness, or slowe lykeness of sleepe." In days gone by, when the mandrake was an object of superstitious veneration by reason of its supernatural character, the Germans made little idols of its root, which were consulted as oracles. Indeed, so much credence was attached to these images, that they were manufactured in very large quantities for exportation to various other countries, and realised good prices. Oftentimes substituted for the mandrake was the briony, which designing people sold at a good profit. Gerarde informs us, "How the idle drones, that have little or nothing to do but eat and drink, have bestowed some of their time in carving the roots of briony, forming them to the shape of men and women, which falsifying practice hath confirmed the error amongst the simple and unlearned people, who have taken them upon their report to be the true mandrakes." Oftentimes, too, the root of the briony was trained to grow into certain eccentric shapes, which were used as charms. Speaking of the mandrake, we may note that in France it was regarded as a species of elf, and nicknamed main de gloire; in connection with which Saint-Palaye describes a curious superstition:-- "When I asked a peasant one day why he was gathering mistletoe, he told me that at the foot of the oaks on which the mistletoe grew he had a mandrake; that this mandrake had lived in the earth from whence the mistletoe sprang; that he was a kind of mole; that he who found him was obliged to give him food--bread, meat, and some other nourishment; and that he who had once given him food was obliged to give it every day, and in the same quantity, without which the mandrake would assuredly cause the forgetful one to die. Two of his countrymen, whom he named to me, had, he said, lost their lives; but, as a recompense, this main de gloire returned on the morrow double what he had received the previous day. If one paid cash for the main de gloire's food one day, he would find double the amount the following, and so with anything else. A certain countryman, whom he mentioned as still living, and who had become very rich, was believed to have owed his wealth to the fact that he had found one of these mains de gloire." Many other equally curious stories are told of the mandrake, a plant which, for its mystic qualities, has perhaps been unsurpassed; and it is no wonder that it was a dread object of superstitious fear, for Moore, speaking of its appearance, says:--

"Such rank and deadly lustre dwells,
As in those hellish fires that light
The mandrake's charnel leaves at night."

But these mandrake fables are mostly of foreign extraction and of very ancient date. Dr. Daubeny, in his "Roman Husbandry," has given a curious drawing from the Vienna MS. of Dioscorides in the fifth century, representing the Goddess of Discovery presenting to Dioscorides the root of the mandrake (of thoroughly human shape), which she has just pulled up, while the unfortunate dog which had been employed for that purpose is depicted in the agonies of death.

Basil, writes Lord Bacon in his "Natural History," if exposed too much to the sun, changes into wild thyme; and a Bavarian piece of folklore tells us that the person who, during an eclipse of the sun, throws an offering of palm with crumbs on the fire, will never be harmed by the sun. In Hesse, it is affirmed that with knots tied in willow one may slay a distant enemy; and according to a belief current in Iceland, the Caltha palustris, if taken with certain ceremonies and carried about, will prevent the bearer from having an angry word spoken to him. The virtues of the dittany were famous as far back as Plutarch's time, and Gerarde speaks of its marvellous efficacy in drawing forth splinters of wood, &c., and in the healing of wounds, especially those "made with envenomed weapons, arrows shot out of guns, and such like."

Then there is the old tradition to the effect that if boughs of oak be put into the earth, they will bring forth wild vines; and among the supernatural qualities of the holly recorded by Pliny, we are told that its flowers cause water to freeze, that it repels lightning, and that if a staff of its wood be thrown at any animal, even if it fall short of touching it, the animal will be so subdued by its influence as to return and lie down by it. Speaking, too, of the virtues of the peony, he thus writes:--"It hath been long received, and confirmed by divers trials, that the root of the male peony dried, tied to the necke, doth helpe the falling sickness, and likewise the incubus, which we call the mare. The cause of both these diseases, and especially of the epilepsie from the stomach, is the grossness of the vapours, which rise and enter into the cells of the brain, and therefore the working is by extreme and subtle alternation which that simple hath." Worn as an amulet, the peony was a popular preservative against enchantment.

———————————————

Footnotes:

1. Fraser's Magazine 1870, p. 709.
 2. "Plant Lore Legends and Lyrics," p. 224.
3. See Miss Busk's "Folklore of Rome."

Also Available from Samhain Song Press

No study of occult philosophy is possible without an acquaintance with symbolism, for if the words occultism and symbolism are correctly used, they mean almost one and the same thing. Symbolism cannot be learned as one learns to build bridges or speak a foreign language, and for the interpretation of symbols a special cast of mind is necessary; in addition to knowledge, special faculties, the power of creative thought and a developed imagination are required. One who understands the use of symbolism in the arts, knows, in a general way, what is meant by occult symbolism. But even then a special training of the mind is necessary, in order to comprehend the "language of the Initiates", and to express in this language the intuitions as they arise.

There are many methods for developing the "sense of symbols" in those who are striving to understand the hidden forces of Nature and Man, and for teaching the fundamental principles as well as the elements of the esoteric language. The most synthetic, and one of the most interesting of these methods, is the Tarot.

-- From *The Symbolism of the Tarot: Philosophy of Occultism in Picture and Numbers,* by P.D Ouspensky

View the Complete Samhain Song Press catalog
of classic witchcraft and pagan quality reprints at

www.SamhainSong.com

Also Available from Samhain Song Press

Ritual Witchcraft... embraces the religious beliefs and ritual of the people known in late mediaeval times as 'Witches'... and appears to be the ancient religion of Western Europe... The deity of this cult was incarnate in a man, a woman, or an animal... Such a god is found in Italy (where he was called Janus or Dianus)... The feminine form of the name, Diana, is found throughout Western Europe as the name of the female deity of the so-called Witches, and for this reason I have called this ancient religion the Dianic cult.

-- From The Witch-Cult In Western Europe, by Margaret A. Murray

This in-depth study of ancient European pagan belief is derived from examination of legal records of "Burning Times" trials, pamphlets giving accounts of individual witches, and the works of Inquisitors and other writers. In equal parts informative, disturbing and inspiring, The Witch-Cult In Western Europe forms the true Historical cornerstone upon which Gerald Gardner and others built the 20th Century Wicca/Witchcraft revival.

View the Complete Samhain Song Press catalog
of classic witchcraft and pagan quality reprints at

www.SamhainSong.com

Also Available from Samhain Song Press

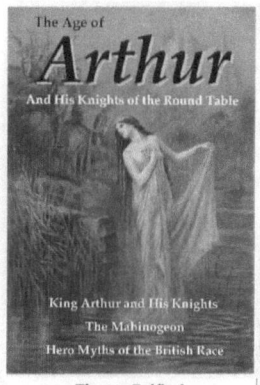

This classic collection of Arthurian Tales includes both the complete British adventures of King Arthur and His Knights and their generally more mysterious and magical Welsh counterparts, as recounted in the famed Mabinogeon. Here, also, are the sagas of many great heroes of the British race, including the Danish monster-slayer, Beowulf, Cuchulain, the Champion of Ireland, and the beloved Anglo-Saxon archer/bandit/hero, Robin Hood. Recounted as exciting adventure stories, in plain English (no degree in ancient dialects required!), Thomas Bulfinch's *The Age Of Arthur And His Knights Of The Round Table* is far and away the most complete compilation of Arthurian lore available in this or any age.